Constituting Modernity

The Islamic Mediterranean

Programme Chair Robert Ilbert
Series Editor Randi Deguilhem

Published and forthcoming

1. Writing the Feminine: Women in Arab Sources
   Edited by Manuela Marín and Randi Deguilhem

2. Money, Land and Trade: An Economic History of the Muslim Mediterranean
   Edited by Nelly Hanna

3. Outside In: On the Margins of the Modern Middle East
   Edited by Eugene Rogan

4. Crafts and Craftsmen of the Middle East: Fashioning the Individual in the Muslim Mediterranean
   Edited by Suraiya Faroghi, Sadok Boubaker and Randi Deguilhem

5. Constituting Modernity: Private Property in the East and West
   Edited by Huri İslamoğlu

6. Standing Trial: Law and Person in the Modern Middle East
   Edited by Baudouin Dupret

7. Shattering Tradition: Custom, Law and the Individual in the Muslim Mediterranean
   Edited by Walter Dostal and Wolfgang Kraus

CONSTITUTING MODERNITY

Private Property in the East and West

Edited by

Huri İslamoğlu

I.B. TAURIS
LONDON · NEW YORK

Published in 2004 by I.B.Tauris & Co Ltd
6 Salem Road, London W2 4BU
175 Fifth Avenue, New York NY 10010
Website: http://www.ibtauris.com
in association with The European Science Foundation, Strasbourg, France

ISBN 1 86064 996 3
EAN 978 1 86064 996 7

A full CIP record for this book is available from the British Library
A full CIP record for this book is available from the Library of Congress
Library of Congress catalog card: available

Typeset in Baskerville by Dexter Haven Associates Ltd, London

Contents

Preface and Acknowledgements

Huri İslamoğlu

This volume was conceived at a time when the primacy of central state administrations was being challenged both politically and intellectually. Responding to the *zeitgeist*, in the early 1990s, the European Science Foundation (ESF) undertook a project entitled 'Individual and Society in the Muslim Mediterranean World' (ISMM). One of the objectives of the project was to re-direct the historical and social-scientific research on the Muslim Mediterranean world towards societal dynamics, towards the lives of social groups and individuals. Traditionally, research on this part of the world had focused on what were assumed to be oppressive states or Oriental despots and on Islam, a religion understood to be equally oppressive and encompassing all aspects of life. In this sense, the ESF project sought to bring forth the society, the economy and the individual that were hitherto subsumed in the histories of states and of Islam. All but three of the chapters included in this volume originated in the workshops organised within the context of the ESF project. The focus of the workshops had been to trace the development of private property in the Mediterranean Muslim world, where conventional historiography assumed that the emergence of private property, as was the case for civil society and the market economy, had been stunted by state intervention. Most dramatic of such interventions was assumed to have been state ownership of land, considered to be a defining feature of society not only in the Mediterranean Muslim world but also in Eastern empires in general.

The original research presented in the ISMM workshops indicated, however, that in the nineteenth century private property had indeed developed in the Ottoman Empire, which dominated the Eastern Mediterranean, and that, significantly, it was instituted through the practices of a specific kind of state: the modern Ottoman state. In fact, the development of private or individual property had been inseparable from the formation of modern administrative states in the Ottoman Empire as well as in British India and China and Great Britain.

These states sought to establish their control over resources to the exclusion of certain groups, including members of religious hierarchies and feudal interests with which the pre-modern states shared that control. From the perspective of this volume, what started out as a project concerning the formation of private property within the Mediterranean Muslim world and, in particular, within the Ottoman domains developed into a project containing a conceptual opening towards the analysis of state–society relations regarding the development of property and market in the age of modern state formation during the nineteenth and the twentieth centuries (until the 1980s). This led to a decision to extend the comparative scope, which was initially limited to comparing developments in different Ottoman regions, to include developments in two major Eastern empires: China and India (late Mughal and British). Lastly, the inclusion of a study on the re-formation of individual property in Great Britain in the late nineteenth century through administrative techniques of indexation and cadastral mapping was important in questioning understandings which designated private property as belonging in the West to the domain of civil society freed of state intervention. This isolation of society from the state is believed to have been a privilege which Oriental despotism had denied to the East.

Consequently, individual authors in this book, each in their own way and some more self-consciously than others, pose a challenge to liberal understandings which assume that activities of state and society are irreconcilable and reject the notion that state intervention disables civil society and/or market economy, the most important institution of which is private property. Rather, they view the state as enabling and as constitutive of social reality. The volume, however, reveals a tension between two constitutivist perspectives. First, the Foucaultian perspective points to the ways in which state administrative practices constitute social reality and, in doing so, subject it to the control and surveillance of an all-encompassing leviathan. The second perspective identifies different constitutive practices, including law, administrative rulings and cadastral surveying and maps, as domains in which different actors, including state actors, negotiate the terms of their existence. This perspective emphasises the responsiveness of administrative actors to the expectations of social actors. In doing so, it paves the way for an analysis which is not simply content with transcending the binaries of state and society and of state and economy; it introduces social actors or social dynamics into the domain of the state and of its constitutive practices. It amounts to introducing the notion of politics and of the struggles of social groups and individuals into the domain of administration. Such an understanding seeks to politicise state administration and points to its responsiveness rather than depicting it as impenetrable and controlling.

The perspective on administration as a political process raises important issues, both methodological and political, which need to be addressed. First, the understanding of central administrations as political domains where society and economy are constituted in relation to the deliberations of multiple actors appears to approximate more closely historical realities of modernity both in the East and the West, as represented in this volume, than do the idealised images which depict state and society as separate spheres of activity often existing in opposition to each other or the Foucaultian perception of the all-controlling Panopticon states.

Second, an approach to administrative practices as domains of political activity raises questions about the perceptions of present-day constitutions of modernity in terms of global market environments. For the most part, new constitutions of market economies largely exclude the central bureaucracies, while the process of market-making is entrusted to transnational bodies of governance which are assumed to be autonomous from central states. The most significant of these bodies are the IMF, the World Bank and the European Union, and market reform packages introduced by them stress the technical and apolitical character of market rules and institutions. Conversely, from the perspective of market reform packages, the central bureaucratic states and their politics of distribution have been restrictive of the development of markets and of private property. Thus, the Smithian notion of the separation of state and society and the relegation of the state to the domain of the enforcement of market rules and property rights, and of ensuring security, is refashioned to fit the conditions of a new market environment in the late twentieth and early twenty-first centuries. By identifying politics strictly with the redistributive politics of central administrative states and by arguing that this kind of politics had impeded market development, the new liberalism dismisses politics, or any possibility of contestation, deliberation and negotiation together with the central states. In doing so, new liberalism distracts attention from the fact that present-day practices of governance are domains of politics just as the administrative practices of central states had been. Yet, if governance practices (like the administrative practices of central states studied in this volume) are viewed as political fields, then it may be possible not to accept what is introduced as 'reform' or economic development as being absolute and incontestable, but as negotiable and open to contestation. Such a perception, in turn, may provide a sense of a political opening for those who are excluded from the benefits of market development, which conceptions of governance as a technical and absolute imperative do not.

Finally, the project which started as a modest exploration into the development of private property and civil society in the Eastern Mediterranean world through a comparative study of different Ottoman regions moved towards studying the unfolding of shared modernities not only in the Ottoman East, in India and China, but also in the West, in particular in Britain. This, however, implies an understanding of modernity which departs from a perspective based on broad mystifications about civil society as the site where market activity flourished unimpeded by the state and its politics, or about the culture of Enlightenment sweeping away religious cultures. Such mystifications often rest on a dichotomous conception of world history which depicts the West as the domain of civil society, private property and individual will and the East as the domain of deprivations, where neither civil society, nor private property nor individual free will capable of challenging religious dogma could flourish. Instead, contributions to this volume look beyond the 'clash of civilisations' towards an understanding of modernity shared by East and West that is far more modest and relates to ways that central bureaucratic states have constituted social entities since the nineteenth century through their administrative practices and in terms of their taxation and military imperatives. These central states were responding to the challenges of ever-intensifying military, political and economic competition among nation-states. At the same time, formation of central bureaucratic states took place in environments of commercial or market expansion. Establishment of the domination of central bureaucracies implied that they reconciled, eliminated and refashioned diverse interests: in Gramscian terms they became sites for hegemony-building. A number of the chapters in the volume show that different administrative practices, including administrative rulings and regulations in addition to registration and surveying practices, were locations for the politics of mediation, exclusion and refashioning in which the hegemony of central bureaucracies was subject to continuous negotiation and renegotiation.

In sum, the present volume presents a picture of modernity – referring to social realities constituted through administrative practices of central bureaucratic states in historical environments of inter-state competition and commercial expansion – not only as shared but also as political and as contested and, therefore, as historically contingent. Chapters in this volume dealing with different world regions describe the multiple trajectories of modernity rooted in the political processes involving diverse social groups and individuals. In this sense, it may become possible to speak of shared modernities rather than a shared modernity.

This volume evolved over a period of nearly six years. Its lengthy development is partly explicable by the fact that these years coincided with a particularly nomadic phase in the life of its editor. As a result, multiple institutions and individuals, wittingly or unwittingly, contributed to the final product. I would like to take this opportunity to acknowledge my debt at least to some of them. The original idea for the volume was conceived in the workshops organised within the framework of the 'Individual and Society in the Mediterranean Muslim World' project of the ESF. I am grateful to the participants at the meetings held at the Middle East Technical University in Ankara in December 1996 and in Istanbul in August 1998 for the stimulating discussions, especially to Alain Pottage for his inspiration and warm friendship; to Robert Ilbert, who chaired the ESF ISMM project, and to Randi Deguilhem, who chairs the publication series of the project, for their unceasing support through the various crises which the volume underwent. A particular source of inspiration, both for my own understanding of property, state and law and for the input that these represented in this volume was the year that I spent as a fellow at the Wissenschaftskolleg in Berlin during 1997/98. I would like to express my deepest appreciation and thanks to my friends and colleagues at the Kolleg, especially to Eberhard Schmidt-Assmann, Peter Behrens, Eric Jones, Jürgen Kocka, Stephan Leibfried and Ekkehart Schlicht for very stimulating and often heated exchanges on 'property'.

To Roger Owen I owe a particular debt of gratitude for his incisive reading of the final draft and suggestions for revisions, but more importantly for his unwavering support and critical engagement in this project and many others throughout the years.

Finally, one institution and its rector contributed greatly, both tangibly and intangibly, to this volume: I thank Yehuda Elkana, rector of the Central European University in Budapest, whose intellectual support, warm friendship and social grace made academic life bearable in the last couple of years.

Budapest, 2003

Contributors

ELVAN GÜLÖKSÜZ received her PhD in city and regional planning from the Middle East Technical University, Ankara. She currently teaches in the Department of Humanities and Social Sciences at Istanbul Technical University. Her fields of research include urban policy and planning with a focus on property rights.

HURI İSLAMOĞLU has taught at the Middle Eastern Technical University, Ankara, the University of California, Berkeley and New York University. She currently teaches at Bogazici University, Istanbul, and at the Central European University, Budapest. Her publications include *State and Peasant in the Ottoman Empire* (1994); as editor, *Ottoman Empire and the World Economy* (1987); and recently, as co-editor with Peter Perdue, a special issue of the *Journal of Early Modern History* (2001) on 'Shared Histories of Modernity in China and the Ottoman Empire'.

MARK LEVINE teaches at the University of California, Irvine. He was a Mellon Postdoctoral Fellow at the Society for the Humanities and the Department of History at Cornell University and a Jean Monnet Fellow at the Robert Schuman Centre of the European University Institute in Florence. His publications include: 'The "New–Old Jaffa": Tourism, Gentrification, and the Battle for Tel Aviv's Arab Neighborhood', in Nezar Al-Sayyad (ed.), *Global Norms/Urban Forms: On the Manufacture and Consumption of Traditions in the Built Environment* (forthcoming); 'Conquest Through Town-Planning: The Case of Tel-Aviv, 1921–48', *Journal of Palestine Studies*, 27/4 (1998); 'A Nation from the Sands? Architecture, Planning and the Evolution of National Identities in Jaffa and Tel Aviv, 1880–1948', *National Identities*, 1/1 (1998); 'The Discourses of Development in Mandate Palestine', *Arab Studies Quarterly*, Winter 1995; *Overthrowing Geography: Jaffa, Tel Aviv and the Struggle for Palestine* (2004); *Why They Don't Hate Us: From Culture Wars to Culture Jamming in the Age of Globalization* (tentative title) forthcoming (2004).

MARTHA MUNDY grew up in New York City. She studied Greek, Latin, Arabic and geography before completing doctoral work under the supervision of Jack Goody at the University of Cambridge. She has taught history at UCLA and anthropology at Yarmouk University, the American University of Beirut, Université Lyon 2 Lumière and the London School of Economics. Her publications include 'The family, inheritance and Islam: a re-examination of the sociology of fara'id law', in A. al-Azmeh (ed.), *Islamic Law: Social and Historical Contexts* (1988) and *Domestic Government: Kinship, Community and Polity in North Yemen* (1995). The article published in this volume forms part of a research project on 'Property, family and administration: an historical anthropology of Islamic jurisprudence and the modern Ottoman state'.

PETER C. PERDUE is the T.T. and Wei Fong Chao Professor of Asian Civilisations at MIT. His PhD (1981) is from Harvard University in the fields of history and East Asian languages. He is the author of *Exhausting the Earth: State and Peasant in Hunan 1500–1850A.D.* (1987) and several articles, including: 'The Qing State and the Gansu Grain Market, 1739–1864' (1992); 'Technological Determinism in Agriculture' (1994); 'Military Mobilization in 17th and 18th century China, Russia, and Mongolia' (1996) and 'Boundaries, Maps, and Mobile People: The Chinese, Russian, and Mongolian Empires in Early Modern Central Eurasia' (1998). His research interests lie in modern Chinese and Japanese social and economic history. His forthcoming book from Harvard University Press examines the Qing Dynasty conquest of Central Eurasia from 1600–1800AD.

ALAIN POTTAGE teaches law and social theory at the London School of Economics.

RICHARD SAUMAREZ SMITH studied at the University of Cambridge and at the Delhi School of Economics. His doctoral research undertook the reconstruction of agrarian relations in a contiguous group of villages in the Punjab from the first nineteenth-century land registers in order to analyse critically the British system of land registration and its construction of knowledge about Indian society. He is the author of *Rule by*

Records: Land Registration and Village Custom in Early British Panjab (1996). He has done parallel research with Martha Mundy on late Ottoman administration and village systems in north Jordan. He teaches at the American University of Beirut.

DAVID WASHBROOK (MA, PhD, Cantab.) was educated at Trinity College, Cambridge, where he was also a research fellow. He has taught at the University of Pennsylvania, Warwick University and Harvard University and is presently the Reader in Modern South Asian History at Oxford University and a Professorial Fellow of St Antony's College. His principal interests lie in the history of South India between the eighteenth and twentieth centuries. He has published *The Emergence of Provincial Politics: the Madras Presidency 1870–1920* (1976) and, with C. Baker, *South India: Political Institutions and Political Change* (1975). He has contributed extensively to learned journals and essay collections.

Part One

CHAPTER 1

Towards a Political Economy of Legal and Administrative Constitutions of Individual Property

Huri İslamoğlu

The idea for this volume germinated within the intellectual climate of the 1980s and 1990s, which was suffused with the experience and conceptualisations of the expansion of world-wide market activity, including the formation of market societies in the former socialist regions of Eastern Europe and the former Soviet Union. The most dramatic and visible aspect of market expansion has been the introduction of private property in the former socialist world, as well as changes in property relations in both developed and less developed countries evidenced by the privatisation of public-sector enterprises, tax cuts and de-regulation measures. The experience of the new market order meant a 'world turned upside down', depriving many of their sources of livelihood, and for those able to enjoy the blessings of the new order signalling new ways of negotiating their existence, a new kind of politics.

Yet the new market order is premised on a rejection and demonisation of politics and the identification of the political with activities of central bureaucratic states, including taxation, protectionist tariffs and social welfare programmes, all of which present-day market advocates view as impediments to the self-regulation of markets in labour, capital and commodities. Adopting an individualistic/naturalistic understanding of the market closely akin to Smithian formulations of the eighteenth-century political economy, this perspective argues that if individuals, unimpeded by privilege and state regulation, were allowed to act with their self-interest in mind, markets could be trusted to allocate resources in the form of wages, rents and profits.[1] State regulatory practices, in preventing markets from doing their job of allocating resources efficiently, impinge on private property rights of individuals, which include full access to the use of their income not limited by taxes, and of their labour power not restricted by work hours or by downward limits on wage levels in the form of a minimum wage. The outcome, according to market advocates, is that self-interested individuals cannot optimise their gains and, as a result, production and economic growth falters. Thus, economic growth presupposes the banishment of the state from the autonomous domain of the market or the economy; the state, in turn, is assigned the role of watching over society, i.e., the domain of exchange activity.

From the liberal-market perspectives of both the nineteenth and late twentieth centuries, the ability of individuals to optimise their gains rests on the fact that individual freedoms and rights, especially those relating to private property, are assured. At this point, the understanding of a self-regulating market society becomes inextricably linked to a certain understanding of the 'rule of law' which refers to a definition of individual rights and freedoms in terms of general laws. The generality of law is expected to shield universal rights and freedoms from the laws of the state. The latter, it is argued, in their particularistic thrust, are protective of special interests as opposed to the 'general' interests of individuals engaged in market transactions. The general formulations of rights and freedoms in law provide certainty and predictability in market transactions, while institutional autonomy ascribed to law imparts a sanctity to the general formulations.

Historically, however, the development of market societies has been inextricably linked to the formation of central bureaucratic states and to orderings of social reality that developed in the context of power configurations which these states represented. That is, notwithstanding passionate pleas on the part of market ideologues for self-regulation and self-creation, markets were made through the legal and administrative practices of centralised states throughout the nineteenth and twentieth centuries. The demands of market actors for generality and uniformity were subsumed in the struggles of central bureaucracies to achieve generality and uniformity in administrative practice. The latter amounted to an assertion of the general claims of central governments, most notably in relation to taxation, to the exclusion of multiple particularistic claims of other groups, and the establishment of the hegemony of the centre. This was especially the case in relation to individual property in land which, by eliminating multiple claims on revenues and use of land, rendered land an 'object' of state taxation, as well as of exchange in the market. Similarly, notwithstanding claims to autonomy, throughout the nineteenth and twentieth centuries, courts of law represented a highly contested domain whose autonomy was largely dependent on power configurations in historical environments where the formation of centralised states coincided with the development of market relations.[2]

However, present-day market society cannot count on central bureaucratic states as 'makers' of markets. This is primarily because power configurations shifted to exclude central bureaucracies from their hegemonic position in favour of groups representing capitalist enterprise. Struggle for a new hegemony also implies the exclusion from the 'politics of the market' of groups, most notably workers and peasants, formerly included in the 'politics of central states'. The 'makers' of present-day market society target the 'politics of central states' and look to governing bodies outside central bureaucratic administrations. At the same time, 'makers' of the market are unable to rely on parliaments for general and unequivocal formulations of market rules, as these bodies are no longer dominated by the propertied middle classes but represent multitudes of interests, including workers or environmentalists who seek to place limits on private-property rights. As a result, there is an increasing reliance on courts of law and on jurists in the governing of the market; these, however, tend to govern through appeals to natural law systems, as evidenced by the practice of the European Court of Justice.[3] Parallel to what might be termed the governmentalisation of the judicial process is the tendency to make law into a 'technique of rule', especially in the post-socialist world and the developing regions of Asia, Africa and Latin America, where there is no historical institutional commitment to the rule of law or where courts or judges cannot be trusted with the business of the market. In these instances, ready-made packages of general rules defining individual rights and freedoms are handed over to governmental bodies to be implemented in new market environments.[4]

Casting of law as a 'technique of rule' coincides with a new statism,[5] largely inspired by the new institutionalism which, pointing to imperfections in the allocation of resources on the part of the markets, sees central administrations as agents enabling the institutions – most importantly private property – that would eliminate those imperfections and achieve economic efficiency and growth. This understanding has become salient since the 1990s, when the actual and arduous tasks of creating market societies in the former socialist regions and of reforming the existing ones in the developing world led to a dampening of the earlier market euphoria. Institutionalism was also responding to the successes registered by state-directed economies in East Asia. On the one hand, the notion of the state as enabler of market activity differs from that of orthodox market advocates who view the state as a disabler. On the other hand, the two understandings concur in situating the state outside the economy and in isolating the economy from politics.

Most significantly, the institutionalist perspective imbues the state with an autonomy and an objectivity; in doing so, it reduces the state to a reservoir of techniques which includes law and which is instrumental in achieving the efficiency that markets cannot achieve by themselves.[6] Focusing on the decisions of maximising individuals as determinants of market activity, and by pointing out the transaction costs resulting from the imperfect allocation of resources in the markets, the institutionalist perspective distances itself from naturalistic conceptions of self-regulating markets. But it does so without problematising the imperfections or the costs incurred from these imperfections. What institutionalists characterise as transaction costs may be described as confrontations, resistance, negotiations or deliberations among groups or individuals when confronted with a social reality premised on market interests. That is, transaction costs may point to the politics of the market or property in any given environment. In that sense, attempts at removing transaction costs amount to attempts at transcending politics and abstracting the market, state and law from politics or from power relations that are constitutive of them.

Present-day understandings of the market, law and state as idealised and absolutised abstractions form the substance of 'reform' packages, be it those of the IMF and the World Bank or the Maastricht criteria; they are part of liberalisation projects articulated independently of centralised bureaucratic states. While the evangelical tone appears universalistic, the market rhetoric has a particularly shrill ring of a 'civilising mission' when non-European societies are addressed. In this respect and in its substance, liberal discourse as it has taken shape during the late twentieth and early twenty-first century harks back to a self-understanding of the European middle classes in the latter part of the nineteenth century.

This liberal self-understanding also viewed the separation of state and society as a precondition for economic growth; it assigned the role of sentinel to the state and saw the guarantees for the order of the market in the rule of law or *Rechtsstaat* (rule-of-law state). The latter promised equality of all before general laws and upheld the sanctity of private property. Both present-day and nineteenth-century liberalisms place law and the state in the service of the market and instrumentalise them to its purposes. Thus, while the state is to watch over or facilitate what existed independently of it, positive law is assumed to represent or formalise what had taken place in the society or the economy. There is, however, a difference between the earlier and present-day rule-of-law formulations, possibly deriving from the difference in the relative leverage of central administrations in the two periods. During the late twentieth century, there appears to have been less emphasis on the law's autonomy or its institutional insularity and sanctity as a way of affording protection to market activity from the state and its particularistic definitions of privilege. What is stressed is the law's proximity to administration, referred to as governance, and its technical insularity. This approximation of law to governance in late twentieth-century rule of law formulations, however, points to a tendency towards a blurring of the earlier distinction between public and private law and towards appropriations of what had been the domain of the central bureaucracy by agencies of private law or the courts. By contrast, bifurcation of law into private and public law is central to nineteenth-century *Rechtsstaat* formulations; it consecrates the oppositional relation between state and society. Private law, referring to the law of contracts (with definitions of legal subjects and objects) and formulations of private property in civil codes, is perceived as a formalisation of what takes place in society or the sphere of exchange, thus making possible certainty and predictability in market transactions.[7] Public law defines administrative rules and procedures; most importantly, from a liberal perspective, it derives the rules of conduct of the state from general norms and, in so doing, subjects the state to the rule of law, which, imbued with an objectivity and institutional insularity and sanctity, stands apart from the domains of both policing and of exchange.

Private property, or individual ownership, has been central to liberal understandings of separations/autonomies and of objectifications of the market and of law. From a liberal perspective, private property belongs to the societal domain. Naturalistic understandings of its origins prevail, while commercial impulses are assumed to motivate the individual to remove all obstacles to his/her enjoyment of his/her property or to exchanging that property, including labour power and land, in the market.[8] Hence, property, assumed to be natural, is individual and absolute; a property relation is represented as between a person and a 'thing' which he or she owns. In the nineteenth century private law formalised this relation,[9] and in so doing it was assumed to have 'objectified' what had already taken place in society or what market activity had helped recover from nature.

The contributions to this volume challenge the paradigm of autonomies and separations in relation to the formation of private property in land. Countering the liberal argument, they reject the contention that private property belongs to the domain of society. Nor do they subscribe to a statist perspective which, pointing to the importance of the state's role in steering the economy and enabling its institutions, ascribes an autonomy and technicality to the state that sets it apart from society. Market liberalism and its statist/institutionalist critique concur in their evasion of politics. By contrast, authors in this volume reject the separation of state and society (some more self-consciously than others) and, in doing so, situate the formation of private property in land as neither within the state domain nor within society, but within power relations which characterised the formation of central administrative states. Chapters in part one address the formation of private property in different regions of the world during the nineteenth and twentieth centuries and the politics of property in relation to the power configurations which described the modern state. The substance of such politics comprised the struggles and confrontations among different actors, including administrative ones, for control over the use as well as the revenue of the land.

The perception of property as a set of power relations and not as a natural state to be freed from these relations reflects to a degree the Marxist perspective, which also rejects objectification of property in nature, in exchange or in law, and points rather towards politics of property, pitting individual ownership claims against multiple claims which formerly constituted property relations.[10] However, this perspective, assuming the separation of state and society, views the development of private property as an outcome of struggles waged in society among classes, and the state, its administrative practices and law as superstructures that rubber-stamp the outcome of these struggles. By contrast, chapters in part two subscribe to an understanding of administrative constitutions of social reality and show the ways in which individual property was constituted through state practices, including law, land registration and cadastral mapping, as well as through urban planning registration. The perspectives of individual chapters vary, however, as to the nature of the politics involved in the constitution of property, ranging from the politics of mastery – subjecting land or property to the oversight of the central state – to the politics of administrative mediation of, or responsiveness to, multiple interests.

The politics of administrative constitutions presuppose contexts of power configurations which underlie given orderings of social reality. Historically, states in various forms represent such contexts, appropriately called hegemonic contexts in the Gramscian sense, where a dominant group establishes its hegemony through exclusions, deliberations and reconciliation of different interests. Modern central states are one such historical hegemonic environment. The ability to govern or order social reality, on the other hand, refers to state power, while groups which hold that power at different times in different places imbue it with different understandings or definitions of what constitutes a state. These definitions or legitimating idioms impart a unity to multiple orderings, making it possible to talk about the state as a singular entity.[11] In fact, they provide a grid, a set of categories in relation to which different orderings or practices of governing take place, which are constitutive of social reality. Law is one such practice, just as are administrative rulings and procedures.

However, this understanding of law as governance and of social reality constituted through practices of governance departs in two inter-related ways from Foucaultian perceptions which confine governmental constitutions of social reality to its subjection to the all-embracing surveillance of the centralised leviathan.[12] The Foucaultian perspective, while transcending the liberal separation of state and society, in reducing the state to its governmental practices, abstracts these practices from the context of power relations in which they are exercised. The result is an autonomisation or objectification of the governmental state which controls or, rather, annihilates society through its constitutions of it. This spells an end to politics, an end to all possibility of persons or groups negotiating the terms of their existence. By contrast, the constitutivist perspective, partly suggested in this volume, points to the character of administrative orderings and/or of law as power fields in which multiple actors, including different state agencies, confront each other to negotiate and to contest, and thus to cast and re-cast the very terms of domination and subjugation.[13] In doing so, it internalises power relations into the very processes of constituting social reality. In the case of property relations, it is possible to speak of resistance or contestation as being part of the constitutive fabric of the very rulings which defined these relations: the struggles of different groups leave their imprint on law and administrative practice. What is suggested here is not only a politics of property and of the market, but also politics of administration, with openings and possibilities for action and initiative on the part of individuals and groups.

Thus, law and/or administrative practice do not simply formalise or rubber-stamp what has already taken place in the autonomous and separate domain of the economy or society. Instead, they represent power fields in which property is constituted. As such, it is possible to speak about the socially and politically constituted character of property. At the same time, in the power fields represented by law and/or administrative orderings, the hegemony of groups which hold state power is negotiated, cast and recast in the course of negotiations. In this sense, it is not possible to view administration or administrative orderings simply as practices of surveillance or of control, with the agent of control mystified and concealed through the metaphor of Panopticon. Nor is it possible to speak of a separation or an autonomy of the state. Put differently, the state refers here to a context of power relations; it represents a hegemonic environment in which a group or groups, through persuasion and through use of force, establishes domination over others. The state also refers to a system of orderings of social reality; the different orderings are constitutive of that reality and are domains where hegemony is continuously deliberated.[14]

The emphasis on constitutions of private property and market relations in historical environments of power relations also points to possibilities of its constitution in hegemonic environments where central states are no longer dominant power actors. Since the late twentieth century, there is indeed a tendency in the direction of 'freeing' the constitution of property and of the market from an environment of politics that focused on central bureaucratic states and relocating their constitution in political environments (or contexts of power relations) where actors other than central bureaucracies, most importantly capitalist entrepreneurs, prevail. This should not mean an end of politics, as we are often told, but simply another kind of politics which goes into the making of property and of market relations.

Discussions of the formation of private property in land in this volume pertaining to an earlier period, however, indicate that this development was part of the process of the formation of centralised states; that is the politics of property was inseparable from the politics of central administration. Three concerns that were central to the process of state centralisation can be said to have motivated the administrative constitutions of individual ownership. The first concern relates to fiscality or the channelling of all tax revenues to the coffers of central administrations and the elimination of revenue claims of former ruling groups. Individual ownership recast property relations in land in terms of the singular claim of the central state on tax revenues and in terms of the absolute claim to access by the owner to the exclusion of multiple claims to land use. This enabled the appropriation of tax revenues by the central administration not solely through its elimination of other claimants to taxes, but also through its simplification of multiple claims to land use facilitating central administration's access to revenues.[15]

Individual ownership was also part of a productionist concern on the part of central administrative states. Since the sixteenth century, centralised states developed within the context of inter-state competition and of increasingly limited territorial space for individual states to expand. State centralisation was not limited to the European continent: in non-European areas such as China and India it was interrupted only in the late eighteenth and early nineteenth centuries through local resistance and/or colonial interventions. In India, it was resumed under British colonial rule, whereas in the Ottoman Empire, responding to the exigencies of European inter-state competition, centralisation led to a radical transformation of the state. In those regions of the Ottoman Empire which subsequently came under European colonisation, colonial administrations continued with the centralisation measures which the Ottoman government had introduced earlier, for example, in Palestine. State centralisation also coincided with commercial expansion, to which it contributed significantly, as was the case with European colonial expansion. On the other hand, given the tendencies for widespread commercialisation in both agriculture and industry, responding to population growth as well as to external demand, individual states no longer saw the generation of wealth simply in terms of extensive measures. These had included territorial conquests, which enabled access to new sources of revenue as well as appropriations of resources controlled by rival political groups within individual territories.[16] Beginning in the eighteenth century, taxation came to be perceived in more intensive terms, that is those of the central administration's regulation or, more appropriately, its constitution of economic activity to increase productive capacity, which would result in an expansion of taxable incomes. French physiocratic convictions germinated as part of this mental climate. The belief that land was the chief source of value, that it was an economic asset or a factor of production seems, in Europe and elsewhere, to have stimulated attempts at cadastral mapping as the scientific basis for the improvement of this most important asset[17] and for the assessment of its taxes (in this volume, this is treated by Richard Saumarez Smith and Huri İslamoğlu). This was coupled with orderings of property relations on land in terms of individual rights, furthered by the understanding that individual ownership was essential for economic growth in that only those who controlled surplus production could be expected to invest in capital improvements.[18] This was the juncture at which productionist concerns of central administrations converged with concerns of commercial groups for exchangeability of land in the market, which individual property facilitated.

In addition, individual ownership was formed in the process of the mediation of different interests on the part of centralised states. Critiques of political economy in the late eighteenth and early nineteenth centuries were concerned about the effects of unconstrained market activity on society. From the perspective of English utilitarians, most notably Jeremy Bentham (1748–1832),[19] as well as German social economists, including Lorenz von Stein (1815–90),[20] unless market society was actively 'constituted' there was a danger of its disintegrating into an arena of self-interest and divisiveness with a potential for self-destruction. As such, it was not enough simply to remove the obstacles of obsolete privilege and the restrictive policies of mercantilism of the *ancien* state. For Bentham, the new economic order required positive state intervention; government was inseparable from an 'art of directing the national industry to purposes to which it may be directed with greatest advantage'.[21] Von Stein identified the 'social problem' as the main obstacle to economic progress or market development; he proposed that injustices and inequalities which that development generated be eliminated through the state's administrative activity. Thus, market society represented an outcome of collective struggles and clashes among divergent interests that were mediated through the state's administrative practices, so that for von Stein, as for Bentham, the state was not the *Rechtsstaat* that stood outside civil society or the economy, but the *Sozialstaat* (social state), representing processes whereby the economy was continuously formed and re-formed. At the same time, market society, its actors, its activities and the economic relations that characterised it were viewed as being inseparable from their legal and administrative formulations. Market society entailed the creation of legal and administrative entities, including trade unions, corporations, the family and the household, as well as of voluntary and charitable associations which, while autonomous from the state, remained within the bounds of its administrative–legal vision.[22] Yet, the state, 'objectified' in its administrative and legal practices, was understood to stand apart from civil society and the economy and to mediate divergent interests and needs. Hence, historically, the success of market society was predicated upon the abilities of central governments to mediate by means of diverse governmental practices as broad a range of interests as possible, for example those of workers, employers, farmers, landowners, paupers, pensioners and the unemployed.[23] The legitimacy and responsibility of centralised administrative states lay in this ability to mediate as well as their ability to steer society and the economy in international competition. The mediational concern, in turn, accounted for a responsiveness of the administration which indeed contradicts the conception of its autonomy both in the Foucaultian sense and in the sense of the technicist states of present-day institutionalism. With respect to property and in line with this thinking, Bentham referred to property as an expectation on the part of individuals which developed in environments of exchange and was to be realised in law, which, for him, was inseparable from administration.[24] Thus, by responding to expectations, the administration sought to achieve the utilitarian ideal of 'the greatest happiness of the greatest number'.

Finally, a European self-understanding of social reality in terms of autonomies/separations/objectifications has pervaded vocabularies of European domination over non-European areas since the nineteenth century. These vocabularies represent collusions of the dichotomous and oppositional perception of social reality with a spatial bifurcation of Europe or the West and non-Europe and the East. Thus, European history is cast as the privileged realm of exchange or of market, of private property, of the circumscribed state presence and of the rule of law. Non-European history, by contrast, describes a sphere of stunted commercial development or economic stagnation, of despotic states and of the absence of the rule of law. The histories of the Ottoman Empire, of China and of Mughal India have long been fashioned in the image of the East, in which state intervention in society or the economy, most dramatically manifested in the form of state ownership of land, was understood to be a feature of Asian despotism and has been held responsible for stunted market activity, for the inability of private property to develop, and for the consequent absences of commercial classes, of bourgeois revolutions, of liberal constitutional states and of the rule of law.[25]

All but one of the chapters in this volume address the issue of the formation of individual ownership in non-European societies, in China, India, the Ottoman Empire and modern Turkey. All but the two chapters by Alain Pottage and Elvan Gülöksüz address the high drama of absences and presences as this is played out in relation to binary conceptions of the histories of the East and West. However, instead of producing revisionist histories of these regions premised on a defensive posture of 'if Europe had it, Asia also did', the authors seek to problematise the arguments about market society, property, law and state which a bifurcated conception of world history assumes. In particular, setting aside the idealised and essentialist images about East and West, the chapters addressing the development of individual ownership in non-European societies do so in the context of power relations and idioms of rule which characterised the different societies.

This emphasis on the historical specificity of the development of individual ownership is not simply an exercise in multiplying discrete histories of property relations. The cases presented here point to a shared history of formation of individual ownership in land in both the East and the West. In the context of power relations which characterised the nineteenth century, that history was inseparable from a shared history of central administrative states that developed in environments of interstate competition and commercial expansion.

These states and their orderings of social or property relations represented a rupture with what had gone before. In fact, the practices of central administrative states and the social realities they set out to conjure were aspects of modernity which were universally shared and which transcended the bifurcation of East and West. As such, one can speak of constitutions of individual property in different areas as part of the project of constituting modernity.

The chapters in part one examine the constitutions of landed property in relation to power relations which characterised the formation of central administrative states in India, the Ottoman Empire and British Palestine in the nineteenth and twentieth centuries. Chapters in this section challenge the two main assumptions of the liberal creed. First, chapters dealing with both colonial and non-colonial empires question the assumption that state ownership in land impedes the development of individual property as well as security of tenure. They argue that the reassertion of state ownership in this period was a precondition for the administrative and legal constitution of individual ownership. It meant the establishment of the control of the central bureaucracy over land and signalled an elimination of multiple claims to land revenues and the establishment of the singular taxation claim of the central state over the income or property of the individual owner. Second, these chapters question the understanding that courts of law enjoying autonomy were privileged domains for the formulation of individual or private property rights. They analyse different contexts of power relations in which courts and central governments overlapped and/or stood in tension with each other in the formulation of individual ownership. Moreover, the autonomy of courts varied greatly in different historical contexts of power relations, underlining the historically contingent character of such autonomy, absolutised in the *Rechtsstaat*.[26]

Peter Perdue questions the ingrained perceptions in European social theory that in China state ownership in land and the absence of rule of law or normative formal categories of law prevented the development of market capitalism, above all by impeding the security of tenure in land. Perdue first underlines the fact that individual tenure was in no way insecure in Qing China. Chinese law provided security in terms of the 'two lords to one field' system, whereby landlords had permanent access to topsoil rights as long as they paid taxes to the state; tenants acquired usufruct or subsoil rights after payment of a fixed rent. 'Two lords to one field' provided incentive for economic investment, as did any other system of tenant security in Europe. As importantly, this system was consecrated in a highly developed body of contractual law transacted at the magistrates' courts. Perdue shows that magistrates' courts were part of a hierarchy of courts, not simply arenas for negotiations of local customary law or practice. China had a well-established appeals system extending from the locality to the emperor, procedures for processing cases and for amending statutes, reasoning by analogy, and, most significantly, rules that were uniform and did not vary from locality to locality. Perdue challenges the European perception of a division between bureaucratic and customary 'primitive' law in China, examining the ways in which the two types of law interpenetrated, and showing that bureaucratic law, in many instances, represented the recasting of custom. At the same time, he draws attention to the historically contingent character of law, whereby legal formulations seeking to achieve security of tenure varied with the social and political environment. In the case of Qing China, Perdue advises that before establishing absence or presence of security of tenure or other sacred representations of European modernity, one must look beyond the normative legal categories and consider how law constituted property relations on the ground in different contexts.

David Washbrook addresses the politics of property rights in South India, beginning in the eighteenth century, and analyses the historically contingent character of the development of individual ownership in this region. In doing so, he counters the liberal contention that state ownership in land under Mughal rule in India impeded the development of private property rights in land, and that these rights were only introduced under British rule. Focusing on the different contexts of power relations during the eighteenth and nineteenth centuries in South India, Washbrook shows that the presence or absence of private property rights in land was not essential to any given context of rule, British or Indian. Washbrook first notes (as does LeVine in relation to Palestine) that while British rule followed local rules and customs, these rules and customs were continuously reinvented in accordance with the changing objectives of the British government in different regions at different time periods. Thus, in the eighteenth century the colonial government of the East India Company, claiming to restore the Hindu Golden Age, reconstituted the communal rights and privileges of the old landed gentry. This policy, primarily effected through the courts of law, reversed the effects of commercialisation in agriculture which had made dents in communal rights and had encouraged a market in rights in land revenues that caused land to be exchanged in a commodity-like manner. In this early period, British policy was also countering centralisation attempts on the part of Indian states directed towards undermining the privileges of the old gentry, so that permanent settlement in South India – far from encouraging a commercial order – endowed landholding rights to old elite families to protect them from the central states or the sultanates. In fact, the policies of the British colonial government, coupled with a waning of Indian trade in textiles in the early nineteenth century, might have been responsible for stagnation and de-commercialisation with respect to property rights in land.

Beginning in 1810 with the successes registered against centralising Indian states and the mounting requirement for tax revenues, there was a shift in British policy to the *ryotwari* system that assumed the sovereign's ownership of all lands, which the sovereign then leased to holders of individual possession rights. Thus, state ownership in land allowed individual holdings to be assigned to every peasant who could occupy the land and who was responsible for payment of taxes to the central state. It meant a radical shift in the politics of property in South India, from one of deliberations of revenue and communal rights to one of the elimination of those rights (or of 'non-real' property) and the constitution of 'real' property or physical property as a measured, fixed and bounded entity which was an object of state taxation. As the chapter by Richard Saumarez Smith shows, cadastral mapping and land registration had been central to this process. It meant a shift in the location of the constitution of property rights from the courts of law to central administration, to which former rights holders had to adjust.

Mark LeVine's chapter also studies the constitutions of individual ownership in land under British rule, in this case in Palestine. LeVine focuses on those aspects of the politics of property which relate to the development of Tel Aviv from its beginning as a suburb of the Palestinian town of Jaffa into an urban centre. First, emphasising the continuity in land legislation between the Ottoman period and under the British Mandate, LeVine challenges liberal perceptions which claim that Ottoman rule impeded the development of market activity and private property. Starting with the premise that the introduction of individual ownership was part of the project of the formation of central bureaucratic modern states, with their concern to monopolise all taxes from the land, LeVine sees the Ottoman and British Mandate governments as having engaged in a similar effort to establish their control over land and extract its revenues. State ownership in land, reformulated in the Ottoman Land Code of 1858, was central to this effort; it enabled both the Ottoman and the British governments to increase their revenues through sale of state lands to individual owners, as well as to establish more direct access to land taxes with the elimination of multiple claims to revenues. Moreover, LeVine shows that the Mandate government expanded the scope of state ownership in land to include urban lands and to establish tighter control over unclaimed or communal and public lands by opening them to state allocation.

Yet the Ottoman and British governments represented different contexts of power relations, and thus they differed in their approaches to the politics of property, which were inextricably linked to Jewish migration to Palestine. Under Ottoman rule, the politics of property represented multiple negotiations of the precepts of the Land Code in ways which sought to stem the tide of Jewish land purchases and to prevent dispossession on the part of the indigenous population. Moreover, under the Ottoman administration, the extent of state-owned lands (*miri*) was limited by the presence of *mülk* (freehold) and *vakıf* (religious foundation) lands, which opposed their claims to revenues from these lands against the claims of the central government. The presence of multiple categories of land corresponding to multiple claims, however, created problems in land transfers to the new Jewish settlers. The Mandate government appears to have been more successful in doing away with multiple categories of land and in generalising state lands. This success no doubt facilitated the transfer of land to Jewish immigrants. Yet the Land Transfer Ordinance of 1920, which prevented transfers of immovable property to protect small landowners and tenants from dispossession in an effort to put an end to land speculation, indicates that political constraints on the actions of the Mandate government prevented unequivocal support of Jewish immigration.

LeVine argues that land surveying and town planning were more effective than land legislation in constituting individual ownership and in facilitating Jewish purchase of land. Surveys set out to establish 'proper settlement rights' to land by defining the boundaries of plots, the categories of tenure and of registrable rights to plots of land which were then to be recorded in land registers. LeVine points to the effects of the 'settlement', which encouraged fragmentation and dispossession of landholdings as well as social dislocation, and he mentions the revolts of the Arab population in response to it. Finally, town planning, together with security concerns following the Arab revolts, provided the prime justifications for Jewish reclamation of lands. Under the Mandate, decisions regarding building of roads on rural lands and reclamation of rural land for urban use were increasingly removed from the jurisdiction of the Jaffa municipal council and became part of the jurisdiction of the High Commissioner. This was a shift in the politics of property which, LeVine suggests, tilted the balance towards Jewish reclamation of land for urban use.

The chapters in part two address the questions of law, administrative processes and/or techniques through which individual property was constituted. Chapters by Saumarez Smith, Pottage and Mundy focus on land registration and/or cadastral mapping, which they either perceive as tools to achieve governmental mastery by affixing the object of mastery spatially or, allowing the historically contingent character of these practices, they focus on the variability of social and political expectations which administrative technique seeks to capture. The final two chapters, by Gülöksüz and İslamoğlu, describe the constitutions of individual property through law and land-*cum*-income surveys, identifying law and surveys as arenas where the politics of property were waged.

Richard Saumarez Smith's chapter focuses on cadastral mapping in British India in the 1820s as a process through which land was constituted as individualised parcels that were fixed and measured in standard measurements, forming the basis for an assessment of tax revenues. Field maps which were constitutive of individual plots represented abstractions from particular contexts of the village or the region. Saumarez Smith indicates that prior to the introduction of field maps, revenue demand was set for a village on the basis of information provided by villagers, and distribution of taxes within the village was subject to negotiation among villagers. Cadastral mapping extended the definition of taxable land to the entire territory beyond the village; its justification rested on its claim of scientific accuracy in taxation, which was to be achieved on the basis of standardised measurements and recording procedures. In the nineteenth-century world of administration such scientific accuracy, Saumarez Smith argues, held the promise of efficiency and prosperity for the agricultural economy.

Saumarez Smith sees the administration of revenues through representations on a map as a form of government which allowed administrators to distance themselves from particularities, that is to acquire a 'bird's-eye view' which, in the case of British rule in India, made it possible to invent India out of multitudes of diverse regions and localities. Administrators ruled using reports which they were able to concoct on the basis of representations provided by statistical information distilled in maps. He contrasts this with another form of government: rule by record, which he identifies with Ottoman Syria during the latter part of the nineteenth century. In the Ottoman case, individual ownership or possession rights introduced by the Ottoman Land Code of 1858 were constituted through the registration of title. For Saumarez Smith, the registration process in this context relied heavily on face-to-face interactions in a given locality whereby different actors deliberated the amount of land registered in the name of an individual. Thus, land registration and the property relations it engendered were rooted in local power relations, without reference to the standard measurements of land represented on a map that in itself signified power relations which stood outside localities and which belonged to the domain of the empire.

Saumarez Smith views mapping as a technology of power, a technique of establishing control which enabled what Pottage calls a perspectival mastery, whereby the map is part of the process related to disciplining by the empire, of the normalisation of imperial fiscal ambitions. Here Saumarez Smith's analysis leans towards what has become a Foucaultian orthodoxy in studies of cadastral mapping and land registration, and which explains the introduction of these practices in terms of the exercise of governmental power.

Alain Pottage's chapter challenges the instrumentalisation of modern cadastral mapping and land registration in the service of administrative programmes in pursuit of governmental mastery or control. Such instrumentalisation expects the map or the registration to achieve a spatial correspondence between the land and the rights or claims over it. Instead, Pottage describes techniques of cadastral mapping as referring to different sets of expectations on the part of different groups with interests in the land, and he argues that these techniques, in fact, constitute property. In this sense, cadastral maps represent and describe terrains (or practices of ordering or of patterning the social fabric) which are continually adapting to changing expectations. This amounts to an historicisation of, or the introduction of the temporal dimension into what have been strictly spatial understandings of cadastral mapping, which tend to focus on techniques establishing control over territory and not on techniques seeking to accommodate expectations that are variable in time.

Pottage explains the rise of the distinctively cadastral map form in England at the end of the nineteenth century by emphasising the fact that property maps which had previously identified locations under the system of conveyancing no longer responded to the practical expectations of the landed class. In the course of time, this class had diversified and called for techniques which freed property from dependence on practical local knowledge and on documents of title where validation rested on networks of reputation and confidence which had historically met the expectations of an aristocracy with stable inheritance and management practices. On the other hand, translation of topographical figures into an abstract index, implying a bureaucratisation of property, was a response to the complex problem of indexing multiple interests on land at a time when social and economic expectations were diversifying. Finally, while Saumarez Smith sees in the abstract representations of cadastral mapping a way of achieving imperial rule or mastery which claimed that accuracy of measurement ensured equitable taxation, for Pottage, the abstraction which the cadastral index provided allowed for a distancing of the bureaucratic process of title registration from the particularity which the ordinary property map represented. Such distancing, for Pottage, enabled an adaptability or a responsiveness by the administration to changing expectations.

Martha Mundy addresses the problem of administrative constitutions of individual ownership in the nineteenth-century Ottoman Empire. Like Washbrook and İslamoğlu, she situates the introduction of individual ownership within the context of the revenue requirements of a central administrative state, and sees in this form of property an opportunity for the central state to identify its subjects, their properties and their corresponding tax liabilities.

Mundy identifies local administration as the site of administrative constitutions of property where the legal or administrative *personae* meet the social and economic actors. For Mundy, a signifier of property is the granting of title, and whoever administers property rights on land becomes the determiner of the kind of property. In the Ottoman context, constitution of individual ownership entailed replacement of one type of property administrator, *sâhib-i arz*, who formerly held the right to manage revenues and issued titles to use-rights on plots of land on behalf of the *fisc*, with another type, those of representatives of the central state administration. She traces this process of replacement for the district of 'Ajlun in southern Syria between 1875 and 1918, which went through phases of village political institutions, for example elected councils, taking over the task of the former revenue managers as interlocutors between the central state and villagers, to be subsequently replaced by district and municipal councils as administrators of property.

The bureaucratisation of the registration process implied that more and more administrators were appointed from the top. While in the initial stages elected persons possessing local knowledge were included in the process of title certification, in the later stages these elected figures were either eliminated or assimilated into state administration. Thus, what Mundy refers to as politics of administration is one of subjection to a certain kind of state or a 'set of formal rules or techniques of knowledge and enunciation in hierarchically ordered institutions composed of legal *personae*'. Such subjection took place through appropriation of local knowledge by the administration. But not visible in Mundy's analysis are traces of encounters between legal local *personae* and non-legal local actors, such as the former managers of revenues, whose knowledge was superseded in the administering of property. The kind of politics to which Mundy appears to be referring aims to end all politics in the spirit of a Foucaultian governmental state, representing a transcendence of power relations.

The last two chapters emphasise the political character of the constitutions of individual property through state law and administrative practice. In doing so, they identify law and administrative practice as domains of struggle over establishing property claims, revealing a kaleidoscopic view of the politics of property, of administration and of law that is constitutive of property.

Elvan Gülöksüz's chapter studies the constitution of individual property on urban land in two districts in the city of Istanbul. These districts form part of illegal settlements which have developed in the outskirts of the city since the 1960s, when massive migration from the countryside began. Gülöksüz focuses on the politics of property in these areas as it was waged in relation to property and urban-planning laws. The central argument of the study is that these laws were constitutive of individual ownership and that they provided a context and a vocabulary in the struggle for establishing claims over land on the part of different actors. For one of the districts, which was part of the estate of a member of the Ottoman royal family, Gülöksüz identifies these actors as descendants of the original owner, whose title deeds dated back to the late nineteenth century, the state Treasury, the Ministry of Forestry, and migrants from the countryside. Gülöksüz points to the cadastral surveying of the 1940s and rural–urban migration as the factors initiating the struggle over the land of this estate. First of all, Ottoman title deeds issued for the plots on this estate represented imprecisely defined claims, largely due to the fact that the Ottoman administration, in face of resistance by landed groups, had not been able to carry out cadastral surveying of its territories (c.f. İslamoğlu's chapter in this volume). Furthermore, owners of the estate lands were forced to leave the country after the collapse of the empire, and the central treasury of the Turkish Republic took the opportunity of the cadastral survey in the 1940s to appropriate these lands. Beginning in the 1960s, migrants who had bought the land from the original owners on the basis of notary contracts not recognised by property law were contesting in the courts the claims of the state agencies.

Gülöksüz points out that new arrivals to the city were not only seeking shelter but, in an attempt to exploit the possibilities of rents from urban real estate, which became a primary form of investment in the inflationary environment of the 1970s and 1980s, fought to have the lands that they had purchased brought under the jurisdiction of urban regularisation plans, and to be recognised as urban property, thus fetching high prices. These struggles were waged in the courts, in municipal councils and in the commissions of the national parliament. In the process, property laws and urban regularisation plans were continuously cast and recast, carrying the imprint of struggles waged in relation to them. Thus, for instance, responding to pressures from electoral politics, laws were passed by the parliament redefining forest lands, making room for new arrivals. This also indicates a process whereby boundaries of the public and private were continuously being drawn and re-drawn. The urban regularisation plans were another arena of struggle. In the 1980s, the granting of autonomy to local municipalities placed the drafting of urban regularisation plans under the jurisdiction of the municipalities. In the municipal councils, these plans were fiercely negotiated to set high numerical limits for populations to be settled in a given district and to increase the number of storeys allowed for individual buildings. Gülöksüz shows that in the second district that she studied, located in the water catchment area of the Elmalı Dam (an important source for the water supply of Istanbul), the law's responsiveness to the demands of rent-seeking residents in this settlement brought another set of actors into the picture, expressing environmental concerns. These included the Istanbul Chamber of Architects and the Water and Sewage Department of the Istanbul Metropolitan Municipality.

Similarly, in Chapter 9 I address the political processes which characterised the 'makings' of individual property in the nineteenth-century Ottoman Empire, primarily in terms of the surveying and registering of landed property. I argue that nineteenth-century Ottoman land regulations and surveys recording land and agricultural resources introduced categories ordering property relations on land which were aimed at establishing the singular claim by the central bureaucratic state to tax revenues, to the exclusion of the claims of religious endowments and/or former tax-farmers. It also meant an elimination of all use claims to land, including communal claims, in favour of claims by the individual owner. The new rules and regulations, as well as the procedures, were contested and resisted. I identify the categories for classifying information included in the surveys, as well as the methods of surveying and registering landed property, and the choice of personnel responsible for gathering information and for registration, as political power fields in which different actors, including those representing the central government, struggled to realise their claims. From the perspective of the central government, the objective was to achieve legibility (in the sense of Scott), which included recording all land and resources in the possession of individuals, and the measurement of the land and resources in standard units of measurement in order to tax them effectively and equitably. Yet the achievement of that objective presupposes political processes which I characterise as concessional politics. In relation to methods of surveying and registering lands, and the choice of personnel responsible for these tasks, the politics of concession involved a trend of bureaucratisation, with central government officials assuming a central role but acting in a continual dialogue with (and responsive to) local actors, who were incorporated into the new state environment through the formation of commissions or councils on all levels of provincial administration. On the one hand, who these were varied over time in relation to changes in power relations between the central government and different local power networks. To realise its objective of knowing and thereby taxing, the central government remained, however, dependent on the flow of information from the local society. On the other hand, organisation of the 'local' around commissions or councils significantly altered its character, casting it in terms and categories of the hegemony of the central bureaucracy. Finally, concessional politics left its imprint on the nature of individual ownership which the administrative and legal practices set out to constitute. While individual ownership was defined in law, the very processes of evading central government taxation which were built into procedures for assessment of land and resources left their imprint on individual ownership in terms of imprecise definitions of the land that was owned. I attribute the apparent absence of cadastral maps in the nineteenth-century Ottoman Empire to the concessional politics of Ottoman administration, which did not allow for a standardisation of the measurement of land and its division into individual parcels. One outcome was that taxes were assessed not on the basis of plots of land, measured and parcelled, but on the basis of income from assets, including land. Similarly, the tithe – or the tax on grains and other produce which amounted to one-tenth of the value of the produce – was not replaced by an exclusive land tax, and estimates of land under cultivation were largely achieved on the basis of the produce of the land subject to the tithe.[27]

Lastly, addressing the issue of why the Ottoman government did not succeed in introducing cadastral or field maps while the British colonial government did, I suggest that the politics of administration which characterised the British and Ottoman Empires may have accounted for the difference. It may be that the Ottoman administration felt more compelled to concede to demands by those who resisted its registration measures than did the British colonial administration. In doing so, I raise the question of different legitimacy requirements of colonial and non-colonial governments in the nineteenth century, and challenge Saumarez Smith's view that differences in scale between the two empires largely accounted for the fact that the British Empire succeeded and the Ottoman Empire failed in introducing field maps.

In closing, it is important to draw attention to the implications of this volume for the writing of comparative history. As noted earlier, the volume addresses the constitutions of individual property in societies ranging from Britain to China – with India, the Ottoman Empire, Palestine and Turkey in between. It also tackles head-on understandings of comparative history since the ascendancy of European domination over much of the rest of the world in the nineteenth century, which cast world history in terms of binaries and of separations of the modern from the traditional, of the civilised from the uncivilised, and which define the 'great transformation' as the moment when the market was liberated from the shackles of feudal politics or states. This instant, most dramatically identified as the moment of modernity, is perceived as belonging to Europe. This volume suggests to the contrary that the 'great transformation', represented as one of multiple state transformations, belonged both to the West and the East. For both, it signalled re-orderings of social realities and represented radical ruptures with what had been before. The formation of centralised leviathans remained the centrepiece of the experience of worldwide modernity in the nineteenth century and most of the twentieth century. Development of individual property on land was part of the process of formation of the centralised states. On the one hand, the understanding that individual property was politically constituted through the practices of central administrations signifies a problematisation which emphasises the historically contingent character of both European and non-European developments. It calls into question the casting of world history as one of contrasting ideal images. Pottage's chapter represents such a problematisation of the history of land registration in England, while others, including Gülöksüz, LeVine, Washbrook and myself, attempt a similar exercise for non-European areas. On the other hand, examination of the orderings of social reality by central administrations, and of the categories in which these orderings were cast, underline a history that was widely shared by different world regions, cutting across the East–West divide. It points to shared but troubled histories of modernity.

Notes

1 Smith, 1974.

2 For a discussion of the case in post-revolutionary France, see Kelley and Smith, 1984, which highlights the contested character of the law's (or the courts') autonomy, pointing to a close affinity between the landed aristocracy and the judges who were responsible for the legal formulations of private property in the Civil Code. In these formulations Kelly and Smith see a juridical 'religion of property'. They go on to argue that in order to keep the lid on rural unrest arising from court rulings on landed property, the central administration had to intervene by setting up tribunals which, in turn, were responsible for deliberations on property rights on the ground.

3 See Neumann, 1990, for the very enticing idea that, in the age of liberalism in the nineteenth century, the German bourgeoisie was satisfied with the state (that is with the share that it received in legislation under Bismarck) and 'judges and jurists no longer had to appeal to a natural law system in order to fight a system of positive law which was hostile to them'. Using this idea to shed light on contemporary developments, it can perhaps be ventured that an increasingly globalising bourgeoisie may not have been satisfied with the state (that is with its share in legislative activity and its marginalisation by other groups), and that the formulation of general laws is increasingly entrusted to courts (for example the European Court of Justice) which base their formulations on natural law systems: Neumann, 1990.

4 For such instances, see Jayasuriya, 1999.

5 For the new statism, see Evans, 1997.

6 North, 1981; North, 1994.

7 For this liberal perception of law as one responding to and expediting commercial expansion, see Maine, 1920. Present-day institutionalists prefer not to get involved in private-law debates. To the extent that they are at all concerned with law, they refer to administrative rulings by the state which formalise the decisions of individuals who seek to maximise their gains in different markets. Also see North, 1981 as well as his more recent work (1994) which focuses on the state.

8 In the nineteenth century, liberal jurists, among them Maine (1920) and Bentham (1931), were highly critical of natural law formulations regarding private property. They saw the

development of private property within the historical context of commercial expansion. For them, private law represented a formalisation of that development: Bentham, 1931. The historicist perspective has recently been taken up by the new institutional economists, most notably North (1981) and Jones (1981). Both North and Jones point to the determination of private property in terms of decisions or choices made by individuals seeking to maximise their economic gains in an environment of commercial expansion. They argue that environments of commercial activity are characterised by 'market failures' or impediments (for example communal property rights) to exchange activity by individuals. Market failure implies transaction costs. Private ownership, in this context, is an institution which achieves a reduction of transaction costs and, in so doing, generates efficiency. It is an outcome of cost–benefit analysis undertaken by maximising individuals to reduce transaction costs.

9 See Cotterell (1987), who focuses on the ways that legal formulations accommodated and guaranteed inequalities implied by private ownership which excluded all claims to property except those of the individual owner. Cotterell argues that, through the separation of legal subjects and the assets that they own, the law could allow for an equality of the legal subjects while inequality becomes an attribute of the distribution of assets. This was important in view of the fact that equality of all persons before the law was a central precept of the rule-of-law formulations in the nineteenth century.

10 See also Macpherson (1978) for a discussion of the rights perspective which views property as a power relation and a bundle of rights which are formed out of these struggles. See also Singer, 1998.

11 Abrams, 1988.

12 For a discussion of Foucault's work in this context, see Gordon, 1991; Hunt and Wickham, 1994. Foucault himself was well aware of the problem of political closures implied in his conception of governmentality: Foucault, 1982.

13 For an excellent example of the constitutivist perspective which is very sensitive to the legal subtleties and which does not reduce the process to that of subjection to administrative surveillance, see Brigham, 1991; Brigham, 1996.

14 For a detailed discussion of the state from this perspective, see İslamoğlu, 2000.

15 For the administrative simplifications of the modern state, see Scott, 1998.

16 The notion of the state's generation of wealth in terms of extensive measures would also apply to mercantilistic policies.
17 Kain and Baiggent, 1996, pp.343–44.
18 Genovese-Fox, 1976, pp.113ff.
19 Bentham, 1931.
20 Pasquino, 1981.
21 Bentham, 1931.
22 Neocleous, 1996.
23 Bentham, 1931.
24 Bentham, 1931.
25 For a discussion of an East–West problematic in relation to the Middle East, see Asad, 1973; for an evaluation of the liberal as well as Marxist (Asiatic Mode of Production) treatments of Ottoman history, see İslamoğlu-Inan, 1987. In relation to China and the Ottoman Empire, see İslamoğlu and Perdue, 2001 and İslamoğlu, 2001. In the case of the Ottoman Empire, liberal historians argued that state ownership of land was the primary obstacle to the development of individual ownership rights in the Ottoman context: Baer, 1969, pp.62–78. In relation to Egypt, Kenneth Cuno, subscribing to a similar liberal reasoning, underlines the development of private property in land in the late eighteenth century in the context of commercial expansion and the weakening of controls by the Ottoman state over the economy. According to Cuno, this process was interrupted by the rise of a strong state under Mehmet Ali, which intensified state intervention in agriculture: Cuno, 1980.
26 For an excellent exercise in the relativisation of the autonomy of the courts in England in the nineteenth century, see Arthurs, 1985.
27 For a discussion of this point in relation to Ottoman agricultural statistics of 1909, 1913 and 1914, see Güran, 1997, pp.xvii–xix.

Bibliography

Abrams, Philip, 'Notes on the Difficulty of Studying the State', *Journal of Historical Sociology* 1/1, March 1988, pp. 58–89.

Arthurs, H.W., *Without the Law: Administrative Justice and Legal Pluralism in Nineteenth Century England*, Toronto, University of Toronto Press, 1985.

Asad, Talal (ed.), *Anthropology and the Colonial Encounter*, London, Ithaca Press, 1973.

Baer, Gabriel, *Studies in the Social History of Modern Egypt*, Chicago, University of Chicago Press, 1969.

Bentham, Jeremy, *The Theory of Legislation*, ed. C.K. Ogden, London, Routledge and Kegan Paul, 1931.

Brigham, John, *The Cult of the Court*, Philadelphia, Temple University Press, 1991.

– *The Constitution of Interests: Beyond the Politics of Rights*, New York, New York University Press, 1996.

Cotterell, Roger, 'Power, Property and the Law of Trusts: A Partial Agenda for Critical Legal Scholarship', in Peter Fitzpatrick and Alan Hunt (eds), *Critical Legal Studies*, Oxford, Basil Blackwell, 1987, pp. 77–90.

Cuno, Kenneth M., 'The Origins of Private Ownership of Land in Egypt: A Reappraisal', *International Journal of Middle East Studies* 12, 1980, pp. 245–75.

Evans, P. (ed.), *State–Society Synergy: Government Action and Social Capital in Development*, Berkeley, University of California Press, 1997.

Foucault, Michel, 'The Subject and Power', in Herbert L. Dreyfus and Paul Rabinow (eds), *Michel Foucault: Beyond Structuralism and Hermeneutics*, Brighton, Harvester, 1982, pp. 208–26.

Genovese-Fox, Elizabeth, *The Origins of Physiocracy: Economic Revolution and Social Order in Eighteenth Century France*, Ithaca, Cornell University Press, 1976.

Gordon, Colin, 'Governmental Rationality: An Introduction', in Graham Burchell, Colin Gordon and Peter Miller (eds), *The Foucault Effect: Studies in Governmentality*, Hemel Hempstead, Harvester, 1991, pp. 87–104.

Güran, Tevfik (ed.), *Osmanlı Dönemi Tarım İstatistikleri 1909, 1913 ve 1914*, Ankara, T.C. Başbakanlık Devlet Istatistik Enstitüsü, 1997.

Hunt, Alan and Gary Wickham (eds), *Foucault and Law: Towards a Sociology of Law as Governance*, London, Pluto Press, 1994.

İslamoğlu, Huri, 'Property as a Contested Domain: A Reevaluation of the Ottoman Land Code of 1858', in Roger Owen (ed.), *New*

Perspectives on Property and Land in the Middle East, Cambridge, MA, Harvard University Press, 2000, pp. 3–61.

– 'Modernities Compared: State Transformations and Constitutions of Property in the Qing and Ottoman Empires', *Journal of Early Modern History* 5/4, 2001, pp. 353–86.

İslamoğlu, Huri and Peter Perdue, 'Introduction', *Journal of Early Modern History* 5/4 (2001), special issue, 'Shared Histories of Modernity in China and the Ottoman Empire', pp. 271–81.

İslamoğlu-Inan, Huri, 'Introduction: Oriental Despotism in World System Perspective', in Huri İslamoğlu-Inan (ed.), *The Ottoman Empire and the World Economy*, Cambridge, Cambridge University Press, 1987, pp.1–26.

Jayasuriya, Kanishka (ed.), *Law, Capitalism and Power in Asia: The Rule of Law and Legal Institutions*, London, Routledge, 1999.

Jones, Eric L., *The European Miracle: Environments, Economics and Geopolitics in the History of Europe and Asia*, Cambridge, Cambridge University Press, 1981.

Kain, Roger J.P. and Elizabeth Baiggent, *The Cadastral Map in the Service of the State*, Chicago, University of Chicago Press, 1996.

Kelley, Donald R. and Bonnie G. Smith, 'What was Property? Legal Dimensions of the Social Question in France (1789–1848)', *Proceedings of the American Philosophical Society* 128/3 (1984), pp. 200–30.

Macpherson, C.B., 'The Meaning of Property', in C.B. Macpherson (ed.), *Property: Mainstream and Critical Positions*, Oxford, Basil Blackwell, 1978, pp. 1–14.

Maine, Henry James, *Ancient Law*, London, John Murray, 1920.

Neocleous, Mark, *Administering Civil Society: Towards a Theory of State Power*, London, Macmillan, 1996.

Neumann, F., 'The Change in the Function of Law in Modern Society', in William E. Scheuerman (ed.), *The Rule of Law under Siege: Selected Essays in Honor of Franz L. Neumann and Otto Kirschheimer*, Berkeley, University of California Press, 1990, pp. 101–41.

North, Douglass C., *Structure and Change in Economic History*, New York, Norton, 1981.

– 'Economic Performance Through Time', *American Economic Review*, June 1994, pp. 359–68.

Pasquino, P., 'Introduction to Lorenz von Stein', *Economy and Society* 10/1 (1981), pp. 1–6.

Scott, James C., *Seeing Like a State: How Certain Schemes to Improve the Human Condition Have Failed*, New Haven, Yale University Press, 1998.

Singer, Joseph W., 'Property', in David Kairys (ed.), *The Politics of Law: A Progressive Critique*, New York, Basic Books, 1998, pp. 240–58.
Smith, Adam, *The Wealth of Nations*, Harmondsworth, Penguin, 1974.

CHAPTER 2

Constructing Chinese Property Rights: East and West

Peter C. Perdue

Several studies in this volume examine property rights in specific local contexts within two Asian empires, and several others look at the interaction between British property concepts defined by law and political theory and the social realities of England or colonial India. They describe how new imperial laws and changes in the economic power of local actors transformed claims to land. If we shift our attention to the contemporaneous Qing Empire of China (1644–1911 CE), we can also find analogous changes. A number of scholars have recently begun to publish studies that pursue these themes.

Here, however, I look at a different but related question: how Western observers from the eighteenth century to the present have represented Chinese property rights. Even though Europeans never fully colonised China, they shared with British colonial administrators underlying assumptions about the nature of Asian societies which determined their conceptions of Chinese property rights. These stereotypes of imperial property rights, like cognitive maps, imposed static simplifications on unruly practice. Like imperial cadastral surveys, they served as tools in significant political debates and supported European mastery of the East. I aim to criticise the flaws in these conceptions, and demonstrate the lineage that links them to imperial concerns. Showing the disjunctures between these schemes and the complexities of practice while recognising multiple forms of property definition in both East and West might lead some contemporary theorists to be more modest, more accommodating and less imperial in their mappings, as Alain Pottage recommends.[1]

The following two quotations display a glaring paradox in common conceptions of the relationship between property rights and economic growth in imperial China:

> [China] was a centralized state in which the decisions over property rights emanated from the center and could be and were changed by the whims of an emperor... Chinese history is replete with arbitrary alterations in policies that fundamentally influence opportunities. In his *Oriental Despotism* Karl Wittfogel had the wrong explanation for the centralization [a consequence of an irrigation system], but the right intuition that centralized controls are antithetical to development in the long run.

> Highly competitive factor and product markets allowed for the exchange of resources and the production and distribution of goods and services by households... households increasingly contracted with each other to exchange resources of all kinds of procedures based on what I have termed customary law... the imperial state looked upon this activity with approval – even consenting to adjudicate violations of contracts between private parties – these private contracts served as an effective device for greatly reducing transaction costs... The state combined the role of noninterference or slight modulation of the private sector with very limited authoritarian allocation of resources so as to create a fairly beneficent economic environment for private enterprise.

The first quotation comes from the Nobel Prize winner in economics, Douglass North.[2] The second comes from an essay by Ramon Myers, North's student, in a *Festschrift* for Douglass North.[3] How can two distinguished representatives of the institutional economic history school come to such contradictory conclusions about imperial China?

We could resolve this question easily by looking at the evidence. The first view does not rely on any empirical research and cites Wittfogel's long discredited theoretical work. The second, along with many other recent studies of Chinese legal institutions, relies heavily on detailed examination of archival and published primary sources in Chinese, especially land contracts and legal cases in Chinese courts concerning land tenure. On empirical grounds alone, viewpoint two wins hands down.

But I would like to pursue the question further. This radical division of views about imperial China's property-rights regime has a long lineage, extending back at least two hundred years, to when Westerners first came into contact with China. Since the eighteenth century, there has been a continual opposition between a theory of 'Oriental despotism' that suppresses and ignores inconvenient evidence about Chinese social realities and an idealised theory of a *laissez-faire* state which has its own limitations. Neither of these abstract models, derived from Western concepts of the 'Oriental other', fully captures imperial China's social complexity. How can we bring theory and empirical research closer together? Although a related critique can be made of the *laissez-faire* perspective, I focus here on the 'Oriental despotism' view because it still is the dominant one in popular and much scholarly discourse.

The question of the relationship between property rights and economic growth lies at the intersection of three distinct theoretical and historical perspectives: those of legal scholars, economists and social historians. All three address the central paradox in different ways. This question is a vital site of convergence of three distinct approaches, but work in each of these areas mostly goes on separately from the others. Ships pass in the night far too often in academic discourse. My goal is to position these three in relation to each other conceptually, so as to provoke new research in all these fields.

First, I argue that a highly misleading assertion about the absence of secure property rights in China is surprisingly influential among a variety of Western social theorists who focus on differences between the long-term historical evolution of Asian and Western societies. Second, recent studies by historians of Chinese legal institutions have severely undermined the once-accepted premises on which these theories are built. The empirical scholars, however, have not directly confronted the social theorists, and the social theorists have neglected the significance of this new research. By bringing these two literatures together, I hope to point the way toward more productive investigation of these important questions.

Inadequate theories cannot be refuted merely with 'nasty, ugly facts'. They need conceptual challenges to their underlying presuppositions. Without such challenges, the same theoretical assumptions persist despite inconsistencies. Misunderstanding of the 'Oriental other' is deeply imbedded in Western theory and may even be necessary to it. But recent developments in legal theory, economic theory and social history offer some hope for convergence at the cost of unbundling or dismantling a coherent parsimonious model of economic growth.

Theories of Oriental Despotism

The notion that there is no private property in land in Asia, by contrast with the West, is deeply rooted. We could trace it back as far as Herodotos's contrast between the Greeks and the Persians, but the most systematic exposition of the idea comes from the French Enlightenment. Montesquieu relied on this claim to support his model of 'Oriental despotism', one of the essential building blocks of his theory of laws and states. Following him, Hegel, Marx and many others elaborated different versions of the model, culminating in Wittfogel's notorious book of the same name, which blamed the success of Soviet communism on the spread of the Oriental despotic state from its roots in ancient Asia, transmitted by the virus of the Mongol conquest, to imperial Russia. Wittfogel found the malignant traces of the despotic 'hydraulic state', purportedly based on absolute control of water supply, in Africa, Asia, Russia – everywhere except Western Europe and the US.[4]

The ludicrously overblown Wittfogel theory, so clearly a product of the Cold War, no longer carries much conviction except for the ideologically committed, but less strident versions of the 'Oriental despotism' argument have popped up in surprising places. Chinese intellectuals, during the reform period before 1989, invoked 'Oriental despotism' in its Marxist guise, the 'Asiatic mode of production', to explain the extremely destructive totalitarian mobilisation of the Maoist period. They linked the lack of individual freedoms and the complete suppression of civic autonomy to the heritage of the imperial bureaucratic state, which, they argued, provided no grounds for individual property rights and no basis for autonomous civic associations. A prize-winning dissertation in political science by a Chinese author trained in the US has revived much of the despotism model in terms of modern political theory.[5] I have criticised these arguments elsewhere as excessively determinist and not based on the best available knowledge about the social processes of late imperial China.[6] It is one thing to argue that the weakness of autonomous civic institutions made possible the communist takeover in 1949 and another to claim that the Communist Party actively built on the despotic legacy of the imperial state, a state, we should remember, which they regarded as completely stagnant, backward and nothing but an obstacle to a modern revolutionary socialist movement.

The influences of this kind of thinking, however, go beyond China. Quite a number of grand social theorists have invoked or alluded to imperial China in attempting to explain the special characteristics of the modern West. Below, I examine briefly a few of their assertions. They all focus on a comparative analysis of legal, economic and social institutions in early-modern Europe (c. 1500–1800 AD) and imperial China (ranging variously over the time period c. 600 BC–1800 AD). Only part of any one theoretical model relies on arguments about property rights in imperial China, but I think that there is a common thread running through these discussions that, in effect, unproblematically accepts the Montesquieu to Wittfogel line of argument. These theories themselves are part of a time-honoured Western tradition counterposing China or the Orient to the West. We may note here two points that link them to their Enlightenment forebears: they are mainly interested in examining the nature of Western capitalist society, not in an accurate portrayal of China, and they have implicit or explicit political aims in their critiques for which the Orient serves as a foil, usually a negative one. Montesquieu used China as his image of a despotism which *ancien régime* France must avoid. Wittfogel used China and the Soviet Union as the nightmare that threatened Western liberal society if it did not awaken to the communist menace. Chinese intellectuals take China's backward 'feudal' past as the legacy to be destroyed by rapid Western-style modernisation. Economic historians tend to describe China as the over-regulated state *par excellence* whose giant bureaucratic apparatus strangled the potential for economic growth. Legal theorists single out China as a place without a Western-style 'legal order', one where bureaucracy, custom and arbitrary justice reigned.

So, although it is rather easy to refute the schematic model of 'Oriental despotism', its traces are powerful enough to create a forcefield that deflects other more sophisticated theories. As a historian, I normally mobilise evidence first and theoretical abstraction second in the service of critique. Here, I can only allude to some of the recent studies that demonstrate the rich complexity of imperial Chinese property rights. Although this study has primarily a deconstructive tone, we may only be able to move forward toward a more nuanced dialogue of social theory and Chinese history after a detailed critique. Although many other facets of these theories deserve discussion, I focus here mainly on the question of property rights, both in the broad sense of the overall relationship of political and social orders to property and in the narrow sense of legal cases and procedures concerned with (primarily landed) property.

Montesquieu: *L'Esprit des Lois*

Let us begin with Montesquieu. The political theory of despotism did not begin with *L'Esprit des Lois* (*The Spirit of the Laws*), published in 1748. The contrast between the free West and the despotic East goes back to Herodotos's contrast between Greeks and barbarians during the period of the Persian Wars.[7] R. Koebner has traced the changing meanings of the word 'despotism' from Aristotle to the Renaissance.[8] Lucette Valensi, in a fascinating little book, argues that modern conceptions of the despotic Oriental state originated in Venetian ambassadors' reports from the Ottoman Sultan's court in the sixteenth and seventeenth centuries. They fixed, in the European mind, the memorable image of an all-powerful, unbelievably wealthy sovereign, irredeemably alien to European religion and culture and determined on its eradication. Most appalling, native-born Christians themselves were bred by Ottoman rulers to be converted to Islam and made loyal slaves of the despot in the notorious Janissary system.[9] But Montesquieu was the theorist who systematically enunciated the basic principles of the despotic state.

Montesquieu, of course, was also a significant point of reference for the founders of the American Constitution.

Both federalists and anti-federalists referred with respect to Montesquieu in support of their arguments. Alexander Hamilton thought that Montesquieu provided 'a luminous abridgment of the principal arguments in favour of the Union'.[10] Anti-federalists, on the other hand, cited 'the celebrated Montesquieu', one of 'the greatest and wisest men who have ever thought or wrote on the science of government', to show that 'so extensive a territory could not be governed, connected, and preserved, but by the supremacy of despotic power'.[11] And the despotisms that Montesquieu and his disciples had primarily in mind were imperial Rome and imperial China.

Regarding China, Montesquieu rejected a competing line of argument, that of the physiocrats, who viewed China as a despotism, to be sure, but one where the power of the sovereign was restrained by natural law and custom. The physiocrat François Quesnay stated, 'I have concluded from the reports about China that the Chinese constitution is founded upon wise and irrevocable laws which the emperor enforces and which he carefully observes himself'.[12] Physiocrats also praised the light level of taxation, the apparent absence of venality in government service, and the tradition of care for the people embedded in Confucian moral values of 'benevolence' and put into practice by institutions and rituals. They cited the emperor's annual ritual of ploughing the soil to show his concern for agriculture, they noted the high productivity of Chinese agriculture, and they recognised the value of the ever-normal granary system which stored large quantities of grain around the empire for the purpose of famine relief. Voltaire, Montesquieu's greatest rival, attacked *L'Esprit des Lois* directly for its distorted conception of despotism:

> Recent writers seem to enjoy, I really do not know why, calling 'despotic' the sovereigns of Asia and Africa. One used to mean by 'despot' a petty European prince who was a vassal of the Turk ... This word 'despot' originally meant in Greek master of a household, paterfamilias. Now we grant liberally this title to the Emperor of Morocco, the Great Turk, the Pope, the Emperor of China.[13]

Montesquieu was unimpressed. To him, China had been and always would be a pure despotism where the population lived in poverty and slavery:

> Our missionaries tell us of the vast empire of China as an admirable government, which mixes in its principles fear, honor, and virtue. If this is so, I have created a useless distinction of principles between the three types of government. I do not know what kind of honor they are speaking of in referring to a people who will never do anything unless they are driven to it by clubs ... China is thus a despotic government, whose principle of rule is fear.[14]

Because of climate and topography, he argued, there were no restraints on the autocratic power of the emperor. (The inconvenient fact that China does have large mountain ranges and river systems and spans both tropical and temperate zones made no impact on the theory.) As this quotation shows, Montesquieu realised that if China could not be described as a despotism, the fundamental classifications of his theory could not stand.

Montesquieu clearly ignored some obvious evidence about Asia that did not fit his model. He argued, for example, that there could be no dowries in despotic governmental systems because women, like all Asiatic subjects, were nothing but slaves themselves and became the complete property of their husbands after marriage. He surely must have known about the tremendous importance of dowries in both China and India which travellers and Jesuits reported, but he omitted this and other contrary evidence.

In the debate between Montesquieu and his opponents, both sides relied on essentially the same evidence: the voluminous reports by Jesuits from the court at Peking collected in the *Lettres Édifiantes*; other travellers' reports; the general history of China compiled from Chinese sources and translated by du Halde; and a few limited translations of portions of Chinese classic texts. Both sides had political points to make at home, and they were certainly more concerned with reforms of the French state than with objective descriptions of China. Physiocrats pushed for lighter taxation and more rational allocation of office based on the Chinese ideal, despot theorists warned that the French state could turn into a crushing Asiatic juggernaut if steps were not taken to protect the autonomy of the nobility and to institutionalise checks and balances within the state. China was a mirror on which were projected Western fears and aspirations, and the reflections were viewed with distorting lenses.

Yet, other comments by Montesquieu reveal more favourable attitudes toward imperial China. The clear precepts of his abstract model, which assumes that governments lacking the restraints of aristocratic or republican institutions can only exhibit arbitrary power based on force, contradict his awareness that the formal despotic structure of the Chinese empire, in fact, had produced remarkable cultural and economic achievements. The secular Montesquieu faced the same paradox as his Catholic enemies. They knew, especially the Jesuit observers of the Chinese court, that here was a country without the Christian religion which, nevertheless, maintained moral and cultural order at least as well as if not better than the *anciens régimes* of Europe. The Chinese paradox was an essential element fuelling the rational scepticism of the French Enlightenment.[15] But the same Chinese paradox implicitly undermined the breathtaking clarity of Montesquieu's political theory.

Montesquieu himself seldom referred to the absence of property rights in Asiatic despotism, but other writers took it for granted. Nicholas-Antoine Boulanger, for example, described the Orient as the land of

> the man who has no will kissing his chains, *the man with no property or safe* fortune worshipping his tyrant, the man with no knowledge of man or reason and whose only virtue is fear; and what is truly surprising and puzzling is that it is there that men take their servitude to heroic extremes, numb themselves to their own existence and with pious imbecility bless the savage whim that often takes their lives, the only thing they might be said to possess but which, according to the law of their prince, belongs to him alone to do with as he pleases.[16]

Montesquieu and his supporters connected the purported absence of private-property rights in land to personal lack of civil rights and economic backwardness, in wilful defiance of readily available evidence about the reality of life in the Chinese empire.

Roberto Unger: *Law in Modern Society*

The work of Roberto Unger, one of the founders of the school of Critical Legal Studies, is of course much more familiar to legal scholars than to historians of China. Unger's focus is 'the place of law in modern society'.[17] By law, he means the specific form of legal order established in the post-Renaissance West. In his analysis, the Western legal order consists of general, autonomous, public and positive rules. It stands apart from other social institutions; it has its own specific style of reasoning and its own occupational autonomy. By contrast, customary law does not make clear distinctions between choosing rules and making decisions under rules, and bureaucratic law consists only of explicit rules made by centralised governments.

Unger rightly rejects social theories that posit a universal human nature and argues for the need to respect historically grounded accounts of society. The Western legal order emerged in early-modern Europe from two developments. First was the development of group pluralism, which forced the state to recognise society as the reign of conflicting interests as community solidarity declined. Sovereigns created rules cutting across class and rank lines which claimed general allegiance, so it was in the interests of all classes to support them. But the early-modern state-builders could not create a pure bureaucratic law governed only by their own expediency because the nobility and the third estate opposed them. The structure of the *Ständestaat* (estate order) in Europe ensured that each estate fought for its own interests to curb governmental power, but by a process of compromise in dynamic balance they created the liberal state.

The second crucial element in the creation of the Western legal order, according to Unger, was the heritage of natural law derived from Greco-Roman and Judaeo-Christian civilisation. This fostered the idea of universal regularities both in nature and in social life. The higher law, seen as transcending the human order, made possible radical criticism of society, going beyond the following of rules to the evaluation of their rightness. Only in the modern West could the secular order be influenced by sacred God-given natural principles. Thus liberal society was the result of sacred higher law combined with interest-group pluralism, the two tempering each other.

Unger's perspective has much in common with that of Max Weber, and many of the same defects. Weber, in analysing the religion of China, stressed the contrast between the transcendental religion of the West and the Chinese concept of immanent natural order. According to both Weber and Unger (falsely), the Chinese immanentist theory made radical criticism of existing social conditions impossible. Unger, like Weber, also finds that neither ancient India, Islam or Israel contained the crucial prerequisites for legal order.

In Unger's analysis, even though the Chinese had achieved the separation of state from society and created public-positive bureaucratic law, their society was alien to the rule of law. Chinese religion contained both transcendent and immanent elements seen in the two concepts of deity in ancient China: *shangdi*, a personified transcendent being, and *tian* ('heaven'), an immanent cosmic impersonal force. The transition to a bureaucratic state in the third century BC proceeded concomitantly with a shift from transcendent *shangdi* to immanent *tian*, removing the possibility of outside critique. Thus ancient China lacked universal laws, it lacked a priesthood which could check governmental power, and it lacked a notion of a personal relationship to God that could support individualism. *Fa* ('law') expanded to become positive and public state law, completely subject to the rulers' use, lacking any autonomy from the ruler's commands. *Li* ('custom' in Unger's mistranslation) remained only a commitment to particular social relations, and did not form the basis for positive rules. Both Confucian philosophy, which insisted on the return to *li*, and Legalist philosophy, which demanded faith in coercive regulation, were incompatible with the 'rule of law'.

William Alford has subjected Unger's conception of ancient China to a sharp critique which I will only briefly summarise here and add a few comments of my own. As Alford notes,[18] Unger totally misinterprets the meaning of the term *li*, which means much more than primitive custom, and he completely neglects the significance of other key elements of ancient Chinese political thinking: the Mandate of Heaven, Taoist and Moist philosophy and the existence of written public law before the sixth century BC. Public law as far back as the twelfth century BC was not confined to penal law, but also included international treaties, tax regulations, family codes and monetary policy. *Li* are better seen as public rituals that define 'due process' behaviour: they do not simply merge what happens and what ought to be done. Confucians did not oppose public law, but insisted that formal rules had to be supplemented by moral suasion. They were not always subject to arbitrary commands by autocratic rulers, but frequently took an independent stance. Even the Legalists, worshippers of a powerful state, stressed not only absolute state power, but stability and predictable order, which applied as much to the ruler as to his subjects. And 'Taoists seem to have had an intense faith in the capacity of men, and perhaps of all human beings, to transcend the limitations of social arrangements within which they found themselves'.[19]

Unger, despite his ambition to transcend the limitations of Western liberal theory, remains solidly within it and shows little respect for the contributions of non-Western philosophy. His discussion of China relies almost entirely on rather old secondary literature and he never analyses any primary Chinese sources in detail, even though all the major philosophical works are available in translation. Most important for our purposes, he never discusses Chinese legal practice because his discussion is pitched at such a high level of abstraction. Alford, by contrast, has shown by detailed analysis of a single legal case that Chinese law was not merely an instrument of state control. The law codes never uncritically supported a local magistrate's decision, which was always subject to review by higher authorities, and the appeal process was, in fact, invoked frequently all the way up to the emperor himself through direct 'capital appeal' (*jingkong*).[20]

Even if we look only at procedural aspects, we should note that an alternative tradition of interpretation of Chinese law in the West focused not on its despotic arbitrariness, but on its carefully structured process of bureaucratic review. Western observers in the eighteenth century had noted with admiration the Autumn Assizes review process, which required that all capital sentences be reviewed yearly by the emperor and his councillors. Imperial pardons spared many criminals sentenced to execution. Early-modern European rulers, although they might give individual pardons, had no such institutionalised review process.

This abstract discussion takes us far away from the issue of property rights, but it indicates some of the problems with this level of theoretical analysis. These models typically focus on ancient Chinese philosophy, fail to examine original texts in critical detail, neglect social practice and assume that nothing significant changed from 200 BC to 1911 AD. Their excessively high level of abstraction fails to capture the most important insights of comparative analysis. Imperial China fits very poorly into the schematic tripartite analysis of societies into tribal, aristocratic and liberal used by Unger and others. Instead of Procrustean efforts to force China into Western typologies, we need a form of analysis that critically reflects on the limitations of Western theorising by seriously respecting the categories of a different time and place.[21]

The implications for property rights, although Unger does not develop them, are clear. With no standpoint of critique outside the state, there could be no security of tenure. If all land belonged to the state, rules for land transfer could only be devised for bureaucratic convenience, not for private gain. The state might want to assist the advance of production in order to increase its tax income, but it would certainly ensure that it gained the lion's share of any surplus created by individual investment or technological advance. Some historians who look at large-scale economic change have drawn out the specific implications of these assumptions.

Eric Jones and the economic historians

Eric Jones is an economic historian who is not afraid to tackle the big questions. He boldly addresses the contrasts between East and West in two books: *The European Miracle: Environments, Economies, and Geopolitics in the History of Europe and Asia*[22] and *Growth Recurring*.[23]

Jones incorporates environment, population, technology and, loosely speaking, culture into his comparative analysis of why Europe grew so rapidly in the early-modern era, and Asia, in his view, did not. He also discriminates between different Asiatic empires: the Turkic, the Indian and the Chinese, although, clearly, the Chinese Empires (Ming [1368–1644] and Qing [1644–1911]) seem to fit his model least well. The basic model is one of an Asiatic predatory state, one which monopolises control of all economic and political resources, extracts them ruthlessly from its subject populations for purposes of war and wealth, and does not redistribute the resources in any institutionalised form to its people. Europe, he argues, had superior devices for redistribution of food and for quarantine against disease when Asiatic empires did nothing. Again, it is the lack of individual property rights in land in Asia that made possible this super-exploitation, while the geographical and social fragmentation of Europe created pockets of autonomy where local authorities or subjected peoples could resist the juggernaut of bureaucracy. Jones quotes with approval the terse summary: 'property is insecure. In this one phrase the whole history of Asia is contained',[24] and, once again, puts forth Montesquieu's conclusion that 'there reigns in Asia a servile spirit'.[25] Differing only slightly from his predecessors, he argues that the Ottoman, Mughal and Manchu empires 'were not timeless despotisms. They were regimes of conquest originating from the steppes, unable to survive efficiently without fresh land and spoils, and terrifyingly prone to inhibit development.'[26]

Jones's work, though it includes many provocative insights, provides an incredibly rich catalogue of misconceptions about Asian empires. Despite frequent assertions of insecurity of property in Asia, he never bothers to examine property laws in practice. He contents himself with the usual random anecdotes that describe savage rulers amassing extravagant wealth and the confiscation of goods from their subjects. (A telling omission is that even larger European royal confiscations such as Henry VIII's seizure of monastic lands or the French expulsion of the Huguenots never appear in these macroeconomic accounts.) He claims that private merchants lived 'on sufferance' because they had no independent legal system to shield them from state demands. Therefore, imperial China, despite its dramatic technological gains up to the fourteenth century, lapsed into stagnation under Malthusian pressure thereafter because of the blighting effect of its despotic imperial state, which was nothing more an 'imposed military despotism, revenue pump, and plunder machine'.[27]

Jones's thesis has severe empirical deficiencies, as a few simple facts demonstrate. This Asiatic 'revenue pump' extracted only 3–4 per cent of the GNP in official tax levies; even doubling this figure to allow for 'informal' levies hardly amounts to devastating impositions. The Qing state bureaucracy governed 300 million people with a salaried official class of no more than

20,000 men. Imperial China, in the eighteenth century, had by far the most extensive and elaborate institutions in the world for redistributing food to people in need.[28] It not only recognised but promoted security of tenure, making great efforts to regulate land markets and to return famine refugees to their lands. The individual landholder, self-sufficient on his plot, able to pay taxes in cash to the state, was the ideal of Qing imperial administration. Famine-relief measures aimed to overcome social disruption by returning uprooted peoples to their land. It was not imperial authorities who engaged in land grabs but powerful local elites; these were the people whom imperial authorities suspected the most and attempted to restrain. Like officials of the late Roman Empire, they recognised the dangers to the state of large landless populations and of land concentration by local elites, but they intervened far more effectively than their European contemporaries, who took, at best, local palliative measures, but had few state-wide institutionalised civilian provisioning policies.[29]

We can recognise common styles of analysis that link the political theorist, the legal analyst and the economic historian. The excessively high level of abstraction, the lack of concern with how institutional orders and legal statutes affected social practice, the airy binary generalisations about 'Europe' and 'Asia' all betray the unmistakable marks of Orientalism. We have not progressed very far, it seems, in the 250 years since *L'Esprit des Lois*. The economic historian, above all, should be interested in the real impact of states and laws on economic behaviour in the long run. The sources are available for such investigations. Jones's use of rather bizarre and outmoded sources on China which have little grounding indicates more casting around for useful tidbits for a predetermined argument than serious investigation.[30]

North and Thomas: the rise of the Western world

Much of the comparative analysis by Jones and other economic historians builds on the premises outlined by Douglass North and Robert Thomas[31] on the causes of the rise of the Western European economies. Although North and Thomas never mention Asia, they endorse the principle that Europe distinguished itself in the early-modern period from the rest of the globe by its ability to generate efficient allocation of labour, capital and natural resources (Imperial Spain often stands in for the Orient in this model). The enforcement of individual property rights was the essential factor in allowing the creation of price-forming markets, and it was particular policies of certain early-modern European governments, particularly England and the Netherlands, that first made possible the establishment of secure property rights. Once property rights were secured, incentives to individual investors ensured sustained long-term growth of per capita income.

What specific legal changes do North and Thomas point to? In fact, they say little about specific legislation regarding the use of landed or commercial property. By 'property rights' they mean a much broader climate of protection for possessors: the establishment of international peace and domestic social order, reduction of barriers to mobility of factors of production, limited confiscation and taxation by organised governments, and active measures by governments to free up factors of production, especially labour. But, all of these measures could well be accomplished by many other states without creating a special realm of 'legal order' and without passing particular items of legislation. Several scholars who view China from North's perspective have found that imperial China also had most of the features claimed to exist in Europe for the securing of property rights. Chang Fu-mei Chen and Ramon Myers point to the very elaborate array of contracts used to negotiate transfers of land, water, goods and persons, the absence of serfdom and the high mobility within the expanding commercial empire, and the positive effects on commercialisation of the Pax Sinica of the mid-seventeenth to the end of the eighteenth century. No specific sphere of contract law was necessary as long as merchants had sufficient confidence that their agreements would be honoured and could be enforced in the courts. Chen and Myers analyse in detail a few of the voluminous printed records of Chinese contracts to demonstrate their sophisticated use in commercial and family transactions.[32]

Thomas Buoye also notes the adaptability of the Qing magistrates to changing commercial conditions.[33] In handling disputes over landed property, local officials upheld ideals of harmonious interpersonal relations as paternalist overseers of their subjects. In practice, they had to develop a body of case law to guide them in resolving conflicts. Among other questions, they had to determine which land sales were enforceable: only those with officially stamped written contracts? Those with written contracts, but without official stamps? Oral agreements? They had to decide when an owner who pawned land had the right to redeem it at the original price and whether the term of redemption had to be specified in the original contract. If it was not specified, what was a reasonable time period? Up to five years after yielding possession? Ten years? In a time of rising land values, land pawners inevitably would struggle with land recipients over the terms of redemption. Magistrates who had to handle these sorts of problems in their courts gradually developed useful precedents, which were recorded in provincial legal codes.[34] These studies demonstrate the flexibility, pragmatism and evolution toward standardised procedure of Chinese land law as it was developed by local magistrates in the process of settling disputes. Could we not call this the functional equivalent of 'common law' for landed property?

Ad van der Woude and Jan de Vries dub the seventeenth-century Netherlands 'the first modern economy', and they cite as characteristic features of property rights in the Netherlands just those attributes described above for both late-imperial China and early-modern England. They argue that tenant leases in the Netherlands ensured incentives to improve agrarian productivity because tenants were relatively invulnerable to confiscation by landlords or the state. China's customary law provided the same feature in the form of separate topsoil and subsoil rights. Landlords owned the subsoil rights permanently if they paid taxes and obtained official seals on their contracts, but tenants had full rights to topsoil (usufruct) after paying a fixed rent, and they could either lease or alienate this right independently. China's 'two lords to one field' and the Netherlands' non-feudal property system, in different ways, provided the same incentives for economic investment.[35]

Once again, the abstract property-rights model is too stereotyped to lead to productive comparative analysis by itself. We need to look at actual cases to test whether or not Europeans or Chinese had functionally equivalent property systems that encouraged commercial growth and investment. When we look at examples of legal systems in social practice, imperial China does not come off badly by comparison.

Empirical scholarship on Chinese law

Social theorists espousing the despotism model of China have found support in older Sinological scholarship on Chinese law. Derk Bodde and Clarence Morris's classic work *Law in Imperial China*[36] contains an overview of the basic principles of Chinese legal thinking that fortifies the Orientalist perspective. They state:

> the written law of pre-modern China was overwhelmingly penal in emphasis... it was limited in scope to being primarily a legal codification of the ethical norms long dominant in Chinese society... it was nevertheless rarely invoked to uphold these norms except when other less punitive measures had failed. Chinese traditional society, in short, was by no means a legally oriented society despite the fact that it produced a large and intellectually impressive body of codified law... Matters of a civil nature were either ignored by it entirely (for example contracts), or were given only limited treatment within its penal format (for example, property rights, inheritance, marriage). The law was only secondarily interested in defending the rights – especially the economic rights – of one individual or groups against another individual or groups and not at all in defending such rights against the state.
>
> The official law always operated in a vertical direction from the state upon the individual, rather than on a horizontal plane directly between two individuals [A did not bring suit directly against B, but brought it to authorities]... no private legal profession existed... [Chinese behaviour was shaped much more by the] pervasive influence of custom and the usages of propriety [than by] formally enacted system of law.[37]

Bodde and Morris's work is most useful for providing translations, commentary and excerpts from a casebook of imperial court decisions. This Conspectus (Xing'an Huilan) contains over 7600 penal cases, covering the period from 1736 to 1885. These cases provide valuable evidence on how officials interpreted and applied the code in China's highest-level courts. These cases, however, are not a reliable guide to the daily operations of local courts, nor can they serve by themselves as a valid basis for generalisation about the legal system as a whole. David Buxbaum discovered how misleading it is to focus only on imperial court cases when he examined a local archive from one district in Taiwan which contained 1164 files of cases from 1789 to 1895.[38] In the first place, civil cases did not show up at the highest courts because the highest court of appeal for civil cases was at the provincial level. The Qing code did recognise the difference between civil and criminal cases, and local magistrates handled significant numbers of civil cases covering, for example, family law, marriage contracts and land and water rights. These cases were disputes between individuals, not 'vertical' relations between one subject and the authorities. About 15–20 per cent of the files in the Taiwan archive were civil cases, and each file could include up to three or four separate civil cases combined together. Magistrates tried to make it easier for farmers to gain access to the courts by refusing to hear civil cases during the busy farming season. Even rather poor farmers could get their day in court. The vast majority of cases were resolved within a year. The courts did not terrify the population in this district, and many people made use of them.

Buxbaum also argues that the Qing system fits quite well into Weber's criteria for 'rational' law. Qing China had a coherent law code, a hierarchy of courts and a well-established appeals system from the locality to the emperor; it had procedures for processing cases and for amending statutes, reasoning by analogy, and rules that were 'uniform and unvarying in application'. The main difference between Qing and modern legal practice was its inefficiency: communication was slow, court officers could not easily catch defaulters, and those who lived a long distance from the court could not always afford to attend its sessions regularly.

Was nineteenth-century Taiwan exceptional? In the 1980s, foreign researchers gained access to the Qing dynasty archives in Beijing, which included a vast quantity of legal cases from the entire empire. Research on these materials has only just begun, but the overall picture, presented most recently in the volume edited by Kathryn Bernhardt and Philip C.C. Huang, confirms Buxbaum's picture. The model cases translated by Bodde and Morris, by design, excluded civil cases, but civil cases were in fact a major part of the caseload of the local courts. 'Those who assumed that the formal court system of the Qing dealt little with civil matters were simply wrong.' Chinese law was not, to be sure, 'liberal assertions of a civil society' or 'formalistic reasoning from universal abstract principles'. The system comprised adaptations to changing social realities by a state mainly concerned with administration and control. But the Chinese as a whole did not see law as an 'arbitrary and terrifying presence to be avoided at all costs'. They 'turned to that system to assert legally protected rights over property, debt, marriage, and inheritance'.[39]

Hugh Scogin, a legal historian, argues that in looking at China, Western scholars cannot 'view as universal categories historically contingent patterns found in their own legal culture'.[40] The 'tunnel vision' of Western lawyers until recently only studied articulated legal concepts in order to defend the ideal of an independent legal order. Not until the twentieth century did newer schools of legal history, such as 'legal realism', consider legal concepts as historically contingent phenomena influenced by social forces. A positivist approach that views law as a body of rules flowing from the sovereign, or a focus on normative aspects of law rather than historical categories, becomes problematic for China. Not all Chinese law came from the sovereign. Law was seen as part of a broader natural order encompassing both local custom and cosmic principles. Henry Maine, the sociologist who opposed 'custom' to 'law' as a basis for a typology of societies, would define China as backward, but it is not useful to classify China as advanced or backward on this kind of scale. Nor can we draw conclusions about economic effects of law from the predominance of custom. Chinese commercial activities outstripped those of early-modern Europe in scale, yet they were based mainly, then and now, on personal relationships (*guanxi*). The 'customary' codes of Chinese guilds formed a more than adequate substitute for commercial law.

Contract law has been seen as the quintessential expression of the independence of the Western legal order. Finding no autonomous sphere of contract law in China, Western observers concluded that trade and investment could not possibly flourish. But the privileged position of contract as a series of principles independent of the status of the parties was severely undermined in the twentieth century:

> In twentieth-century practice, many of the elements downplayed by the classical will theory and associated with traditional, non-progressive societies have been reintroduced as contract law has continued to develop. Such factors as status of the parties, officially mandated elements of contracts, reliance as a basis for enforceability, and the role of commercial custom have been resurrected as important determinants of contractual obligations. When one finds elements such as these at work in traditional China, to maintain that they demonstrate the absence of 'contract law' says a great deal about one's analytical framework, but very little about Chinese practices.[41]

The very influential article by Lon Fuller and William R. Perdue[42] substantially altered the view of contracts in Western legal thinking by introducing the concept of 'reliance interest'. By showing that law and society are intertwined like *yin* and *yang*, it resurrected ideas formerly associated only with 'traditional' societies. In social practice, China and the West were not so far apart.

Thus Western contract law itself turns out not to be so autonomously rational as claimed. And in China, too, there were functional equivalents to contract conceived as 'legal effects of consensual transactions giving rise to a relationship of obligation'. Promises and compacts (*yue*) were widely recognised and enforced in China ever since the Han dynasty. Valerie Hansen's recent work *Negotiating Daily Life in Traditional China: How Ordinary People Used Contracts, 600–1400*[43] is a superb exploration of the extremely pervasive influence of contracts in Chinese daily life. The oldest extant Chinese land contracts date to the first century AD. They are probably some of the oldest in the world. Documents preserved in the desert and in Buddhist caves dating from the eighth and ninth centuries show that contracts were used by all strata of society, even the poorest, for a great variety of purposes: transfers of land and goods, marriages and family matters. They appear in religious documents and in fictional tales as well as in government archives. The state switched its *de facto* approach to the registration of land as contracts spread: while land tenure was officially recognised only on the basis of land registers in the seventh century, by the tenth century only officially stamped contracts could provide proof of tenure in court cases. People went to court so frequently to assert rights under contract that officials attempted to draw up model contracts so as to resolve ambiguities and prevent litigation. Officials tried to collect significant tax revenue from the growing volume of contracts by imposing a stamp tax, but many evaded paying the tax. They had sufficient confidence in the enforceability even of non-stamped 'white' contracts that they felt official registration was unnecessary. These practices, originating in the tenth century, were still actively promoted in provincial legal codes in the eighteenth.[44] All of this is powerful testimony to the pervasive influence both of written contracts and of the idea of contractual arrangements in Chinese culture. The Chinese even extended the notion of contract to areas that Westerners would consider out of bounds: they drew up large numbers of contracts with the dead and with supernatural beings. The Chinese treated their gods and ancestors as beings with whom one could bargain and whom one could hold to agreements in other-worldly courts.[45]

In the Qing dynasty, local magistrates protected private ownership rights, even endorsing the Lockean notion that the investment of labour created rights to wasteland. Although the Qing state regulated market exchange and interest rates, its main interest was in the stability of business practice, not in exploiting the market for rent-seeking gain. A quantitative analysis of several hundred land, marriage, inheritance and debt cases in Taiwan, Sichuan and north China demonstrates that 'magistrates almost always adjudicated civil matters in accordance with the code', following consistent principles.[46] They generally delivered judgements and did not merely mediate. We must also not forget the very common 'third realm' of justice: cases neither settled by kin and community nor finally adjudicated at court, but settled before coming to trial. This 'third realm' of out-of-court settlement, after all, is not so rare in the West either.

Ordinary Chinese, in short, were not simply victims of a mythical Oriental despotism, deprived of legal guarantees and subject to the whims of an autocratic state; they lived in a growing commercial-agrarian society governed by a complex mixture of legal provisions and informal procedures not so different from early-modern Europe.

Republican China, in the early twentieth century, built on the productive inheritance of the imperial past. One example is merchant dispute mediation in twentieth-century Zigong, the centre of the Sichuan salt industry.[47] For at least two hundred years, Zigong had an active share market, constant investment in salt-well drilling and frequent bankruptcies that produced litigation. Usually merchants settled their disputes by mediation or the local government intervened to assist, but not enforce, debt settlement. Even Chinese commercial culture, so tightly intertwined with family relationships, could be highly litigious. Mothers could sue to recover debts from their son's wife. Although all parties aimed to maintain an atmosphere conducive to investment and the expansion of production, violence often threatened business activity, just as in the Qing.

The legal profession did make reasonable progress in the early twentieth century. At least in Shanghai, modern lawyers, despite very diverse origins and qualifications, did achieve some independence and reasonably high social status, and tried to establish basic professional norms. Many women used the new divorce law of the 1930s, one of the most liberal in the world, to escape from unhappy marriages. Most did not employ lawyers, but an 'affordable, efficient' court system offered them new opportunities.[48]

The consequences for theory and social analysis

T.H. Huxley once described tragedy as a beautiful theory destroyed by a nasty, ugly fact. Social theorists should not stop writing about imperial China, but they should abandon the claim that imperial China had only bureaucratic law and primitive 'custom' (*li*) and no private law, and the argument that only the West produced the form of property rights considered essential for economic development. I detect encouraging signs of convergence between new trends in legal scholarship and social theory in the West and studies of Chinese legal institutions. If the old approaches which focused on norms and ideals, and not on practices, stressed the ideal of an independent legal order and remained concentrated on the figure of the sovereign central power which creates law as a body of rules, the new approaches find law embedded in multiple dispersed social practices and locations intertwined in historically contingent ways with the regulations of legislators, emperors and courts.

Unger's objective is to recast Western social theory fundamentally. Mine is more modest: to make theorists aware of the need to interpret carefully imperial China's experience. I will not devise a comprehensive new comparative theory of the West and China in this space.[49] But these maxims may offer some useful guidelines. Although the following precepts may be all too banal, they seem to be violated frequently in practice.

First, pay close attention to scale. China is a continent, not a nation. Typical East–West comparisons contrast all of imperial China with one or two European nations, usually the most advanced ones. The proper ratio of comparison for economic or social analysis is all of Europe west of the Urals with all of China or one region of Europe with one region of China. If we compare Southern England or the Netherlands with the Jiangnan (lower Yangzi valley) region of China, China comes out as quite comparable in transport costs, degree of urbanisation, commercialisation of agriculture, monetisation, and even development of industry, even into the nineteenth century.[50] Placing all of Europe against all of China reveals vast diversity and large gaps between advanced and backward areas in both regions.

Second, allow for contingency. The economic historian N.F.R. Crafts has argued that the Industrial Revolution in England may have been a 'stochastic event', i.e. a chance occurrence resulting from the fortuitous combination of a special array of factors at a given time.[51] Singularities are a poor basis upon which to build general theories, but the usual practice is to take industrialising England's experience as the model against which to measure all other developing countries. Just like Marx and Smith, Western and Chinese scholars continue today this misguided form of analysis.

Third, keep up with recent scholarship. Theories and theorists do improve with time as they take account of new interpretations or catch up with unfamiliar work. Both Jones and Unger have substantially revised their early crude accounts of China in their later work. Promoting dialogue between different disciplinary traditions, in a spirit of mutual respect, is the best way to ensure broad understanding and the highest critical awareness. History, legal studies and economics all have productive insights to share with each other.

Encouraging news comes from recent economic history. Joel Mokyr's *The Lever of Riches*[52] is a considerable advance on its predecessors in this genre. Mokyr is concerned with the wellsprings of technological innovation in the early-modern world which paved the way for the subsequent Industrial Revolution. He focuses on early-modern Europe, but he also has a chapter on imperial China. Unlike Jones's *The European Miracle*, but similar to Jones's *Growth Recurring*, he is aware that imperial China led the world in technological creativity for many centuries up to around 1400 CE.[53] In rice cultivation, iron ploughs, seed drills, blast furnaces, spinning wheels, water power, water clocks, maritime exploration, paper, porcelain and silk – to name only a few fields – China advanced faster and further than any other civilisation up to the thirteenth century. The real mystery for Mokyr is why China slowed down and even went backward in technological progress after 1400. He cogently rejects most of the current explanations based on culture, political factionalism, 'equilibrium traps' and social structure. Mokyr is aware that the effect of institutional structures on economic growth varies with time and place, that both China and Europe transformed themselves in many ways during this period, and that no simple dichotomies will do. Although there is reason to doubt many of Mokyr's assertions – not all technical change stopped completely after 1400 – on the whole he is quite attentive to scholarship on China published through the 1980s. Notably, he does not endorse either the general property rights explanation or the parasitic Oriental state paradigm in their pure form. Fewer traces of the old binary dichotomy of stagnant East and dynamic West are left. This gives grounds for hope and a challenge for comparative historians to push ahead.

Mokyr, however, does endorse one of the most common explanations for the ceasing of technological innovation in the early Ming: the notion that the Ming emperor, by cancelling further investments in the great tribute fleets that reached as far as the coast of Africa, single-handedly stopped Chinese technological growth. This assertion is, to be sure, widespread in the historical literature on Ming China. Now it is time for Ming–Qing historians to respond, by demonstrating how misleading this notion is. First of all, the Ming emperor's decision was strategically and economically rational. Since there was a rising threat from Mongolian state-builders on the northwest frontier, he and his advisors wisely chose to divert scarce resources from the southeast coast to the much more critical northwest. Second, the emperor did not stop technological or economic growth. Despite his prohibitions, coastal trade continued and grew in the sixteenth century (even though the government castigated these traders as 'pirates'), monetisation of the economy proceeded as silver imports from the Philippines and Japan grew and the Single-whip Tax Reform responded to this process by changing many local tax collections from in-kind to money. State-directed technological investment was re-directed from ships to the extraordinary logistical network required to supply the garrisons along the Great Wall. These civil-engineering achievements deserve just as much credit as nautical engineering, but economists neglect them. Third, the assumption that overseas voyages must be the key engine of economic growth rests ultimately on a giant geological contingency: the presence of another continent between the west and east coasts of Eurasia, one completely unanticipated by European explorers. If Columbus and his ilk had found what they expected to find, a westward sea route to the riches of the Orient, their tiny ships would have been quickly marginalised by the much vaster Asian coastal trade, just as the Portuguese, Dutch and other traders had already discovered. With no gold to bring across the Pacific, the Spanish would have had nothing to offer Asia.

Legal institutions and case law may not, however, be the best place to look for explanations of technical change. The law tends to be conservative; it responds to, but seldom anticipates, rapid technological change. One may argue that efficient property rights redirect factors of production toward their most efficient uses, but except in the case of patent law, a relatively recent innovation in a meaningful sense, there has not yet been a clear demonstration of how property rights induce innovation. As Mokyr notes, either the government or private individuals may promote new inventions or block them, depending on which interest groups gain or lose from new technology. It all depends on the time and place. He thinks that China, in contrast to Europe, was excessively dependent on imperial support for invention and lost its dynamism when the state turned against new technology after the fifteenth century. This argument is only partly convincing, since the eighteenth-century emperors were, in fact, quite interested in new military technology, at least, and the state dominance over the private economy was much weaker in the eighteenth century than in the fifteenth.[54]

If I were to sketch speculatively the outlines of a more satisfactory explanation, I would focus on the contrast between the competitive European state system and the Chinese imperial structure. This idea has been often thought, but ne'er so well expressed as in Mokyr's analysis, though only in passing.[55] Britain became the world's leading power in the eighteenth century not because of its private-property rights, but because of its war machine.[56] In incessant competition with absolutist France, the British drove both technical change in the military sphere and fiscal policy so as to mobilise the maximum amount of resources for economic and military competition. China, too, faced extremely serious military threats from the mid-seventeenth to mid-eighteenth centuries, which also impelled military and economic innovation, but after the successful crushing of the last major nomadic empire in 1760 CE, the dynamism went out of the system. For much more on this subject, see my forthcoming book.[57]

Constructing Chinese property rights today

Finally, the legacy of oversimplified dichotomies between East and West persists in the discussion of China's recent economic reforms. The Chinese themselves and Western observers misleadingly polarise the alternatives as a choice between collectivist and completely individualist property regimes. This view relies on a stereotypical image of Western capitalism as based only on a purely individual property regime. It also misrepresents the current status and future directions of property-regime changes in China. Zhiyuan Cui, collaborating with Roberto Unger, has argued that new forms of property are now emerging in China, in the form of the township and village enterprises (TVEs) which form the most rapidly growing part of the Chinese economy.[58] These are neither individually owned nor state-owned, but they have developed diverse forms of ownership structures ranging from partially representative local government, to partnerships, to joint-stock corporations. Cui has also been informing his Chinese colleagues that the modern West cannot be characterised as an exclusively individual-property-rights regime. He points to regulations and constraints on individual property uses and the dominant presence of corporate organisation.

He has also noted, like Carol Rose, the paradox of Locke's story of the origins of property. Although in the posited state of nature, individual owners sought only their own self-interest, somehow they conceived of the need to co-operate to create an individual-property-rights regime.[59] They broke out of the prisoners' dilemma. Where did this impulse to co-operate come from? Setting up the regime itself required psychological attributes that are not present in the individual self-maximiser model. I would suggest that classical Chinese philosophy, which sees the self as social, deals more adequately with this paradox than the exclusively egoistic psychology of classic Western political theory.

China today, however, has lost touch with its classical past. It is almost at the stage of Locke's state of nature, where the characteristics of a future property-rights regime are highly unsettled, but the cultural and political forces encourage only short-sighted individualism. In this situation, there are no clear boundaries defining what should and should not be subject to market forces: almost everything is potentially up for sale, including orphans, libraries, works of art, historical treasures, documents, intellectual property etc.[60] The widespread accusations of 'corruption' in China today are a product of inadequate boundaries and unclear enforcement of the line between what is and is not legitimately on the market. Drawing sharp lines between state and individual property, as if there were only two choices, will not lead to enlightenment on these issues. It would be more useful to recognise that both in the

Chinese past and in the modern West property rights are not individual and absolute claims to a thing, but bundles of symbols, texts, narratives and artifacts (e.g. fences) by which possessors persuade a community and state that they are entitled to certain uses of a resource. These claims are dependent on changes in social norms, changing definitions of what is a resource, changing values of resources and state enforcement capabilities and jurisdictions. Such a view sends the social theorist and the social reformer out on uncharted waters because there is no firm anchor of universal reason to be found. It is truer, however, to the historical evidence about how societies, East and West, have developed their characteristic property-rights regimes.

Notes

1 Pottage, 2004.
2 North, 1995, p. 21.
3 Myers, 1982, pp. 280, 296–97.
4 Wittfogel, 1957.
5 Yang, 1987.
6 Perdue, 1994.
7 Anderson, 1979.
8 Koebner, 1951.
9 Valensi, 1993.
10 Rossiter, 1961, p. 5; Rose, 1994, pp. 82–83.
11 Ketcham, 1986, pp. 242, 275.
12 Quesnay, cited in Perdue, 1987, p. 1.
13 Koebner, 1951, p. 275.
14 Montesquieu, 1951, pp. 365–67.
15 Pinot, 1971.
16 Cited in Valensi, 1993, p. 3, my italics.
17 Unger, 1976, p. 44.
18 Alford, 1986.
19 Alford, 1986, p. 961.
20 Alford, 1984.
21 To his credit, Unger has, in later work, moved toward greater respect for Chinese thinking, expressing some admiration for Confucian moralism, but the excessively high level of abstraction remains: Unger, 1987.
22 Jones, 1987.

23 Jones, 1988.
24 Winwood Reade, *The Martyrdom of Man*, London, Watts, 1925, cited in Jones, 1987, p. 165.
25 Montesquieu, 1951, Book 17, Chapter 6, cited in Jones, 1987, p. 166.
26 Jones, 1987, p. 171.
27 Jones, 1987, pp.202–22.
28 Will, 1990, reviewed by Perdue and Wong, 1983; Will, Wong et al., 1991.
29 For Jones's unconvincing response to Wong and Perdue – Will, Wong et al., 1991 – see Jones, 1987, pp. xii–xiii.
30 Jones, like Unger, does provide a more nuanced account of imperial China in his later work, *Growth Recurring* (1988), but many of the basic features of this analysis remain.
31 North and Thomas, 1973.
32 Myers and Chen, 1976; Myers and Chen, 1978.
33 Buoye, 1993; Buoye, 2000.
34 Perdue, 1987; Perdue, 2001.
35 Van der Woude and de Vries, 1997, pp. 160–62.
36 Bodde and Morris, 1967.
37 Bodde and Morris, 1967, pp. 3ff.
38 Buxbaum, 1971.
39 Bernhardt and Huang, 1994, pp. 4, 9, 11; cf. review by Perdue, 1996.
40 Bernhardt and Huang, 1994, p. 41.
41 Scogin, 1994, p. 33.
42 Fuller and Perdue, Jr, 1936; Fuller and Perdue, Jr, 1937.
43 Hansen, 1995.
44 Perdue, 1987.
45 Hansen, 1995.
46 Bernhardt and Huang, 1994, p. 179.
47 Zelin, 1994.
48 Bernhardt, 1994, in Bernhardt and Huang, 1994, p. 195.
49 For the best recent discussion of these issues, see Wong, 1998.
50 Pomeranz, 2000.
51 Crafts, 1985.
52 Mokyr, 1990.
53 Mokyr, 1990, pp.209–38.
54 Waley-Cohen, 1993.
55 Mokyr, 1990, pp.206–8.
56 Brewer, 1990.
57 Perdue, forthcoming.

58 Cui and Unger, 1994.
59 Rose, 1994, p.38.
60 Cf. Alford, 1995.

Bibliography

Alford, William P., 'Of Arsenic and Old Laws: Looking Anew at Criminal Justice in Late Imperial China', *California Law Review* 72/6, 1984, pp.1180–256.

– 'The Inscrutable Occidental? Implications of Roberto Unger's Uses and Abuses of the Chinese Past', *Texas Law Review* 64/5, 1986, pp.915–72.

– *To Steal a Book is an Elegant Offense: Intellectual Property Law in Chinese Civilization*, Stanford, Stanford University Press, 1995.

Anderson, Perry, *Lineages of the Absolutist State*, London, Verso, 1979.

Bernhardt, Kathryn, *Women and the Law: Divorce in the Republican Period*, in Bernhardt and Huang (eds), 1994, pp.187–214.

Bernhardt, Kathryn and Philip C.C. Huang (eds), *Civil Law in Qing and Republican China*, Stanford, Stanford University Press, 1994.

Bodde, Derk and Clarence Morris, *Law in Imperial China: 190 Ch'ing Dynasty Cases*, Cambridge, MA, Harvard University Press, 1967.

Brewer, John, *The Sinews of Power: War, Money, and the English State, 1688–1783*, Cambridge, MA, Harvard University Press, 1990.

Buoye, Thomas, 'From Patrimony to Commodity: Changing Concepts of Land and Social Conflict in Guangdong during the Qianlong Reign (1736–1795)', *Late Imperial China* 14/2, 1993, pp.33–59.

– *Manslaughter, Markets, and Moral Economy: Violent Disputes over Property Rights in Eighteenth-Century China*, Cambridge, Cambridge University Press, 2000.

Buxbaum, David C., 'Some Aspects of Civil Procedure and Practice at the Trial Level in Tanshui and Hsinchu from 1789 to 1895', *Journal of Asian Studies* 30/2, 1971, pp.255–80.

Crafts, N.F.R., 'The Industrial Revolution in England and France: Some Thoughts on the Question: Why was England First?', in Joel Mokyr (ed.), *The Economics of the Industrial Revolution*, Totowa, Rowman & Allanheld, 1985, pp.429–41.

Cui, Zhiyuan and Roberto Unger, 'China in the Russian Mirror', *New Left Review* 208, December 1994, pp.78–87.

Fuller, Lon and William R. Perdue, Jr, 'The Reliance Interest in Contract Damages', *Yale Law Journal* 46, 1936, pp.52–96; 1937, pp.373–420.

Hansen, Valerie, *Negotiating Daily Life in Traditional China: How Ordinary People used Contracts, 600–1400*, New Haven, Yale University Press, 1995.

Jones, Eric L., *The European Miracle: Environments, Economies, and Geopolitics in the History of Europe and Asia*, Cambridge, Cambridge University Press, 1987.

– *Growth Recurring*, Oxford, Oxford University Press, 1988.

Ketcham, Ralph (ed.), *The Anti-Federalist Papers and the Constitutional Convention Debates*, Harmondsworth, Penguin, 1986.

Koebner, R., 'Despot and Despotism: Vicissitudes of a Political Term', *Journal of the Warburg & Courtauld Institute* 14, 1951, pp. 275–303.

Mokyr, Joel, *The Lever of Riches*, Oxford, Oxford University Press, 1990.

Montesquieu, Michel, *De L'Esprit des Lois, ou du Rapport que les Lois Doivent Avoir Avec La Constitution de Chaque Gouvernement, Les Moeurs, Le Climat, La Religion, Le Commerce, etc.*, in Roger Caillois (ed.). *Oeuvres complètes*, Paris, Gallimard, 1951, vol. 2, pp.227–995.

Myers, Ramon H., 'Customary Law, Markets, and Resource Transactions in Late Imperial China', in Roger Ransom, Richard Sutch and Gary M. Walton (eds), *Explorations in the New Economic History: Essays in Honor of Douglass C. North*, New York, Academic Press, 1982, pp. 273–98.

Myers, Ramon and Chang Fu-mei Chen, 'Customary Law and the Economic Growth of China', *Ch'ing-shih Wen-t'i*, 3/5, 1976, pp. 1–32; 3/10, 1978, pp. 4–27.

North, Douglass C., 'The Paradox of the West', in Richard W. Davis (ed.), *The Origins of Modern Freedom in the West*, Stanford, Stanford University Press, 1995, pp. 7–34.

North, Douglass C. and Robert Paul Thomas, *The Rise of the Western World: A New Economic History*, Cambridge, Cambridge University Press, 1973.

Perdue, Peter C., *Exhausting the Earth: State and Peasant in Hunan, 1500–1850*, Cambridge, MA, Harvard University Press, 1987.

– 'Technological Determinism in Agrarian Societies', in Merritt Roe Smith and Leo Marx (eds), *Does Technology Drive History?: The Dilemma of Technological Determinism*, Cambridge, MA, MIT Press, 1994, pp. 169–200.

– Review of Kathryn Bernhardt and Philip C.C. Huang (eds), '*Civil Law in Qing and Republican China*, Stanford, 1994', *Journal of Interdisciplinary History* 27/1, 1996, pp. 177–80.

– 'Property Rights on Imperial China's Frontiers', in John F. Richards (ed.), *Land and Environment in World History*, Oakland, CA, Institute for Contemporary Studies Press, 2001, pp. 71–93.

– *China Marches West: The Qing Conquest of Central Eurasia, 1600–1800*, Cambridge, MA, Harvard University Press, forthcoming.

Perdue, Peter C. and R. Bin Wong, 'Famine's Foes in Ch'ing China' (review of Pierre-Etienne Will, *Bureaucratie et Famine en Chine au 18ème siècle*, Paris, Mouton, 1980), *Harvard Journal of Asiatic Studies* 43/1, 1983, pp.291–322.

Pinot, Virgile, *La Chine et la formation de l'esprit philosophique en France, 1640–1740*, Geneva, Slatkine Reprints, 1971.

Pomeranz, Kenneth, *The Great Divergence: China, Europe and the Making of the Modern World Economy*, Princeton, Princeton University Press, 2000.

Pottage, Alain, 'The Cadastral Metaphor: Intersections of Property and Topography', in Huri İslamoğlu (ed.), *Constituting Modernity: Private Property in the East and West*, London, I.B.Tauris, 2004, pp.180–213.

Rose, Carol M., *Property and Persuasion: Essays on the History, Theory, and Rhetoric of Ownership*, Boulder, Westview, 1994.

Rossiter, Clinton (ed.), *The Federalist Papers: Hamilton, Madison, Jay*, Harmondsworth, Penguin, 1961.

Scogin, Hugh T. Jr, '"Civil Law" in Traditional China: History and Theory', in Bernhardt and Huang (eds), 1994, pp.13–41.

Unger, Roberto M., *Law in Modern Society: Toward a Criticism of Modern Social Theory*, New York, Free Press, 1976.

– *Plasticity into Power: Comparative-Historical Studies on the Institutional Conditions of Economic and Military Success*, Cambridge, Cambridge University Press, 1987.

Valensi, Lucette, *The Birth of the Despot: Venice and the Sublime Porte*, Ithaca, Cornell University Press, 1993.

van der Woude, Ad and Jan de Vries, *The First Modern Economy: Success, Failure, and Perseverance of the Dutch Economy, 1500–1815*, Cambridge, Cambridge University Press, 1997.

Waley-Cohen, Joanna, 'China and Western Technology in the Eighteenth Century', *American Historical Review* 98/5, 1993, pp.1525–44.

Will, Pierre-Etienne, *Bureaucratie et Famine en Chine au 18ème siècle*, Paris, Mouton, 1980 (English translation by Elborg Forster, *Bureaucracy and Famine in Eighteenth-Century China*, Stanford, Stanford University Press, 1990).

Will, Pierre-Etienne, R. Bin Wong et al., *Nourish the People: The State Civilian Granary System in China, 1650–1850*, Ann Arbor, University of Michigan Center for Chinese Studies, 1991.

Wittfogel, Karl. *Oriental Despotism: A Comparative Study of Total Power*, New Haven, Yale University Press, 1957.

Wong, R. Bin, *China Transformed: Historical Change and the Limits of European Experience*, Ithaca, Cornell University Press, 1998.
Yang, Tai-Shun, *Property Rights and Constitutional Order in Imperial China*, unpublished PhD dissertation, Indiana University, 1987.
Zelin, Madeleine, 'Merchant Dispute Mediation in Twentieth-Century Zigong, Sichuan', in Bernhardt and Huang (eds), 1994, pp. 249–86.

CHAPTER 3

Sovereignty, Property, Land and Labour in Colonial South India

David Washbrook

One of the most enduring myths of colonialism is that British rule created private rights to landed property in India.[1] Like most myths, it may contain a grain of truth: land was more securely held and more widely bought and sold after the establishment of colonial rule than before. But that grain is so heavily surrounded by ideological secretions that its real character is easily lost. At least in South India, it would not be true, for example, that prior to colonial rule private rights to property (as opposed to rights claimed in the name of the state) did not exist, nor that these could not be associated with the physical possession of land, nor that they might not be bought and sold, nor even that they might not be held individually rather than as part of a social community. But, equally, it would not be true either that, at least during the first hundred years of colonial rule, freely alienable, individualised private rights to landed property actually came into existence.[2] Indeed, it could be argued that, particularly during the first half-century of British rule, colonial land-settlement policy was strongly geared to preventing such an outcome, and worked against tendencies generated within southern Indian society itself to move history in this direction.

The issues raised by the question of private-property rights in land are extremely complex. Nor are they made any easier by methodological assumptions that the British necessarily held common and coherent views about the nature of landed property and its place in society any more than that the Indians shared common indigenous traditions about it. During the critical 30 years (1790–1820) when the East India Company's government first addressed the problems of land settlement and laid down the institutional bases of landed property ownership, British ideologues were divided between three different and competing theories of right. A 'Permanent Settlement view', borrowed from Bengal, sought both to create and to 'free' private-property rights in land in the marketplace.[3] However, what might be termed an 'Anglo–Hindu law view' held that not only was private-property right in India 'ancient' (and, thus, hardly in need of creation), but that it could not be 'freed' in the marketplace without being destroyed.[4] And a '*ryotwari*-system view' held that as all land belonged to the sovereign, there were no absolute rights to private property and none should be created.[5] All three views existed side-by-side, jostling for provenance and competing for authority – and rendering the legal status of landed property extremely uncertain down to at least the 1850s. Thereafter, a species of consensus was created, but it was born of compromise and contained elements – and contradictions – derived from its multiple origins.

Yet, in this complexity, at least British settlement policy was not entirely out of kilter with the southern Indian society on which it was imposed and where different people also held different views on the appropriate character of private-property rights in land – and contended them, often ferociously, before law courts and tribunals of the state.[6] In very broad terms, these differences corresponded to class positions. Theories favouring the antiquity and inalienability of private rights in land were most commonly advanced by those possessing 'privileged' property entitlements and who might be equated with the established 'landed gentry'. Their critics came from both above and below them in the social hierarchy: from the agents of a state or royal power which had long tried to weaken their control of landed resources and from lower-caste tenant and labouring groups who sought to extend their own rights in the land. Both of these latter groups favoured Permanent Settlement or *ryotwari*-system understandings of property right which broke its associations with social ascription. Moreover, the fortunes of these latter groups had waxed strongly in the century prior to British rule, when economic and political uncertainties had brought the authority of established 'landed gentries' under challenge.

This last point also draws attention to the context in which early colonial land settlements were made and which, perhaps, has not figured sufficiently or prominently in previous accounts of them. This context imposed conflicting imperatives on policy which, in turn, opened up deep contradictions in the ideologies of landed property held by the new British rulers and, scarcely less, among their new colonial subjects. The context was marked by severe social dislocations caused by half a century of intensive warfare. This warfare had acquired novel forms, especially in relation to the economy, in which rival states had attempted to seize each other's assets (including populations) and destroy each other's productive bases.[7] Following its eventual 'conquest', the East India Company had to cope with the detritus of these conflicts: with substantial sections of long-resident populations absent or in hiding, with moneyed adventurers or parvenu claimants 'pretending' to ancient rights and with 'lower orders' of society taking advantage of opportunities created by the removal of their 'betters' in order to occupy land.

Undoubtedly, it can be supposed that land settlements made by the Company – a commercial organisation – always had an eye to profit and to establishing conditions conducive to the development of commerce. However, in southern India, other imperatives also intruded. One was simply to maximise revenue collections in order to meet the escalating military costs of 'conquest'. But another, rather more subtle in nature, involved the restoration of social stability: the recovery of the bases of a 'Hindu Golden Age' which many British ideologues firmly believed had existed in South India, underpinning its legendary medieval prosperity, before the latter-day evils of 'Islamic' tyranny and despotism.[8] The institutions required to (re-)create this stability were not necessarily those most functional to the promotion of market commerce or the extraction of land revenue. Attempts to meet all three imperatives inevitably generated tensions which became in-built to the institutions of the early colonial state and were thence bequeathed to posterity.

Nor were these tensions only manifested in institutions. The situation also brought them out in the 'public thinking' of the new colonialists, where they reflected contradictions buried deep in the ideologies of the eighteenth-century Britons who now found themselves ruling an Asian empire. In his celebrated account of the theories informing the Bengal Permanent Settlement of 1793 – that 'Rule of Property for Bengal' – Ranajit Guha has drawn attention to the influence of Enlightenment and Physiocratic ideas on Philip Francis, who was perhaps the intellectual architect of the Settlement. Guha sees these as particularly important in the making of a settlement designed to convert land into a freely marketable commercial property.[9] However, Guha emphasised much less Francis's other claim to historical fame as 'Junius', the arch-radical critic of Hanoverian despotism in England and the defender both of 'the ancient Anglo-Saxon constitution' and customary rights (including property rights) of 'free-born Englishmen'.[10] If Francis believed (as Junius certainly did) that private-property rights were the guarantors of liberty and foundations on which society was built, it is hard to see how he can also have meant those rights to be placed, vagariously, at the chance disposals of the marketplace. And an often-overlooked feature of the original Bengal Permanent Settlement is that it held the 'new' rights of private property in land which it created only to exist insofar as they did not conflict with any established customary rights.[11]

In the southern Indian context, where social disturbance and uncertainty were much greater than in Bengal, the inherent ambiguity in eighteenth-century British ideologies of property tended to come out even more clearly, giving rise to two different schools of thought among colonial administrators. F.W. Ellis championed the cause of ancient customary rights as the pillars of a stable 'Hindu' social order and urged their defence, even at the expense of market freedoms. Thomas Munro took the other side, advocating a system promoting the more rapid circulation of land through society, albeit more in the form of *ryotwari* revenue tenancies held from the state rather than absolute rights to private property.[12] The two contending philosophies fought their corners through most of the first half of the nineteenth century, leaving southern Indian society in considerable confusion over the nature of its landed property rights, if it indeed had any at all.

From the middle of the nineteenth century, however, something resembling a consensus did begin to emerge, at least at the level of legal practice (theory always remained more problematic). In 1855, a 'new' *ryotwari* settlement was inaugurated, aimed at giving (supposed) government tenants securer rights to the possession of their land: possessionary rights which they could now formally register and alienate in the market without incurring the wrath or, at least, requiring the (corrupt) consent of revenue officials. In 1859, an Inam Commission also began work, surveying the vast congeries of rights to land revenue immunity (which previously had constituted the bulk of what was meant by private property) and reducing them to the ownership of land 'in fee simple'. By this time, too, the law courts had laid down sufficiently firm precedents for them to operate with a broadly agreed set of procedural rules, exemplified in W. Hudleston's authoritative compendium on *mirasi* right, first published in 1862.[13]

What was most striking about the new consensus was the way that it strictly equated property rights in land with rights to the possession of 'real' landed property – bounded, measured and fixed. This did not necessary mean that it 'freed' such property to circulate in a marketplace under rules of complete social anonymity. That was to come, if it ever has come, only much later. In British India, restrictions on alienability associated with Hindu family law and caste and religious practices remained remarkably tight. However, the concept of 'landed property' now referred strictly to possessionary rights over the land itself. This represented a considerable change from the point of departure whence the colonial law had set out half a century before. Then, it had encountered and been prepared to adjudicate also hosts of claims to 'non-real' property rights in the land: multiple claims to shares in its products and/or to parts of the government revenue demand on it. These last had all now fallen into desuetude or become subsumed within the simple division of the land itself.

How, exactly, such 'non-real' rights had come to disappear and to effect a profound transformation in the social meaning of 'land ownership' is not immediately clear. No sovereign power, colonial or other, directly willed it. The new *ryotwari* system and the Inam Commission merely regularised what had grown up in the day-to-day practices of the law courts and revenue department. Equally, at least by this time, very little resistance was put up by southern Indian society itself to the loss of such perceived rights. Rather, the logic of 'real' property in land was rapidly internalised even by those who were the victims of it and who now came to couch their counter-claims in its own terms. By the late nineteenth century, inferior caste groups were starting to contest their rights against the upper castes, not as of old, on the basis of differential claims to shares in a common social product, but rather as 'sons of the soil' whose originary 'real' possession of the land had suffered historical confiscation by the upper castes and ought now to be restored.[14]

To understand this, albeit belated, transition in the nature of property rights, it may be necessary to look not only at the formal and theoretical discourses of the law, but also at its institutional practices and wider social context. Property rights are constituted at the boundary-point between claims to sovereignty made by the state and those to privacy and autonomy made by its subjects. By the mid-nineteenth century in southern India, this boundary point had shifted markedly from that of a hundred years before: the state was differently structured and legitimated; 'civil' society itself was of a different order. It could hardly be that the nature of property rights would not change in these circumstances. Also, property right is exclusionary: it denies access to resources to those not possessing it. In the case of land, this necessarily makes it bound up with the relations of production and labour. In southern India between 1750 and 1850, these relations also had changed – making, for example, land a much scarcer factor of production than had been the case earlier, and giving those with exclusionary possession of it a much stronger dominance over labour. To be fully grasped, the transition needs to be seen not only as a function of the introduction of 'alien' ideas (which, in this case, may not have been entirely alien), but also in terms of southern Indian society's own adaptations to the novel conditions facing it as part of a new imperial state and as a participant in a new kind of global political economy.

Pre-colonial land systems

The status of land rights in pre-colonial southern India has long been the subject of scholarly dispute. Some historians have seen the lineaments of private-property rights dating back to Chola times (ninth to twelfth centuries AD).[15] Others have emphasised the importance of 'royal' authority in distributing rights over land or at least over its products.[16] In the two centuries prior to the colonial 'conquest', claims on the land would appear to have been made with reference to both sources of authority, giving southern India's land systems a 'dualistic' character very similar to that which Frank Perlin has sketched out for Maharashtra.[17]

On one side, claims to a share in the products of agriculture were launched under royal prerogatives derived from kings and emperors. British advocates of the *ryotwari* system understood these to represent claims to direct taxation based on the royal proprietorship of the land. However, in southern India (which lay outside the Mughal imperium until very late) there is little evidence of large revenue flows to central treasuries. Rather, the system may be better understood in the terms seen by Nicholas Dirks as a system of resource redistribution operating under royal aegis. Kings 'gifted' their claims over the surplus to a variety of client groups, priests and temples, who held them on what might be called *inam* tenure.[18] Notionally, these 'gifts' were given in return for service and loyalty, and could be resumed at royal will, albeit only to be 'gifted' to others.

However, and as British theory of the *ryotwari* system notably failed to see, royal prerogative did not represent the only source of claim to rights. There were also 'community' claims based on ancient rights derived from settlement and land clearance, especially in the rich river valleys (although also wherever tank and well irrigation made land highly productive). These claims extended beyond mere entitlement to surplus, but amounted to broad 'lordship' rights over the land as well as its water resources, mineral wealth and the labour of non-members of the original proprietory community (especially that of *adimai* [slave/serf] castes).[19] In support of these claims, community 'territories' were measured out and bounded, in part, in paper records and, in part, through rituals involving 'beating the bounds'. Burton Stein has suggested that, originally, such territories comprised large *nadus*. But, from Vijayanagara times (fourteenth to sixteenth centuries), if not before, they had mostly become reduced to 'village' dimensions.[20] In Tamil, the common term for these lordly rights was *kaniachi* (from *kani*, 'land', *acharya*, 'power'), which properly conveys their meaning. However, the British, following latter-day Persian practice, preferred the term *mirasi* (hereditary landed right). *Kaniachikarrars* (or *mirasidars*) also had the power to 'gift' shares of their own surplus to temples and village servants. These might be described by the Tamil term *manyam*, to distinguish them from the (Persian) *inam* granted by kings.

In addition, there was a third claim to proprietary right, although its incidence was rather limited. Certain gifts of land by kings to Brahmans were held subsequently to inhere in the person of the recipient. By convention, they were not resumable by the king, but were seen to constitute the 'personal' property of the Brahman, with which he could do (including alienate) as he pleased.[21]

Among these three claims to right in the epoch before British rule, undoubtedly the *kaniachi/mirasi* form was the most important in terms of the volume of resources which it commanded. In most areas, the primary *kaniachi* claim was couched in terms of corporate possession, rights being shared equally between the number of families held responsible for the original clearance of the land. However, by the eighteenth century, if not long before, equality in the distribution of real assets had ceased to exist. Although village accounts always divided *kaniachikarrar* villages into equal shares, different families were credited with holding disproportionate amounts of them. Thus in a village consisting of 16 shares, one family might possess five sixteenths and another one quarter of one sixteenth, although all would still claim the collective title and status of *kaniachikarrar*.[22]

The ideology of 'share' (in Tamil *pangu*) also ran through the length and breadth of other village relationships, but in the same asymmetrical manner. 'Inferior' land-occupying 'tenants' and field labourers took their rewards as 'inferior' shares in what was calculated as a corporate village product. The claims of kings and their *inamdars* (especially on wet paddy lands) were similarly formulated.[23] However, it remains unclear how far methods of production, at least by the eighteenth century, were actually corporate or communal. Although certain production functions (such as the maintenance of irrigation channels) were regarded in this light and responsibility for them distributed according to shareholdings, the organisation of cultivation appears generally to have been conducted by discrete farming families operating independently.

Moreover, the most obvious sign of the continuation of a communal production regime was becoming very scarce. That sign was the form of tenure (commonly known as *karaiyedu*) whereby particular village lands were redistributed (according to share) between *kaniachikarrars*, usually every seven years, to even out differences in fertility and proximity to irrigation sources. But even by the time that the East India Company first took over direct administration of the Chingleput Jaghir in 1782, the majority of its villages had ceased to follow this practice.[24] It proved to be equally abnormal in the other riverine districts which the Company acquired over the next 20 years. One reason for this may have been the pressures of intensified commercialisation during the seventeenth and eighteenth centuries, which swelled the demand for high-value garden crops such as betel, tobacco, indigo and sugar. These crops required heavy fixed investments, and tax claims on them were made in monetary, rather than crop-share, terms. Also, periodic redistribution was relatively uncommon in country irrigated by tanks and wells which were the products of royal, temple or 'personal' endowment.

The dual nature of proprietary claims couched between royal prerogative and community privilege naturally raises questions about the relationship between their two sources of authority. Potentially, this relationship could be conflictual and, as we shall see, there is much to suggest a deepening conflict in the years leading up to the British conquest. However, it could also be mutually reinforcing and reflective of extensive accommodations between kingly power and local interests. Documentary expressions of *kaniachi* right invariably invoked the authority of both king and community to attest to the legitimacy of the underlying claim.[25] As both Stein and Dirks have argued, concepts of sovereignty in Tamil culture strongly favoured shared expressions of authority – with local elite groups appealing to connections with kings in order to buttress their superior status over 'inferior' groups, and kings seeking recognition by local elites in order to preclude claims over their territories by rivals.[26] Such relations of mutual support frequently had material implications, for example, in Chingleput, where most *kaniachikarrars* also held tax-free *inam* lands 'gifted' to them by kings.[27] They were further reinforced by the intermediary functions of the temples, where both kings and local elite groups worshipped and where they ritually expressed the joint character of their authority by jointly endowing the gods.[28]

Nonetheless, there was also potential for conflict. Most obviously, this could come where royal demands on surplus exceeded those which local elites were prepared to concede and also where *inams* were 'gifted' to people of whom local elites did not approve. Such tensions achieved a variety of institutionalised forms. For example, from at least Vijayanagara times, kings had sought to impose measurements on crop production, the better to assess the size of their own shares. But local elites resisted these measurements or at least bent them towards their own interests. Thus, in the Tiruvendrapuram farm which the English East India Company took over in the 1760s, there were 14 different weights of *kalam* (a grain measure used for revenue purposes) which corresponded to the different status of the *kaniachikarrar* being assessed for revenue.[29] Thus, there were also regular annual struggles over the commutation price at which paddy grain was calculated to meet revenue claims (which were always expressed in *kalam* but usually collected in cash). In the Kaveri districts, powerful *kaniachikarrar* habitually hoarded grain before the date when commutation prices were set in order to drive them up and thus reduce the amount of grain demanded to discharge them. Afterwards, they flooded local markets with supplies, frequently causing price collapses.[30]

With regard to 'wrongful' *inamdars* and recipients of royal gifts, tensions here were often expressed in the sectarian caste and religious conflicts which were a key feature of Tamil society in the late pre-colonial era. While the origin of the endemic factionalism of the castes of 'the Left' and 'the Right' Hands remains mysterious, in the more heavily commercialised regions from the seventeenth century, there can be little doubt that it partly reflected a confrontation between settled agricultural castes and mercantile and artisanal 'intruders'. Settled agricultural castes of 'the Right Hand' were extremely sensitive to the privileges which kings and temples might accord parvenus of 'the Left Hand'.[31] Equally, in Sri Vaishnava temples, struggles over patronage of the Vadagalai (Northern) school of ritual practice (which accorded lower status to non-Brahman worshippers than the Thengelai [Southern] school) could spill over into the countryside, leading to payment strikes against priests and temples.[32] Rural Tamil Nadu was by no means a society marked by peace and tranquillity before the disturbing interventions of colonialism.

It was also not a society marked by simple subsistence production and lack of engagement in market activities. From Roman times, its long coastline had drawn it into extensive maritime commerce and, as Sanjay Subrahmanyam has seen, from the twelfth century it had experienced long-term secular economic growth and intensified urbanisation. During later medieval times, it became a major centre for the production of cotton textiles, which was linked to 'world' markets stretching from Arabia and the Levant to Southeast Asia.[33] Such developments promoted high degrees of economic specialisation with, for example, most of the weaving villages along the coastline being fed with rice brought from as far away as Bengal. They also promoted a high degree of commercialisation, which impacted on agrarian relations in the interior.

The first known record of a 'sale' of *kaniachikarrar* rights dates back to the eleventh century. Intriguingly, it took the form of a 'gift' to the gods, which the gods then passed on to a third party in return for a donation of money which, in turn, they passed back to the first party.[34] Such divinely mediated instruments of sale remained the norm into the eighteenth century. In addition, complex mortgage systems came to develop, most commonly usufructory in kind with the mortgagee permitted to reclaim his property within 30 years if he ever managed to repay the debt.

Such instruments permitted the substantial accumulation of *kaniachi* rights, often in several different villages, and the emergence of 'gentry' families who were sharply distinguished in wealth and lifestyle from the bulk of the peasantry. Not infrequently, such gentry families also enjoyed close connections with kings, holding, in addition, quantities of royally generated *inam* rights. Such connections breached the walls of local 'community' solidarity. They helped give rise to 'great households' which mediated between royal and local authority and developed an independent influence of their own.

Growth in the use of instruments of sale also introduced *de facto* elements of social 'pluralism' into the relations of land. Although, in broad terms, conventions excluding *paraiyan* ('untouchable') castes from holding *kaniachi* rights appear to have been maintained into the eighteenth century, not least to preserve dominance over a subservient labourforce on which *kaniachi* privilege rested, other connections between social ascription and access to land were loosening. Subrahmanyam has noted the rise of 'portfolio capitalists' during the sixteenth and seventeenth centuries, who invested widely in commodity trades, tax farms and moneylending.[35] Their activities brought them closely into contact with rural society and frequently saw them also invest in *inam*, *manyam* and *kaniachi* rights. Such men usually hailed from mercantile caste backgrounds and could be Muslims or Christians. Also, from the fourteenth century, warrior-farmers from the Telugu country had filtered into the interior districts of Tamil Nadu, practising specialist forms of cotton cultivation on the upland black soils and demonstrating a prowess at martial arts. The growth of the cotton economy and the strength of their sword drew them progressively towards the rich rice-growing river valleys, where they established claims to a share of the surplus, first as traders and 'protectors' (*palaiyakarrar*) and later as the holders of *kaniachi* rights.[36]

In effect, even by the seventeenth century, the idea that the Tamil countryside (especially the rich river valleys) consisted of simple subsistence-orientated 'village communities' cultivating the lands that their ancestors had cleared and worshipping their age-old gods would be largely fictitious. This was now, in practice, a highly commercialised and culturally plural society where *kaniachi* rights and privileges were bought and sold and held by many groups other than those who could claim descent from the original settlers – merchant Chetties, Telugu Balijas and Reddys, both Muslims and Christians. Importantly, however, ideological expressions and ritual forms had not adjusted to practice, creating possibilities of strain. Primary claims to privileged rights over the land still made appeals to corporate institutions and ancestral lineages whose factual existence was now tenuous. Agrarian relations, including even the formal sale of land rights, were mediated through 'divine' institutions in which the participants did not necessarily 'have faith'. Where, for example, Muslim or Christian *kaniachikarrar* (or for that matter Hindus of different sectarian traditions) found themselves having to acknowledge other gods in the course of purchasing their land or having to endow and participate in temple festivals as an obligation of their newly acquired 'lordship' rights, the disjunction between received 'tradition' and effective 'practice' was already becoming extreme.

The crisis of the eighteenth century

Whether such a disjunction, in and of itself, might be treated as evidence of impending structural change is a problematic question. 'Modern' historians are wont to have difficulty in resisting evolutionist assumptions and those of a Marxist bent in not conceiving that blatant contradictions must be moving towards some kind of resolution. Thus, looking at contradictions between forms and rituals of 'traditional' artisanal craft and practices of a highly commercialised society in the sixteenth and seventeenth centuries, Chicherov supposed that southern India must already have been in the course of a transition to capitalism.[37] It would be tempting, similarly, to suppose that the dissonance noted between the ideological structure of claims to rights in land and the practices of an increasingly commercial and pluralist society was leading towards the emergence of secular and, perhaps, even individual forms of right. However, it would be fairer to note that there is little evidence before the eighteenth century of any attempt within southern Indian society to reformulate the nature of land rights. We cannot know what might have happened had history turned out other than it did and, of course, even the most glaring of contradictions is capable of surviving almost indefinitely.

What did happen, however, was that during the eighteenth century the region came under unprecedented pressures (mostly emanating from outside) which directly impacted on its structure of land rights and sharpened the many tensions already inherent in that structure. The first force of impact was felt through the strengthening of royal demands for surplus extraction and the multiplication of *inam* bequests. South India had remained outside the Mughal imperium until very late, and the subsequent expansion of Mughal authority there, after Aurangzeb's 1689 conquest of Golconda, always met fierce resistance from local warrior groups. Also 'Mughlai' rulers, especially the Nizam of Hyderabad, the Nawab of Arcot and the Sultan of Mysore, by no means sought simply to impose a northern Indian revenue system on their new territories. As Susan Bayly has seen, they adapted with great flexibility to southern practices.[38] Nonetheless, there cannot be much doubt that the weight of royal demands for taxation increased substantially from the middle decades of the century.

The period was marked by escalating warfare between various new claimants to regional power and by a huge proliferation in the number of armed mercenaries serving in the regions – Pathan and Maratha cavalrymen and, later, European-style infantrymen. Such mercenaries were extremely expensive and pressed the revenue system for accommodation. In response, hosts of new *inams* were created (locally known as *shrotriems*), existing *inams* (especially to Hindu temples) were either redistributed away from them or simply resumed into forms of direct taxation, and revenue rights were more extensively farmed out to the highest bidders (frequently commercial men from other parts of India, most notably Gujarat) who had less respect for local interests and deities.[39] The privileges and immunities represented by *kaniachi* now came under growing threat from above.

To exacerbate this threat further, the influence of the European trading companies on the coasts also began to increase exponentially. Although long present in the south, there is much to Subrahmanyam's case that, until the turn of the eighteenth century, they were relatively minor players in what was essentially an intra-Asian commercial system.[40] But the political turmoil in the hinterland gave them new opportunities, particularly to make use of that uniquely close 'mercantilist' relationship between political power and commercial wealth which distinguished their practices from those of their Asian competitors.[41] Even before Clive and Dupleix initiated the build-up of European military strength, European trading factors were entering the world of southern Indian 'portfolio capitalism' to buy up notionally royal claims to surplus and taxation. But, once that build-up had started, a new dimension was brought to 'the commercialisation of royal power', as Christopher Bayly has called it,[42] and all royal rights were at risk of being shifted into the portfolios of European capitalists as well as those of their Indian agents and collaborators.

In the hinterland of the main port cities, the commercialisation of royal rights reached remarkable degrees, with *inam*, *shrotriem* and even *palaiyakarrar* rights bought by the highest bidders, almost regardless of their social identity or ability to fulfil the obligations attached to those rights. The celebrated Tamil diarist and *dubash* (commercial agent) of the French East India Company, Ananda Ranga Pillai, for example, who was a humble Idaiyan (shepherd) by caste and had no pretensions to martial prowess, contrived to purchase *palayaikarrar* rights in several villages and, eventually, even a mansabdarship of the Mughal Empire.[43] Moreover, and perhaps inevitably, it was not only 'royal' rights which became caught up in this process, but community rights represented by *kaniachi* privilege, too. Judging by the sales documents deposited in the *choultries* (record rooms) of leading temples, the mid-eighteenth century saw a remarkable growth in the land market, with several 'great households' building up extensive estates composed of bundles of rights in different villages. In his study of 'Nattar' (leadership of local *kaniachi* communities) in the Tamil coastal districts, T. Mizushima has argued that by the second half of the eighteenth century there was no longer very much connection between the possession of Nattar office, caste identity and natal origin in the local territories to which the office was attached.[44] Commercialisation, albeit under the forced conditions which marked the period, had loosened ties between ascriptive social identity and rights over land.

Moreover, the political turbulence of the epoch also added a further dimension to the problem. The escalation of warfare and increased pressure of commercial demands began to have serious implications for the relations of labour. Service opportunities provided by armies and in the construction of fortifications and towns, as well as new employment prospects in the textile industry started to make significant calls on rural labour supplies, especially among *paraiyan* labourers and 'inferior' caste tenants. Wage rates tended to rise and, at least if calculated against grain prices, were substantially higher in these years than at any time in the nineteenth century. All this began to affect agriculture, where a regular cry began to be heard from *kaniachikarrar* concerning 'inability to cultivate' due to lack of labour supply. In many places, *kaniachikarrar* were obliged to improve conditions offered to labour in ways which impacted on the structure of land rights. For example, in many parts of Chingleput, Pallis – an 'inferior' agricultural caste working especially as tenants of Brahman *kaniachikarrar* – were able to acquire full *kaniachi* rights in their villages in order to tie them more closely to the community. The survey of land rights in Chingleput, conducted by Richard Barnard in the 1760s, shows *kaniachi* rights in most of the principal *casbah* (market) villages being shared between high-caste Brahmans and Vellalas and humble Pallis.[45]

The possibility that social inferiors might rise into the elite community of *kaniachikarrar* was even greater in several other places. As the new regional states of Mysore, Hyderabad, Arcot and (on the west coast) Travancore became locked in war, they began to be influenced by mercantilist practices of the Europeans (who, even by the 1750s, were the real power behind the rise of Arcot). Economic strategies became crucial to the objectives of warfare. In particular, Hyder Ali and Tipu Sultan in Mysore sought both to build up the economies of their own domains and to undermine those of their rivals. To these ends, they attempted (by inducement and by force) to attract those possessed of skill and capital to their territories. In certain areas, the result was considerable turmoil. In the northern Kaveri delta, for example, Hyder's 1782 invasion led to the forced displacement of many *kaniachikarrar* to Mysorean land further upriver. In Malabar (on the west coast), it led to the wholesale dispersal of the Nayar and Nambudiri rural elites.[46] Intriguingly, one consequence of these policies was that as established elites were driven out, the land tended to pass into the *de facto* possession of the 'inferior' castes and even *paraiyans* still resident on it. At least briefly, even in 'holy' Thanjavur (the most 'Brahmanical' district in the south), the most demeaned of subjects came to inherit the earth.

Early British settlements

It was in this highly unstable context that the new East India Company state was obliged to address the issues of 'land settlement'. As indicated earlier, its approaches were influenced by three separate concerns: to restore, to commercialise and to tax. But the three were always in tension with one another. The imperatives of 'restoration' were most clearly manifested in the proceedings of the law courts set up under Warren Hastings's dispensation in 1773, which adjudicated questions of right in the territories progressively ceded, thereafter, to the Company's government. The courts were instructed to operate on the basis of Indian law and custom and, hence, very quickly established the existence and legitimacy of the privileged rights of *kaniachi* and *inam*. However, they were inclined to take an extremely 'literal' view of Indian law and custom, demanding documentary evidence of privileged rights and insisting that these be held, in practice, in forms which approximated most closely to their foundational theory. But this overlooked and, in many ways, de-legitimated the effective patterns of change which had developed over the previous century. In particular, it questioned the marketability of land rights.

With regard to *kaniachi* rights, for example, loose conventions that no 'share' in them could be sold without the consent of all other shareholders were now made enforceable at law. Sales could be abrogated if any co-shareholder refused to give his consent, creating vast possibilities of blackmail for co-shareholders over would-be vendors.[47] With regard to *inam* rights, two developments took place. First, the courts were inclined to disallow claims made by families not mentioned in original *sanads* (deeds) of 'gift', thereby also threatening the principle of alienability. And second, as Nicholas Dirks has seen, they were inclined to undercut the rights of resumption previously enjoyed by (royal) donors: *inams*, once given, were assumed to inhere permanently in the families of the original recipients and could not be reclaimed and redistributed subsequently.[48] In effect, here the law extended much more widely that principle of inherence which previously had been confined narrowly to very specific Brahman forms of property. What it also did was to throw back the distribution of privileged rights over the land towards their most ancient and originary forms and to seek to keep them there – changeless and unchanging.

Nor was it only the law courts which interpreted the task of restoration in this very direct way. The legal perspective was strongly endorsed by particular groups of administrators, most notably gathered around F.W. Ellis, who avowedly sought the revival of a 'Hindu Golden Age'.[49] It was also informed by ideas of leading Brahman and upper-caste Vellala *dubashes* of the Company who were associated with the established 'gentry' and who scarcely disguised their ambitions to recover privileges put under threat by turmoil in the previous half-century.[50] Hopes of such a recovery provided a powerful bond between local elite groups and the Company, but one which was very much at the expense of people of 'the inferior sort' who had made recent gains. The application of 'court law' tended to lead to the loss or abrogation of rights recently acquired by low-caste labouring and tenant groups, to the restoration of rights to *kaniachikarrar* families who had been (temporarily) displaced, and to the consolidation of a firm order of caste priority in temple relations and at festivals. Combined with other policies of the 'neo-Hindu' Company state, it was also very damaging to *paraiyan* interests. Attempts were made to force *paraiyan* labour back onto the land by excluding it from many occupations (the military, weaving) and locations (especially the towns) where it had made recent advances. For a brief period, several of the Company's new collectors even utilised resources of the army to capture 'runaway' *adimai* and return them to their 'masters'.[51] Although the criminal courts raised questions about the legitimacy of this practice, the civil courts soon came to the rescue of masters by decreeing that debtors might be returned to the power of their creditors, which amounted to very much the same thing.[52]

Yet, even while Ellis and his followers were attempting to (re-)build a neo-Hindu Brahman Raj in Madras, winds from Bengal brought a change of climate. Under the principles of the Permanent Settlement, a new level of superior rights over the land was meant to be created, parcelled out among large territorial *zemindars* and made marketable. However, these principles found few advocates in the south, Indian or British. Some erstwhile 'portfolio capitalists' from mercantile castes pursued them in areas (mainly Andhra) where commerce was highly developed and closely integrated with the revenue system. But in many other places, confusion over the potential relationship between 'new' *zemindari* and 'old' *inamdari* and *kaniachikarrar* rights undermined interest.

For the most part, the Permanent Settlement in the south was confined to areas where powerful local families of chiefs (*palaiyakarrar*) had survived the political turmoil of the previous half-century with their 'royal' authority relatively intact. Such families came forward to accept *zemindari* rights which, initially, they operated as part of their continuing royal patrimony. Far from heralding a new commercial age, the Permanent Settlement actually, if only temporarily, rescued 'little kingdoms' from the threat of the greater kingdoms and sultanates which had pressured them in the eighteenth century. Admittedly, within a generation it had become painfully clear that royal authority could not fulfil the functions of commercial agency and most of the new *zemindars*/old *palaiyakarrars* had fallen deeply into debt. But then the Company state came to their rescue again, declaring them to be members of an 'ancient aristocracy' whose needs must be sustained as part of the Hindu Golden Age and setting up a much-used Court of Wards to preserve them in perpetuity.[53] As it was implemented, not even the Permanent Settlement went very far towards commercialising the relations of land in the south.

Moreover, from the 1810s, its philosophy was challenged by that of the *ryotwari* system, which reflected other goals. This system was premised on the notion that all land belonged to the sovereign, who could let it out on an individual basis to *ryots* ('peasants') in return for annual revenue engagements. The notion questioned the very existence of private-property rights in land at all. It could just about tolerate the idea of *inam* rights as gifts given by the sovereign strictly in return for service. But it directly abrogated *kaniachi* and *manyam* rights, which it saw as the result of illegitimate claims made by local communities against prerogatives exclusive to the sovereign.

Of course the notion of sovereign possession of the land, intimately linked to conceptions of Oriental despotism, had a long history in Company thought. However, its re-assertion at this time in the context of the south was not just a function of changing fashions in intellectual history. Rather, it reflected new perspectives generated within the Company as a result of its military conquest of the south in the period 1792–1805. Prior to the conquest, the Company had been inclined to conceive itself as defending property and liberty (especially for the Hindu commercial groups with whom it was closely associated) against threats posed by 'Islamic despotisms'. But after it had defeated those despotisms, it came to look more positively on what it took to be their own principles of government, which it now sought to appropriate and utilise for its own ends. Thomas Munro and his mentor, John Reade, openly admitted to having grasped their understanding of *ryotwari* theory from study of the Baramahal districts received from Tipu Sultan's Mysore as an indemnity payment in 1792.[54] What they were proposing was to extend Tipu's system of revenue administration, once considered in Fort St George as the symbol of Asiatic tyranny at its worse, across the whole of 'British' South India.[55]

But, however tendentious its origins and status, the system appealed to the directors and governors of the East India Company for the simplest of reasons. It promised far higher levels of revenue extraction than would have been possible had legitimate rights to *kaniachi* privilege and 'inherent' *inam* property been recognised. And, faced with large debts and rising military expenditures as a result of the conquest, it can hardly be deemed surprising that the directors and governors should have accepted it greedily. Following the celebrated Fifth Report of 1812, the principles of the *ryotwari* settlement were imposed on all territories of Madras not subject to the earlier Permanent Settlement.[56] In 1824, the Board of Control in London also ordered Fort St George to cease granting any future *inams* and to institute procedures investigating existing claims with a view to invalidating and resuming as many as legally possible.

The shift to a *ryotwari* form of settlement carried major implications for the character of state and society in the Company's south. It established the revenue department as the key institution of government, hugely inflating both its size and functions. Every piece of land now had to be surveyed and measured, its fertility assessed and a cash-revenue weight assigned to it. Individual *patta* (certificate of land-revenue payment) also had to be issued to (or withheld from) every peasant who would 'occupy' land. The (often discretionary) powers involved here made the revenue bureaucracy into the practical arbiters of agrarian society, and the heavy weight of the land revenue demand (especially during the price depression between the 1820s and 1850s) made it the determinant of the wealth and poverty of whole communities.

However, where these powers (and the distinctive revenue regulations through which they were enforced) stood in relation to rulings of the law courts (and the different rationality which they applied) remained utterly unclear throughout the next half-century. The two 'branches' of the state were constantly at loggerheads, with revenue-collectors frequently finding their arbitrary abrogation of *kaniachi* and *inam* rights overturned by the courts and, conversely, the courts' own judgements blithely ignored by revenue officials. The courts refused to accept revenue *pattas* as any kind of legal title to land, and the revenue department regularly swept aside court-validated claims on the grounds that they must be fraudulent.

Nor did these struggles only stay in the courts or involve only British officials. Threats to *inam* rights provoked several local rebellions. Furthermore, in the rich river valleys, attempts to impose *ryotwari* principles of settlement on *kaniachikarrar* groups frequently led to revenue and cultivation strikes and fomented social turmoil. The key issue turned on whether the revenue bureaucracy could 'let' uncultivated lands to peasants prepared to work them, or whether *kaniachi* privilege included the right to keep lands uncultivated (and untaxed) at will. How the struggle turned out depended very much on local conditions. In the Kaveri delta, where *kaniachi* authority was deeply entrenched, attempts by Munro's henchman, Collector Thackeray, to confront it came to very little and, eventually, even Thackeray abandoned his advocacy of *ryotwari* in favour of the recognition of *kaniachi* right.[57] But, in the South Arcot district, where the power of upper-caste gentries was much weaker and where lower-caste tenant and labourer groups pressed strongly for access to the land, Collector Ashton was able to find local allies to take the uncultivated lands which he offered on *ryotwari* tenure and to undermine *kaniachi* privilege.[58]

In the context of these repeated shifts in land-settlement policy, conflicts between different institutions within the colonial state, and tensions between gentry, tenant and labouring classes, it remains an open question what, exactly, happened to property rights in land at this time. Moreover, whatever residual elements of a market in land rights there might have been were further eroded by adverse economic circumstances, which began to bite in the late 1820s. South India lost most of its overseas textile markets to the new products of the British Industrial Revolution, and many of its erstwhile centres of domestic demand collapsed as the courts and armies of kings and sultans were either dismantled or subjected to Company-directed parsimony.[59] A major economic depression sat over the region for the better part of a generation, marked by price levels which fell to half of their pre-1820s average. Cultivation expanded ahead of population, but much more in response to the subsistence needs of unemployed soldiers and artisans than the lure of market profits. Land values declined, where, that is, rights in it could be defined sufficiently clearly to be given a meaningful value at all.

Practice makes perfect

Yet, by the 1850s, certain general conventions regarding proprietorship of land had come to be established. It was these which were grasped and regularised by the Inam Commission, the 'new' *ryotwari* settlement and the codification of the law. As noted earlier, the most striking feature of these conventions was the way that they reduced claims to rights in land to claims to the physical possession of particular measured pieces of 'territory'. But exactly how the transformation had come to take place is not entirely clear.

One major influence on it, certainly, was the logic of the *ryotwari* system. The system required that every acre of land under its regulation be measured, assessed for revenue and assigned to a *patta*-holder. Initially, there was resistance to the acceptance of *pattas* in many places, since they implied obligations to pay revenue whether cultivation was undertaken or not. However, there were also incentives, at least, for certain people in certain places. Where 'possession' of the land was under contest, acquisition of *patta* rights could act as a buttress to securing claims. Also, where cultivation was expanding (as it generally was in this period), 'new' farmers could gain access to land without having to pay dues and recognise the authority of existing *kaniachikarrar*. Here, the *ryotwari* system steadily gained acceptance as it facilitated the ambitions of 'inferior' and 'new' farming groups.[60]

But there could also be incentives for established *kaniachikarrar*. As practice developed in the old river valleys, a compromise was reached between *kaniachi* rights and the demands of the *ryotwari* system. Although progressively losing their ability to control village wastes, *kaniachikarrar* were offered both privileged rights to reduced revenue demands on lands which they cultivated and powers to curtail claims made against them by 'inferior' members of their local communities. *Pattas* gave their possessors absolute rights of occupancy and use of the land. This meant that they undercut subsidiary claims for 'customary' shares in the product made by tenants and labourers. In areas where a labour surplus had begun to develop (especially by mid-century), *kaniachikarrar* appear to have been prepared to concede 'lordship' rights which implied fixed obligations to labourers, in favour of *patta* rights which implied none whatever. The transition from *pangu* to *patta* was part of the creation of a new and stronger structure of class dominance in many agrarian localities.[61]

A second aspect of the shift to land rights as individualised claims on 'the soil' came from the progressive decline of 'community' structures. The *ryotwari* system contributed to this in two ways. First, it facilitated the break-up of jointly held *kaniachikarrar* villages. Although it may have been part of *ryotwari* theory from the beginning that all land ought to be occupied by 'individual' *ryot* families, in fact the practice of the settlement did not press this very far. Initially, large amounts of land were registered under the occupancy of joint-*pattadars*. However, the system did permit individual registration of *patta* rights upon request, with the result that intra-village family feuds often gained expression in appeals to separate out land rights once jointly held. Moreover, the system was biased against re-registering as 'joint' what, at any time, might have been established as 'individual' right. Over time, therefore, the system did work against the maintenance of forms of proprietorship held by multiple families. When collective rights were broken up, the most obvious logic of partition involved a final division of the land into separate (and thereafter permanently occupied) fields.

Second, the implications of the *ryotwari* system for irrigation practices were also highly significant. Normatively in pre-colonial times, *kaniachikarrar* had been meant to take responsibility for the maintenance of irrigation channels according to their 'shares' in particular villages. Such responsibility was recognised by the state in reduced revenue payments and, in many senses, functionally legitimated *kaniachi* privilege. However, unwilling to accept the loss of revenue involved, the *ryotwari* system transferred responsibility for irrigation maintenance entirely to the state and raised local levels of revenue demand. Needless to say, the Company scarcely fulfilled this responsibility: between the 1820s and late 1840s, less than a half of 1 per cent of land-revenue collections were actually re-invested in the irrigation system. But what the shift in responsibility and funding certainly did was to undermine the last vestiges of economic logic holding 'community' production systems together. There was now no compelling reason why individual farming families should not concentrate their energies and capital entirely on their own private fields.

A third area where the *ryotwari* system also promoted this outcome concerned the character of *inam* rights. Although the system notionally recognised such rights as immunities from revenue demand, the nature of its administrative logic meant that it had to express them as claims against the revenue due from particular measured fields – not from a collective village product. Inam rights thus became detached from the local community institutions which had originally created them and – bizarrely – were imputed to the soil itself.

Yet, however, bizarre this imputation, there were – again – strong reasons why certain members of local society should be keen to instrumentalise the new system. For example, in the Ceded Districts first settled by Munro between 1800 and 1804, over 40 per cent of the cultivated land and most of the best black soils came to be conceded as *inam* on which little or no revenue should be collected.[62] Munro's initial settlement recorded possession of these *inam* lands to be widely distributed between temples, charitable organisations, village artisans and servants: with village officers (the lowest rung of the revenue bureaucracy) holding only 22 per cent of them. However, these village officers controlled the accounts and, when the Inam Commission of 1859 re-surveyed the area, it found that they had by now transferred 69 per cent of *inam* lands to their own possession.[63] Once more, the realisation of colonial innovations rested on the interested participation of certain colonial subjects.

Yet if the role of the *ryotwari* system in the 'individualisation' and 'territorialisation' of land rights is not difficult to see, the same is not necessarily true of the role of the law courts. These, originally, had recognised rights in land to be much more broadly based and to include claims made on a 'village' product. But, at least by the 1840s, they too seemed to have been drawn towards the same conclusions as the *ryotwari* system and to have taken to treating land rights exclusively in terms of the physical ownership of land. The reason for this may have lain in growing pressures from London and Fort St George to apply juridical rules reflective of current theories of political economy.

The abolition of 'slavery' in 1843 had the effect not only of legally dissolving the power of lords (*dorai*) over their *adimai*, but also the web of customary payments and obligations binding the two together.[64] Henceforth, labour relations were legally established on a strictly contractual basis wherein appeals to 'custom' had no validity. This completed a process, begun in the 1820s, whereby the courts were pressed to abandon their claims to adjudicate in disputes over other matters of 'non-real' property, such as *manyam* and tenancy rights, which were held also to belong to the domain of contract. The domain of 'tradition', supposedly governed by India's own laws as interpreted by the courts, came progressively to shrink until, in effect, it covered only questions of the possession and inheritance of 'real property'. In law, property rights became concretised as land rights less by intention than by corollary. Once the customary rights of labour had been 'de-recognised', all that was left for the law to adjudicate were rights in land. Moreover, as this shift took place in a context where land was becoming scarcer and labour relatively more plentiful, it need hardly be said whose interests it served. Labour's share in the social product started to fall as capitalism finally consolidated its hold on southern India.

Epilogue

By these curious and cross-cutting roads, then, the nature of land rights in southern India had come to be transformed by the second half of the nineteenth century. They now meant, simply, rights to the exclusive and individual possession of a physical piece of land. As argued above, it is unclear that this outcome entirely met the intentions of any of the parties (at least British colonial parties) engaged in the process. If the procedures of the *ryotwari* system were aimed at raising a massive revenue demand, they signally failed to achieve it over time. Not only were the authorities obliged to concede vast amounts of tax-free *inam* land but, as *pattas* progressively became equated with ownership and came to acquire a market value of their own, so the ability of the revenue department to sustain taxation steadily declined. The price rise, which began in the 1850s and lasted until the First World War, continuously eroded the proportion of the agricultural product taken in revenue.

But the actual nature of the transformation scarcely suited Permanent Settlement ideologues either. Although land rights were now equated with 'real' landed property, and a market for them grew (or recovered) in the later nineteenth century, the influence of the Anglo–Hindu law continued to provide strong restraint. While traditional obligations owed to labourers and tenants were undercut, those owed to ancestors, other family and caste members and even 'the gods' continued little diminished. Landed property remained tightly encumbered by other forms of tradition and the development of a fully commercial agrarian society was attenuated.[65]

Yet, while Anglo–Hindu law might claim some kind of victory here in terms of its original mandate to rule India by its own laws and customs, it was very much less successful elsewhere. In conceding its rights to adjudicate matters pertaining to 'non-real' property, it threw away one of its most vital links with history. Rather than preserving 'Hindu Society', it inadvertently presided over and became an instrument in a social transformation taking southern India towards regressive forms of agricultural capitalism in which profits came less from technological innovation than lowering the rewards of labour.

It is this last aspect of the transition which, perhaps, deserves the strongest emphasis. Whatever the new colonial rulers (contradictorily) willed could only be turned into social reality through the agency of southern Indians themselves. Here, the promulgations of the courts, the *ryotwari* system and the Permanent Settlement became tools of strategy in complex and often long-standing social struggles for status and power on the land. As the region became more closely related to the 'global' political economy of the later nineteenth century, as population expanded and as land became scarcer, those struggles increasingly turned to questions of the exclusionary possession of the soil. Labour commanded ever less of a price and the transmutation of land rights became, most meaningfully, part of the elimination of labour's claims on the social product and reduction of that labour's effective status within southern Indian society.

Notes

1 Neale, 1969.
2 Washbrook, 1981.
3 For a summary, see Guha, 1963.
4 Ellis, 1816.
5 Mukherjee, 1962.
6 For debates in Tamil society on the proper nature of its traditions, see Irschick, 1994.
7 On the expansion of Mysore, see Guha, 1985.
8 Irschick, 1994.
9 Guha, 1963.
10 Travers, 2001.
11 Wilson, 2000.
12 Stein, 1989.
13 Hudleston, 1862.
14 Subramanian, 1999.
15 Karashima, 1984.
16 Gough, 1981.

17 Perlin, 1985.
18 Dirks, 1986.
19 Karashima, 1984.
20 Stein, 1980.
21 Stein, 1984a.
22 Sivakumar and Sivakumar, 1993.
23 Ludden, 1985.
24 Sivakumar and Sivakumar, 1993.
25 Sivakumar and Sivakumar, 1993.
26 Stein, 1980; Dirks, 1986.
27 Sivakumar and Sivakumar, 1993.
28 Stein, 1980.
29 'Report on the Tiruvendrapuram Farm, 1775', *Revenue Sundries* (ASO/D), vol. 43. Tamil Nadu Archives, Chennai (hereafter TNA).
30 Tanjore District Records, vol. 3200 (1800), pp. 53-77, pp. 179–80: TNA.
31 Beck, 1972.
32 Stein, 1984b.
33 Subrahmanyam, 1989.
34 Ludden, 1985; Karashima, 1984.
35 Subrahmanyam, 1989.
36 Ludden, 1985.
37 Chicherov, 1971.
38 Bayly, 1989.
39 Bayly, 1988.
40 Subrahmanyam, 1989.
41 Furber, 1948.
42 Bayly, 1983.
43 Kavi, 1948.
44 Mizushima, 1986.
45 Washbrook, 1993.
46 Guha, 1985.
47 Washbrook, 1981.
48 Dirks, 1986.
49 Ellis, 1816.
50 Irschick, 1994.
51 Washbrook, 1993.
52 Masulipatam District Records, vol. 2963 (1816), pp. 683–85: State Archives, Hyderabad (hereafter SAH).
53 Price, 1996.
54 Stein, 1989.

55 Or, at least, extending what Tipu had pretended was his revenue system. There are doubts that the *ryotwari* 'model' found in documents from Tipu's court ever was enforced. Also, it seems clear that Tipu made inflated claims about the revenue yield of the Baramahal which he was obliged to surrender to the Company in 1792 as a war indemnity.
56 Stein, 1989.
57 Tanjore District Records, vol. 3176 (1807), pp. 24–26, 224–32: TNA.
58 Revenue Department Consultations, vol. 538, no 1, February 1841, pp. 565–651: TNA.
59 Raju, 1941.
60 Ludden, 1985.
61 Washbrook, 1993; Ludden, 1985.
62 Stein, 1984a, especially pp. 90–117.
63 Washbrook, 1994.
64 Prakash, 1990.
65 Washbrook, 1981.

Bibliography
Abbreviations

SAH: State Archives, Hyderabad
TNA: Tamil Nadu Archives

Primary sources

Tamil Nadu Archives, Chennai
'Report on the Tiruvendrapuram Farm, 1775', Revenue Sundries (ASO/D), vol. 43
Tanjore District Records, vol. 3200 (1800)
State Archives, Hyderabad (SAH).
Masulipatam District Records, vol. 2963 (1816)

Secondary sources

Bayly, Christopher A., *Rulers, Townsmen and Bazaars*, Cambridge, Cambridge University Press, 1983.
– *Indian Society and the Making of the British Empire*, Cambridge, Cambridge University Press, 1988.

Bayly, Susan, *Saints, Goddesses and Kings*, Cambridge, Cambridge University Press, 1989.

Beck, Brenda E.F., *Peasant Society in Konku*, Vancouver, University of British Columbia Press, 1972.

Chicherov, A.I., *India, Economic History in the 16th–18th Centuries: Outline History of Crafts and Trade*, Moscow, Nauka Publishing House, 1971.

Dirks, Nicholas B., 'From Little King to Landlord', *Comparative Studies in Society and History* 28/2, 1986, pp. 307–33.

– *The Hollow Crown*, Cambridge, Cambridge University Press, 1987.

Ellis, F.W., *Replies to Seventeen Questions Posed by the Government of Fort St George Relative to Mirasi Right*, Madras, Government of Madras Press, 1816.

Furber, Holden, *John Company at Work*, Cambridge, MA, Harvard University Press, 1948.

Gough, Kathleen, *Rural Society in Southeastern India*, Cambridge, Cambridge University Press, 1981.

Guha, Nikhiles, *Pre-British State System in South India: Mysore 1761–1799*, Calcutta, Ratna Prakashan, 1985.

Guha, Ranajit, *A Rule of Property for Bengal*, Paris, Mouton, 1963.

Hudleston, W., *Papers on Mirasi Right*, Madras, Madras Government Press, 1862.

Irschick, E.F., *Dialogue and History*, Berkeley, University of California Press, 1994.

Karashima, Noboru, *South Indian History and Society – Studies from Inscriptions AD 850–1800*, Delhi, Oxford University Press, 1984.

Kavi, Srinivasa, *Anandarangavijayacumpuh* (in Sanskrit), ed. V. Raghavan, Tiruccirapalli, Palaniyappa Bros, 1948.

Ludden, David, *Peasant History in South India*, Princeton, Princeton University Press, 1985.

Mizushima, T., *Nattar and Socio-Economic Change in the Eighteenth and Nineteenth Centuries*, Tokyo, Tokyo University of Foreign Studies, 1986.

Mukherjee, Nilmani, *The Ryotwari System in Madras*, Calcutta, K.L. Mukhopadhya, 1962.

Neale, Walter C., 'Land is to Rule', in Robert Eric Frykenberg (ed.), *Land Control and Social Structure in Indian History*, Madison, Wisconsin University Press, 1969, pp. 3–16.

Perlin, Frank, 'State Formation Reconsidered', *Modern Asian Studies* 19/3, 1985, pp. 415–80.

Prakash, Gyan, *Bonded Histories: Genealogies of Labour Servitude in Colonial India*, Cambridge, Cambridge University Press, 1990.

Price, Pamela G., *Kingship and Political Practice in Colonial India*, Cambridge, Cambridge University Press, 1996.

Raju, Sarada A., *Economic Conditions in the Madras Presidency, 1800–1850*, Madras, Madras University Press, 1941.

Sivakumar, C. and S.S. Sivakumar, *Peasants and Nabobs*, Delhi, Hindustan Publishing House, 1993.

Stein, Burton, *Peasant, State and Society in Medieval South India*, Delhi, Oxford University Press, 1980.

– *All the King's Mana*, Madras, New Era Press, 1984a.

– 'Social Mobility and Medieval Hindu Sects', in Burton Stein (ed.), *All the King's Mana*, Madras, New Era Press, 1984b, pp. 281–302.

– *Thomas Munro: The Origins of the Colonial State and His Views of Empire*, Delhi, Oxford University Press, 1989.

Subramanian, Narendra, *Ethnicity and Populist Mobilization*, Delhi, Oxford University Press, 1999.

Subrahmanyam, Sanjay, *The Political Economy of Commerce in South India, 1500–1650*, Cambridge, Cambridge University Press, 1989.

Travers, Robert, *Contested Notions of Sovereignty in Bengal under British Rule*, unpublished PhD dissertation, Cambridge University, 2001.

Washbrook, David A., 'Law, State and Agrarian Society in Colonial India', *Modern Asian Studies* 15/3, 1981, pp. 649–721.

– 'The Golden Age of Pariah', in Peter Robb (ed.), *Dalit Movements and the Meanings of Labor in India*, Delhi, Oxford University Press, 1993, pp. 68–86.

– 'The Commercialization of Agriculture in Colonial India', *Modern Asian Studies* 28/1, 1994, pp. 129–64.

Wilson, Jon, *Governing Property, Making Law: Land, Local Society and Colonial Discourse in Agrarian Bengal, 1785–1830*, unpublished DPhil. dissertation, Oxford University, 2000.

CHAPTER 4

Land, Law and the Planning of Empire: Jaffa and Tel Aviv During the Late Ottoman and Mandate Periods

Mark LeVine

It is a balmy late-summer day in 1925 and the eminent British town planner Patrick Geddes is moments away from boarding one of the infamous lighters that ferry passengers from Jaffa Port and its treacherous reef to the steamships anchored out to sea. Geddes's mood is ebullient as he addresses the assemblage of local dignitaries there to see him off, for he has just submitted his new town plan for Jaffa, the rapidly developing economic and cultural capital of Palestine, and Tel Aviv, its impetuous upstart sibling to the north.

Reading from the text of his plan, Geddes concludes his address by stressing that 'with all respect to the ethnic distinctiveness and the civic individuality of Tel Aviv... the old town and the modern [quarter] must increasingly work and grow together... for Greater Jaffa'.[1] The mayor of Jaffa, along with the *kaymakam* and their retinue, clap with approval. The leaders of Jaffa's most famous Jewish neighbourhood are less enthusiastic. They had hoped for a plan which would address the needs of Tel Aviv not within the horizon of Jaffa's development, but rather as the autonomous independently developing and thoroughly modern city that they imagined it to be. But they could not complain; they would be lucky if the municipality allowed Tel Aviv to expand to the borders of surrounding Arab villages, as called for in the Geddes Plan.

* * *

Of course, there was no *kaymakam* or any other Ottoman official in Jaffa in 1925. His duties had been assumed by a British District Commissioner several years earlier. Nor was Tel Aviv merely Jaffa's most prominent new quarter. Instead, British rule and a dramatic increase in Jewish immigration had, by 1925, poised Tel Aviv to surpass Jaffa in terms of population and capital growth.[2] Yet Patrick Geddes did deliver his new town plan for the Jaffa-Tel Aviv region in the summer of 1925; the above words are his, the reaction of Tel Aviv's leadership was less than sanguine, and the plan was never meaningfully adopted. I have begun with the above simulacrum of the events of that summer because the moment that it depicts marks an important but overlooked entry point into one of the central questions of the historiography of modern Palestine: the extent to which British rule (and the Zionist colonisation that it facilitated) marked a continuation of or a rupture with the social and political economy of the country during the final decades of the Ottoman era.

Until recently, historiography of modern Palestine was dominated by a liberal or modernisation perspective. This view saw European hegemony in Palestine (that is Zionist colonisation and British rule) as heralding a radical transformation of a country bogged down in centuries of social and economic stagnation, political despotism and an absence of private property and 'the rule of law'.[3] These were the defining characteristics of Ottoman rule (in general and in Palestine) as imagined by British, Zionist and most Western scholars – the antithesis of European energy and progress unleashed by the regime of private property, unhindered markets and states that did not intrude into the business of society.[4] Thus Tel Aviv's first mayor complained that Ottoman rule 'did not know any law and did not have any rules [professional regulations] for building the city. So there was complete anarchy.'[5]

Such dichotomisations of East and West, of state and society, contributed to an understanding of emerging Zionist and Palestinian communities as 'dual societies', autonomously developing at different rates along separate paths.[6] This view exerted a profound influence on the way that Palestine was governed under the British Mandate, particularly in the arena of law and the fields of power that it encompassed, where the contest over land between Palestinian Arabs and Jews was often played out.

Recent scholarship on the political economy of the late-Ottoman state has challenged the privileging of nineteenth-century Europe as a unique realm of private property and market relations. It is becoming increasingly clear not only that both were present throughout Eurasia but, equally important, that they were fuelled by a process of increasing state centralisation and involvement in society that runs contrary to the disentanglement of the two called for in modernisation theory.[7] This understanding of the determinative role of the late-Ottoman state in the expansion of private property and market relations within its realm is supported by research on the political economy of modern Palestine. In fact, it provides a framework for explaining the growth of the country's regional and worldwide trade during this period, the concomitant increase in the capitalisation of land and the 'flourishing' economy of the Jaffa region (home to Palestine's most important port and to the lucrative orange trade) that they helped secure.[8]

Such a picture suggests the need to re-imagine British rule over Palestine not as a rupture with, but rather in many areas a continuation of, the dynamics of Ottoman rule.[9] The research presented here supports the argument for continuity as well as for abandoning numerous binaries separating peoples (Jews and Palestinian Arabs) and social actors (the state from society) that are inherent to the modernisation paradigm. Yet, as I hinted in the dramatisation above, shared vocabularies and technologies of rule did not lead to continuity in the trajectory of Palestine's socio-economic development from the late-Ottoman to the Mandate period.

In fact, my purpose in briefly imagining the development of Tel Aviv and Jaffa under continued Ottoman rule was precisely to highlight the changing fortunes of the two cities under British administration which mirrored the shifting balance of power between the larger Jewish and Arab communities whose hopes and self-image they symbolised.[10] That is, negotiation over the meanings and power of new laws and categories of tenure in late-Ottoman Jaffa were continuous,[11] and if the politics of private property that framed their articulation were not always congruent with the interests of the indigenous population of

Jaffa, neither did they automatically favour the numerous European communities, including Zionist Jews, who lived and did business there.[12]

However, with the arrival of the British and the concomitant rise in Zionist political, economic and demographic power, the discourse of modernist planning[13] contributed significantly to legal transformations that occurred under British rule. These changes benefited the Zionist movement even as they purported to 'conserve' the vocabulary of Ottoman law.[14]

Within this context, the battle over the establishment of Tel Aviv offers an opportune moment to chart how this transformation was being contested and resisted in ways that would no longer be possible under British rule.[15] The goal of this chapter is to determine the nature of these changes by examining the struggles over land in the Jaffa-Tel Aviv region and the arenas of law and planning which defined the parameters of that contest. In order to accomplish this, a three-fold exploration is required: first, of where and how the British 'recodification' of this body of laws signalled a continuity or transformation of the existing body and practice of Ottoman, religious and customary laws in Palestine, and in particular the Jaffa-Tel Aviv region; second, of the extent to which the dynamics of the property market in Jaffa (as exemplified by the purchase of the land on which Tel Aviv was established) reflected the vocabulary of land law articulated by the late-Ottoman state; third, of how a recognition of the centrality of the discourse of planning to this vocabulary can more accurately frame the transformations that did occur.

The choice of the Geddes Plan as my entry point to this discussion highlights the role of planning as an axis of that transformation, and will sensitise the reader to its determinative role in the politics of property under both Ottoman and British rule.

The changing categorisations of land tenure in late-Ottoman and Mandate Palestine

In a previous study, I analysed the consequences of Zionist and British discourses of development in Mandate Palestine, particularly as they played out in the agricultural sector.[16] My examination revealed how the 'modernist' world view underlying both Zionist and British diagnoses of Palestine's (and its population's) problems and these two interests' proposed solutions to develop and modernise the country led inevitably to an understanding of development which – like all colonial-national projects – meant developing the local population off their land.[17]

The importance of this shared discourse of development is clearly evident in the ability of Tel Aviv's leadership to utilise British land and town-planning legislation to gain control of large swaths of land from neighbouring Palestinian Arab villages. In order to understand how Tel Aviv's leaders were able to affect this expansion, this section examines the changes wrought by the British on Ottoman land law in Palestine.

British land law in Palestine was based on the existing body of Ottoman law that emerged from the Land Code, Mecelle (the Ottoman civil code, adopted from 1869-76), Constitution and subsequent rulings extending up to 1914. Six classes of land – *mülk*, *miri*, *vakıf*, *mevat*, *mahlul* and *metruke* – were adopted by the British during their rule of the country.

In fact, as Huri İslamoğlu points out,[18] the Land Code dealt only with state lands: *mevat*, *mahlul* and *metruke*; the categories of *mülk* and *vakıf* were not included. *Mülk* was dealt with in the Mecelle.[19] It is important to note that while *mülk* is generally understood as being 'private' property, this is not an accurate reading of the pre-1858 reality, in which it was specifically a claim to revenue from land which was balanced against parallel and sometimes competing claims to usufruct and title (*rakaba*). That is, it was one of a bundle of often competing rights under constant negotiation by the state and other social classes. However, with the enactment of the Land Code, the state became the outright 'owner' of new state lands, instead of the possessor of the power to distribute various rights to different competing groups within society. Most importantly, as the owner of land, the state could then sell lands to raise money, as opposed to the previous practice of distributing rights to revenue. The buyers of state lands were issued titles of ownership. The *mülk* and *vakıf* were subsequently assimilated into the new ordering through the extension of practices of the issuing of title deeds and of lease contracts which applied on state lands. It is within this context that we must understand the post-1858 categories of land tenure which the British would ultimately inherit and rigidify. Specifically, the reconstituted category of *mülk* encompassed privately owned land, located primarily in urban areas, which could be disposed of as the owner saw fit. *Miri* land was land in which the *rakaba* (the title) rested with the state (and thus was owned by the state outright). Occupiers had permanent usufruct rights as long as they cultivated it and paid the tithe. Until 1913, *miri* owners had to obtain special permission from the state to use *miri* land for industrial purposes or even for vineyards, orchards or dwellings, as the state believed (mistakenly) that these restrictions would keep the largest amount of land available for agriculture.[20] The same year, freehold rights were extended to *miri* land, bringing the process to its logical conclusion and rendering inoperative large parts of the 1858 Land Code.[21] *Vakıf* lands were dedicated to religious or charitable purposes and were divided into two types: those dedicated from *mülk* lands (*vakıf-sahih*) and those dedicated from *miri* lands (*vakıf-ı gayr-ı sahih*). In addition to the six official categories of land, another important classification in use in Palestine was the *musha'* system, which essentially meant collective village ownership or tenure of a plot of land, with the land being redistributed on a periodic basis so that all members of the community had equal access to the best land. *Musha'* came under more criticism than perhaps any other form of tenure in Palestine, as it was believed by the British and Zionist leaders that collective ownership prevented the capitalisation of land that was the prerequisite for privatisation and modernisation of the agricultural sector.

The categories of *mevat*, *mahlul* and *metruke* are of particular importance for our discussion because they were conceived of as being unused or empty and, with the British committed to extending the roots of a new even more generalised concept of state ownership, could be most easily converted into urban land, the precursor for development by Jews.[22]

Mevat lands were unoccupied, marginal agricultural lands that were situated far from inhabited areas and were neither held by title deed nor assigned *ab antiquo* to the use of inhabitants of a nearby town or village.[23] Under Ottoman rule, one could assume possession, cultivate and gain title to *mevat* lands upon payment of a tax on the unimproved value of the land. Many Arab cultivators took advantage of this provision during the Ottoman period, and numerous towns and villages were extended and enlarged this way. However, the British wanted to retain full control of as much state land as possible, and in 1921 the Mevat Land Ordinance was issued, making it an offence to cultivate *mevat* land.[24]

This marked an important change in the understanding of *mevat* land, because it shifted the meaning of the term from emphasising the land's unclaimed status and distance from built-up areas to an understanding of such land as being 'waste' and 'barren' – the perfect *tabula rasa*, for example, upon which to build a modern European city such as the one envisioned by Tel Aviv's founders, for whom the legend of Tel Aviv's 'birth out of the sands' attained the level of ur-myth.[25] That is, as the 1947 Survey of Palestine explains, '*mevat* land should have no significance and should be deemed undeveloped, vacant land proper which cannot be possessed except by allocation from the State'.[26] Deemed to be 'dead or undeveloped',[27] *mevat* land was ripe for development and, being state property, was more easily allocated to those thought capable of developing it, although 'the nature of the reviver' would be considered in any case involving attempts to reclaim *mevat* land.

Mahlul (state land) was land that reverted to government control if left uncultivated for three years.[28] Similar to *mevat* land, until 1921 the previous holder of usufruct rights could redeem the land by paying a tax, while even squatting was recognised in certain circumstances. But here too the British re-interpreted the law so that the High Commissioner could declare *mahlul* land to be public land and thus permanently at the disposal of the state to allocate as it deemed appropriate.[29] During the transition from Turkish to British rule, in 1917, the Tel Aviv Council attempted to claim surrounding *mahlul* (and also *miri*) lands by allocating money to plant trees.[30] Two decades later, the *mahlul* lands (particularly in the north of the city) were still considered to be vital for the city's development because they could be used for building the Tel Aviv port.[31]

Matruke lands were public or communal lands, such as roads or pastures, and were especially important in the Jaffa-Tel Aviv region, where at least three villages had semi-sedentary bedouin populations. It was prohibited for anyone other than the village to which the land belonged to encroach on, cultivate or plough *matruke* land, and ownership was not transferable during the Ottoman period.[32]

During the Mandate period, there were several struggles over whether the High Commissioner had or should have the power to change the categorisation of *matruke* land (which he, in fact, assumed in 1933).[33] The Palestinian Arabs were particularly worried about the High Commissioner assuming this power because in most cases where it became possible to reclaim *matruke* land Arab cultivators would not have the funds to develop such areas themselves, the assumption being that 'the Jews would be allowed to buy up land and develop land which it is impossible for them to obtain under the present law'.[34]

It is clear that under British rule the categories of *mevat*, *mahlul* and *matruke* were brought under tighter control than in the previous period, essentially becoming *de facto* if not *de jure* *miri* (that is state) land.[35] Thus the semi-official 1935 Land Law of Palestine describes a case heard at the Jaffa Land Court in 1926 in which the presiding judge declared that 'cultivation ... must be effective and "maintained". Operations must be carried out which result in a *permanent*[36] and definite change in the quality of the land. The wilderness must be made to blossom.'[37] This new dynamic of permanently altering the 'quality' of land and the concomitant change in its status is in marked contrast to the local experience of marginal or 'unclaimed' land brought into use when needed and left fallow during other times – a dynamic that is not recognised by this more rigid interpretation of land reclamation.

What makes this transformation so important is that traditionally, and even more so during the Mandate period, 'all land situated within the boundaries of towns and villages [was] treated as *mülk*... it matters not whether the land is cultivated or not'.[38] While only the High Commissioner had the power[39] to convert urban *miri* into *mülk* land, the authors of the Land Law of Palestine describe the process as usually being 'automatic with the extension of urban boundaries'.[40]

In fact, this rigidification of what had formerly been (and in the villages outside of Jaffa, at least, continued to be) a more elastic negotiation of bundles of rights to and control over land was an inevitable outcome of the transformation of Ottoman land law, beginning with the 1858 Land Code, and the drive toward outright ownership by the state or private parties that it signified. It is further clear that while the British sought to give Ottoman land law the appearance of being a body of immutable rules and procedures, land law during the Mandate period was, in actuality, 'a contested domain, continually being created and re-created pending the requirements and assertions of the participants in particular historical situations'.[41] In fact, British officials often had trouble finding a copy of the original Ottoman laws, especially in English, and until the late 1920s no one had the requisite knowledge and experience to compose an authoritative and reliable English digest of Ottoman land law. Thus the very foundation of Mandate land law was literally copies of copies or translations of translations[42] of Ottoman laws.

The borders of modernity: the changing dynamics of land tenure in the Jaffa-Tel Aviv region during the final years of Ottoman rule

The above discussion concerning the evolution of land tenure in late-Ottoman and Mandate Jaffa-Tel Aviv helps situate the conflicts over land during this period and the history that they produced. Traditional historiography has described Jaffa as a forsaken district, at least until the latter part of the nineteenth century.[43] More recent studies suggest that the invasion of Napoleon in 1799 and the strengthened Ottoman presence in the region in its wake helped inaugurate a dynamic period of growth during the nineteenth century that lasted till the end of the Ottoman period, one that profoundly reshaped Jaffa's social geography.

This development was not limited to the immediate environs of the old city and its port, but also included small villages and farms in its immediate vicinity which had been settled for centuries.[44] By mid-century, in the wake of the Crimean War, Jaffa was becoming the centre of Arab Palestine's economic life. In the following decades, it would play a similar role in the 'New Yishuv' – that is the specifically Zionist-inspired immigration to the country that began during the century's final decades.[45]

Central to this process was the immigration of significant numbers of Palestinian and non-local Arabs (including bedouin), Jews and Europeans to the region. With them came increased capital, investment and a rapid expansion of the built-up and cultivated area outside the old city, much of it undertaken by peasants and an emerging middle class (including women). Both merchants and peasants understood that investing in Jaffa was a good business prospect.[46]

It is within the context of the increasingly complex social and political economy of Jaffa and its deepening economic ties with Europe (which, it should be pointed out, did not indicate a necessary reduction in trade within the Ottoman Empire[47]) that we must examine the changing nature of land ownership during this period. This was a relationship which caused great consternation to Europeans even as it presented great opportunities for investment. Specifically, local officials were often felt to use chicanery or take advantage of the 'subtlety' of Ottoman land law in order to disrupt property transactions involving Europeans.[48]

There is an alternative understanding of the behaviour attributed to local officials beyond greed and corruption, namely that they were concerned about the ramifications of increased foreign land purchases on the economic and social health of the region, especially its poorer inhabitants. The European perception of these actions as dishonest and labyrinthine reveal a bias against any Ottoman/indigenous attempts at development that would similarly characterise Zionist and British reactions to Ottoman and then local activities.

Perhaps the most important development in the decades after the Crimean War was the increased capitalisation of land in the vicinity of Jaffa,[49] a process which, in fact, had begun two decades earlier, during the mid-1830s.[50] This capitalisation of land was a sign both of the social and economic development of the Jaffa region and of the monetarisation of the local economy which, in turn, challenged and helped transform the system of land tenure in Jaffa even before the better-known 1858 Land Code was issued.

Along with Europeans, Sephardic (and later Ashkenazi) Jews played an important role in the geographical expansion of Jaffa.[51] They purchased land not just for exclusively Jewish purposes, but also in partnership with Muslims and Christians, although these occurred less frequently than Muslim–Christian partnerships.[52] In fact, several of the prominent Sephardi families realised even before the war that converting their liquid capital, earned from commerce and money-changing, into property would prove to have been a wise investment in the future. By the 1870s, for example, the Shloosh family was 'buying vineyard after vineyard' in the sands north of Jaffa, land which would form the nucleus of the pre-Tel Aviv Jewish neighbourhoods of Jaffa.[53]

Already by the early 1880s, Jews had begun building on the lands acquired in previous decades, joining the exodus of Christians and wealthier Muslims from the old city.[54] From one perspective, the Zionist need to purchase land dovetailed nicely with a major objective of the centralising Ottoman state during this period: the constitution of private property and the sale of lands through it to generate tax revenue.[55] Such policies, however, led to conflicting impulses vis-à-vis Zionist activity which spoke in just such a language of productivity and revenue.[56] On the other hand, the Ottoman government in Istanbul was aware of the increasing influx of Jews into and through Jaffa and, as a matter of policy, opposed Zionist-inspired Jewish settlement even before it began in 1881.[57]

Thus, within a decade Jews in Jaffa 'were beginning to incur ill-will' by building houses and vineyards without permission from the government.[58] Nevertheless, by 1906, almost a dozen Jewish neighbourhoods had been founded in Jaffa. That year, 60 prominent members of Jaffa's Jewish community decided to found a society, Ahuzat Bayit ('Estate-purchasing Society') for the purchase of land and the construction of homes in the Jaffa region. Soon other building societies were formed to buy land in the Jaffa region.[59]

The desire to build a modern European-style suburb stemmed from the Zionist concept of 'Arab Jaffa' as ancient and unplanned, suffering from 'filth and ugliness, from a lack of comfort and aesthetic beauty'. This sentiment 'made the arriving Jewish immigrants feel bad and caused them to dream of a new quarter', one 'arranged according to laws, all of it Hebrew', and thus suitable for people who 'possessed energy and vigor'. This quarter would be 'the new, the beautiful and clean – Jaffa of the Jews'.[60]

Tel Aviv, the name given to the Jaffa of the Jews,[61] would play a central role in the drive to constitute both an economic and political force in Palestine. Even before its foundation, however, Zionist leaders talked of having created 'a state within a state' in Jaffa. The success of this enterprise depended on ownership of land,[62] and Tel Aviv would be the instrument with which to 'conquer Jaffa economically'.[63]

The conquest of Jaffa would be made possible in no small part by the modern and planned nature of the new Jewish town against which (what was perceived to be) an unplanned Arab Jaffa and its surrounding villages could not compete. In fact, the period 1909–11 in which Tel Aviv was born and began its development was a pivotal one in the development of modern architecture and even more of town planning in Europe and the US.[64] Together with their knowledge of Ottoman[65] and later British land laws, the discourse of planning would play a principal role in the transformation of the predominantly Arab hinterland of Jaffa into a sphere of urban development, one understood by the British as well as Tel Aviv's leadership as being essential to the health and development of the Jewish town.[66]

Specifically, the members of Ahuzat Bayit sought to design their suburb along the most modern lines possible. Thus they favoured the garden-city model then in vogue in Europe (and especially Great Britain), which was also being used by British planners in the colonies. 'The aim of this group is the founding of a modern Jewish quarter in Jaffa' was how the first paragraph of the charter for Ahuzat Bayit read.[67]

It must be stressed that Jaffa was no less modern or full of energy than Tel Aviv. In fact, one could easily interpret problems of overcrowding or disorder as demonstrating its modernity as they were also the bane of most European cities during this period.[68] More positively, an examination of both the urban expansion of Jaffa and its architecture reveals similarities in style and design to Tel Aviv that continue well into the Mandate era.[69]

Nevertheless, to protect its modernity the leaders of Ahuzat Bayit determined that the new suburb should be spatially and ethnically segregated from the mother town, similar to the *villes nouvelles* of other colonised cities. Thus they searched for land situated at a distance from the city in order to maximise the neighbourhood's autonomy, and only Jews were to be allowed to live there (the bylaws prohibited the sale or renting of houses to Palestinian Arabs).[70]

With this historical background, let us turn to the events surrounding the establishment of Tel Aviv. The plot of land chosen by Ahuzat Bayit was located slightly more than a kilometre from the old city in an area known as Karm al-Jabali (that is the vineyard owned by the Jebali family [in Hebrew Kerem Jebali]). It was owned by numerous heirs, some of whom had entered into contract with three Jewish brokers from Jerusalem to purchase the land.[71] How numerous were the heirs? While the official history of Tel Aviv claims that there were nine,[72] a list of owners written in Hebrew, Arabic and Ottoman Turkish lists an exponentially larger number of heirs: in fact 106 pages of heirs with around one thousand names.[73]

Moreover, an examination of various contracts, maps and surveys relating to Karm al-Jabali reveals that none describes the same borders or even the same geographical landmarks.[74] Nor is the area of the plot the same in each document.[75] In a very tangible sense, then, these documents are not speaking of the same plot of land.

The original Arabic contract of sale stated that the sellers had 'uncontested' ownership of the property, obtained both by inheritance and purchase (and thus the subsequent purchase of Karm al-Jabali by Ahuzat Bayit should also have been uncontested), yet there were many problems with the purchase. To begin with, the land could not be openly purchased by either Ahuzat Bayit or the Anglo-Palestine Bank, but only by an Ottoman subject. This problem was overcome when two Ottoman Jews living in Jaffa agreed to register the land in their name in return for each receiving a plot of land in the neighbourhood (once again demonstrating how Ottoman laws were not so much an obstacle to be overcome as a reference point for negotiation).[76]

Moreover, in the autumn of 1907, the Porte had tightened the strictures on land sales to Jews by prohibiting sales of *miri* (state land) even to Ottoman Jews.[77] This impacted on the purchase of the land when the Jaffa municipality subsequently challenged the sale by claiming that part of the land of Karm al-Jabali was, in fact, *miri* land.[78] There were two specific areas of concern. First, if the Jaffa municipality's above-mentioned claim that a quarter of Karm al-Jabali was *miri* land was sustained, the purchase of Karm al-Jabali even by Ottoman Jews would be prohibited, or in the best-case scenario (assuming that the municipality disregarded the order from Istanbul, which was certainly not unthinkable), Ahuzat Bayit would have to purchase that portion of the land from the municipality, not the representatives of the al-Jabali family.[79] Moreover, a 1909 reference to Karm al-Jabali in the Jaffa Islamic Court records describes the land as 'already having a group of houses on it', owned by one Mr Yakubus bin Morris bin Elizar of the Netherlands, who rented it to a group of Jews for 363 French francs for 18 years.[80] This is perhaps how the sale of Karm al-Jabali to Ahuzat Bayit was recorded in the court records in order to avoid raising the eyebrows of the authorities, or it could indicate that another part of the al-Jabali land already had buildings on it, which is less likely.

Second, Ahuzat Bayit's attorney was having trouble determining from whom he could obtain final title on the land, that is who were the legal heirs of the property. While confident that the municipality's various claims of *miri* or *mahlul* status were *malfondée*[81] and that the land was *mülk* (privately owned) by the seller on record,[82] this caused some consternation, and for good reason. As one of the founders of Tel Aviv describes it, 'suddenly a new fungus [i.e. the bedouins] appeared – a real one – in that new owners announced their ownership of the place ... and inserted their tents and lived in them armed with swords and ready for war, claiming that the land was theirs, and only after compensation and much hesitation in time did we free the land'.[83]

In fact, there were 'numerous conflicts awakened between the heirs and the Jerusalem Jews with whom they signed the contract, and many Arabs ... perhaps bedouins ... set up tents on the land with the claim that it belonged to them ... that they harvested the supposedly "withered" vines'.[84] However, while the local population initially succeeded in halting construction, the leadership of Ahuzat Bayit, confident in their knowledge of and ability to use Ottoman land laws, knew they would prevail, which they did when the local governor, under pressure from the Dutch consul, to whom the Jews brought their complaint, dispatched troops to evict the squatters. Apparently, they were also paid a tidy sum of money to leave peacefully.

Given the complexity and contradictions surrounding the purchase of the land on which Tel Aviv began its development, it is not surprising that Ahuzat Bayit ultimately succeeded in completing its purchase of Karm al-Jabali despite seemingly intense opposition from segments of the local population, the Jaffa municipality and Ottoman authorities. The foundation stone for Tel Aviv was laid on 11 April 1909.

Yet while many Palestinian Arabs opposed the creation of Tel Aviv and saw it as possessing a character that was different from older Jewish quarters,[85] others continued to sell land to and purchase land with Jews.[86] In some cases, Palestinian sellers agreed to parcelise ('mafrouzer' is the French neologism used) land before sale, while one contract states that 'the koushan is legal and the plan confirmed by the non-Jewish neighbours, by the municipal engineer, by the muhtars of the quarter and by the local imam'.[87] Much of the Arab-owned land surrounding Karm al-Jabali was sold to Tel Aviv during the next few years.[88]

Moreover, the Shari'a Court records indicate that the municipal engineer was authorised to create a new map of the town in 1911 and divide the land for registration in the *tapu* (title deed) along modern lines.[89] Around the same time, building activity increased to the north of the old city along the shore (in or near the Manshiyyeh quarter).[90] Jaffa's wealthier Christian families also expanded their holdings of agricultural land in the surrounding villages during this period.[91]

The confusion surrounding the purchase of land upon which Tel Aviv was constructed as well as the larger dynamics of the Jaffan property market in which it occurred (and the relationship of that market to the larger Mediterranean and even the world economy) reveals a level of complexity and fluidity within the field of late-Ottoman land law that challenges any easy determination of the meanings and roles of particular categories of land such as *mülk* or *miri* within the system. The next section will examine the evolution of land law during the Mandate period and the competition over land that it helped to fuel.

Planning to conquer: the struggle for land in the Jaffa-Tel Aviv region during the Mandate period[92]

The events surrounding the establishment of Tel Aviv demonstrate that the transformation from a system based on the distribution of rights to one centred around absolute ownership diminished the state's ability to protect the local population from foreign encroachment. This occurred at a time when Tel Aviv's leaders saw the expansion of the town's territory as the primary means to achieve their desired autonomy from, and ultimately conquest of, Jaffa.[93] Yet, however elastic and malleable, the late-Ottoman system of land tenure and property rights was unlikely to permit the scale of expansion that occurred under British rule when the Land Code underwent further reform and 'recodification'.

As important, the British enacted numerous pieces of town-planning legislation during their almost three decades of rule which had a significant impact on the development of the Jaffa-Tel Aviv region in general, and on the history of Tel Aviv's expansion in particular. This focus on town planning and the usurpation of municipal-planning powers which it occasioned found sympathy with Tel Aviv's leaders, for whom there was a strong link between the need to reform the country's land laws and the need to increase both the power of its Town Planning Committee and the size of its town-planning area.[94]

To begin with, the British prohibited all transfers of immovable property in Palestine during their first three years of rule. In 1920, a Land Transfer Ordinance was enacted, the objectives of which were to stimulate economic growth and capital investment that accompanied the development of land, and to regulate the purchase of land in order to prevent speculation and protect small landowners and tenants against eviction. Whatever its intentions, however, the restrictive elements of the 1920 Ordinance were removed, one by one, during the course of the decade.[95]

In 1928, a Land Settlement Ordinance was enacted, and in 1930 existing town-planning ordinances were consolidated in order to deal with the increasing importance of the land question in the wake of the country-wide violence of 1929.[96] Also resulting from the violence were four reports: the Shaw

Commission, the Passfield White Paper of 1930, and the Hope-Simpson and the French Reports of 1931; all prescribed severely limiting future Jewish immigration and land purchases.

In particular, the French Report called for five steps to be taken to address the issue of Palestinian Arabs displaced by Jewish land purchases, the 'prerequisites for which the Report determined were the acceleration of survey and settling of title to lands, the speedy partition of *musha'* lands, and government control of lands and water resources in areas slated for development'.[97] While these measures were intended to ensure that the *fellahin* most threatened by displacement from Jewish land purchases remained on the land, the colonial pedigree of the ideology underlying 'surveying, settling and partitioning' the land was such that, particularly in urban regions such as Jaffa-Tel Aviv, Zionist leaders and planners were able to use these developments to continue to gain control of Palestinian Arab land in the Jaffa region even in the wake of the restrictions on land purchases ushered in by the 1939 White Paper.

As for the necessity of government control of developable land and water resources, this idea was understood by one senior British official to be so 'distasteful to the Jewish Agency' as to preclude 'successful cooperation with Jews in any scheme of development carried out by Mr. French',[98] and prompted the Secretary of State for the Colonies to suggest not appointing anyone 'too closely connected with actual development work' to committees dealing with land settlement.[99] Thus development and planning were to be guided largely by ideological and political considerations and not the goal of maintaining *fellahin* on their land that motivated the four reports. The subsequent development of Tel Aviv would epitomise this process.

There was a strong link in the minds of Tel Aviv's leaders between the need to reform the country's land laws and the need to increase the power of its Town Planning Committee and the size of its town-planning area. In the administrative structure that was consolidated during this period, the High Commissioner and Central Town Planning Commission on the national level and the District[100] and Local Town Planning Commissions on the regional/local levels (composed of British and local representatives) assumed exclusive powers to designate town-planning areas and regulate planning and development – powers which, until then, had been under the purview of the municipal councils such as the Jaffa municipality, which had enacted its own town-planning legislation as early as 1923.[101]

In fact, the importance of land settlement in the Palestinian context cannot be overstated, particularly because the cadastral survey and newly established Land Registry offices mandated by it facilitated the purchase of land. At the same time, a recession was making it harder for the often debt-ridden Palestinian smallholders to resist speculative prices offered for their lands.[102] The process of settling the land involved use of the cadastral surveys called for in the 1928 Ordinance to determine boundaries, categorisation of tenure and other registerable rights to plots of land,[103] which would then be recorded in land registers. Such settlement of title to land was considered by the British to be the fundamental ingredient for improvement and development;[104] as important was the need, in the words of the Survey of Palestine, to ensure that the idea of land settlement 'not be confused with the settlement of people on the land'.[105]

There was good reason for this admonition. As Scott Atran explains, through the discourse of land settlement British and Zionist interests could continue to converge in practice even when their political interests differed.[106] Thus, the Director of Lands explained to Jewish officials that the proper settlement of rights to land was 'the only way to make lands available for the Jews without political complications'.[107] Not surprisingly, settling the land inevitably 'encouraged fragmentation and dispossession of landholdings as well as social dislocation and disaffection'.[108] The villages surrounding Tel Aviv were particularly affected by this process.

In fact, during the first decade under British rule, conflicts with the local Arab population were mostly over the purchase price of land, not the purchases themselves, as landowners and Jewish brokers sometimes increased the sale price after contracts had been entered into.[109] Even the Mayor of Jaffa, perhaps not wanting to curtail his own power, wrote to the Central Town Planning Commission in support of taking land for public purposes by the Tel Aviv municipality, which he stated was permissible under Ottoman law.[110]

However, in 1927 and again in 1934, ordinances were enacted that separated Tel Aviv from Jaffa and then constituted it as an 'independent local authority no longer in any relation of subordination to the municipality of Jaffa'.[111] At the same time, Tel Aviv ran out of uncontested land onto which it could expand,[112] and with its new freedom attempted to gain control of much of the agricultural land directly east of the city, as well as parts of the Jewish and Arab neighbourhoods on its borders.[113]

The Palestinian Arab revolt that began in Jaffa in 1936 led to close co-ordination between the British and Zionists on issues of security.[114] This added another powerful rationale to the discourse of town planning which justified the annexation of village lands during the remainder of the Mandate period, especially after the 1939 White Paper limited the ability of Jews to purchase agricultural land. Security and planning were thus powerful determinants of how British land law in Palestine was deployed on the ground in Palestine.[115]

The experience of the Arab villages surrounding Tel Aviv during the 1930s and 1940s also provides an opportunity to examine how land settlement worked in practice during this period and why, despite the advice of the Survey of Palestine, it is hard not to confuse settling rights to and people on land. For example, the village of Summel, adjacent to Tel Aviv, was perhaps the oldest village in the immediate vicinity of Jaffa. Despite the crucial role of citrus farming in the region's economy, in 1930 the central Land Settlement Office reported that the part of Summel situated within the Urban Property Tax Area of Jaffa-Tel Aviv was not settled, and the local Land Office was 'accordingly authorized to effect dispositions respecting lands within that area without reference to me [the Land Commissioner]'.[116] The land was thus authorised to be allocated for the new housing and industrial enterprises generated (and necessitated) by the demographic and economic expansion of Tel Aviv.[117]

Again, in September 1933, the Town Planner of Tel Aviv presented a plan to the District Commissioner of Jaffa to develop the lands east of Tel Aviv,[118] claiming that 'the existing population north of [the German colony of] Sarona [i.e. Summel] is very sparse and ... presents the only possibility of expansion of these urban areas'.[119] Summel, in particular, was to be reserved 'for commercial development ... lending additional value to the property to attract investment in its reconstruction.[120]

Here, we see how the terms 'settled' and 'unsettled' were understood simultaneously as involving rights to land and population density on a piece of land, thus creating distinctions and boundaries between and within the lands of a village (registered versus unregistered land, sparsely versus densely populated) that made possible its reclamation and urbanisation by Jews. In fact, in a 1937 meeting of the Boundaries Commission, Tel Aviv Mayor Rokach pressed for the annexation of Summel and the adjoining part of Arab el-Jammasin el-Gharbi, then still part of the 'rural area', into Tel Aviv's boundaries by explaining that 'these lands are rural but have acquired an urban value'.[121]

It is in this that the two meanings of the term 'land settlement', which the authors of the Survey of Palestine admonished readers not to confuse, necessarily become conflated. For, as Atran explained, fixing or settling of rights to the land was the necessary precondition to its physical settlement by Jews, in this case making possible its use for the expansion of housing and industry necessary for the development of Tel Aviv.[122]

The villages surrounding Tel Aviv were continually in the sights of Zionist and British town planners in the 1940s. Thus considered 'practically undeveloped', the incorporation of these villages into Tel Aviv would help the city 'redeem some of these defects which have deformed and stunted its past growth and to prepare for a better planned and more spacious urban future'.[123]

Taking another example, as the population of Tel Aviv swelled to the north in the 1930s, the village of Sheikh Muwannis, because of its size and location on the banks of the 'Auja River directly north of Tel Aviv's built area, became a prime target for annexation by both the government and the Tel Aviv municipality.[124] In 1925 and again in 1929,[125] the government attempted to gain title to the sandy lands lying to the west of Sheikh Muwannis up to the seashore, in the first case claiming that the land was *mahlul*, in the second *rimali* ('sandy') – in both cases waste and uncultivated. The residents of the village promptly sued to prevent the expropriation, and while it is impossible to determine which of the two sides' claims were true (that is whether or not the lands had been under cultivation by the villagers[126]), what is just as important is the fact that the government clearly re-interpreted, if not mis-interpreted, the Ottoman land law in stating that 'nobody has a right to waste uncultivated land', as they claimed in their defence against the villagers' suit.[127]

In fact, preference could have been given to the villagers to obtain rights to the land, as opposed to either leaving it uncultivated state land or transferring it to Tel Aviv for urban and industrial development, which the government considered doing. Instead, the Director of Lands noted that the land was 'a very valuable site for urban development purposes',[128] and it ultimately was incorporated into Tel Aviv.

While the government focused on permanently fixing the status of the land based on its present condition in order to facilitate both urbanisation and land purchases by Jews, permanently determining or 'settling' the categorisation of land was nearly impossible in the case of sandy land or coastal dunes, both because the borders continually changed and because such lands could, when needed, easily be used for planting vegetables or even citrus groves. This was, not coincidentally, the very claim made by the local bedouins regarding the sands on which Tel Aviv was to be built when they tried to block the suburb's construction in 1909.[129]

Moreover, the local population understood, as Sheikh Ragheb pointed out before the Palestine Supreme Court, that 'sand does not make [land] *mevat*', that is dead land,[130] and it is clear from numerous cases in the *tapu* and land files that the British were aware of this.[131] Yet, because such reclaimed land easily 'vanish[ed] from the face of the earth' (as one British judge explained), it was often impossible for Arab inhabitants to obtain rights to it from the government.[132]

Thus, despite or because of the fluid condition of the land, its present state was used to justify Jewish development of the land while specifically excluding the possibility that the local Palestinian Arab population could themselves reclaim such land. In fact, the Jewish Agency touted the transformation of Sheikh Muwannis as a model for the benefits of Zionist-inspired development of the country, claiming that the sale of 1500 of the village's 19,000 *dunums* of land to Jews between 1924 and 1932 fuelled a complete transformation of the village, in which 'all lands without exception [were] cultivated'.[133]

Assuming the figures and analysis are correct, they are quite telling: the claim that all the village's land was being cultivated underscores the stakes involved in the later attempts by the Tel Aviv municipality to annex its land, which would make villagers even more dependent on a town whose mayor confessed to the District Commissioner that he wished he could 'blow up with bombs' a new Jewish market that sold Arab produce.[134]

By 1943, as a result of the 'expenditure of great efforts' by Tel Aviv's Mayor Israel Rokach, the municipality succeeded in having large parts of Sheikh Muwannis incorporated into its town-planning area, 'a great victory for Tel Aviv', as it was described in the city's *Official Gazette*.[135]

Palestinian Arab responses to the discourses of development and town planning

Whatever the beliefs of the Zionists or British, it is clear that villagers were familiar with and utilised the Ottoman and British Land Codes, not just to protect against Zionist encroachments but also as part of their internal battles for control of territory.[136] It is also clear that residents of the Jaffa region began to improve their lands during Ottoman times[137] and that they subsequently worked with the Mandate government to that end, especially to drain swamps.[138]

In fact, from the beginning of the Mandate period, villagers petitioned the government both to reclaim and cultivate *mevat* lands and to prevent encroachments on their land by Tel Aviv.[139] Yet it is also clear that the British were not alone in their ambivalence toward Jewish purchases of village lands. On the other hand, many leading Palestinian Arabs, several of them from Jaffa (including two mayors),[140] were involved in land sales at the same time that they publicly criticised British support of Jewish land purchases.[141]

But such ambivalence over annexation of land to Tel Aviv was absent from the rest of the population, which clearly understood the British changes to the Ottoman land system as being aimed at securing and extending British control over the land and the country as a whole.[142] In fact, British attempts to codify the land system in Palestine met with protests from

Palestinian Arabs from the beginning of their rule, with the 1920 Land Transfer Ordinance being cited as one of the causes of the first revolt of the Mandate era in May 1921.[143]

The Palestinian Arab population also understood the intricacies of town-planning regulations. The consolidated town-planning regulations of 1930 gave a local Town Planning Commission the right to build roads as a first step toward executing a town plan. When the Tel Aviv municipality attempted to build a road on Arab land, the Jaffa-based religious daily *al-Jam'ia al-Islamiyya* complained that

> in reality, the plan in the Town Planning Commission, now including Sheikh Muwannis, is not really a 'plan', but rather a plan to take the land out of the hands of the owners ... We have farmed land north of the 'Auja for a long time and then Jews came and wanted to buy it because it is close to Tel Aviv and we said no and they tried to get it through various means, including using the government to push a plan to open a road through our farmland ... after it proved incapable of gaining ownership through [other] means. [We declare] that this project has no benefit returning to the village, either from a planning or moral perspective.[144]

The villagers clearly had their own quite practical and rational notions of what constituted waste land. More generally, they offered a sophisticated critique of planning practice as it affected them, declaring that

> the essential wisdom in constructing a road is to shorten distances with the least possible inconvenience to property owners, thus helping serve the inhabitants in the best and most economic manner. There is at present a road ... which has and still continues to serve the inhabitants ... The old road passes by the village itself, thus serving the inhabitants to the best manner possible while none of the projected roads pass by the village.[145]

For the Tel Aviv municipality to 'seek and get those facilities under the guise of a town planning scheme amounts to an unlawful and most uncommendable attempt that should never be allowed'.[146]

The contest for lands of the villages surrounding Jaffa and Tel Aviv continued until the end of the Mandate period. In 1947, the Supreme Muslim Council and the Department of Awqaf in

Jaffa wrote to the government asking it to disallow the inclusion of certain *vakıf* lands in Tel Aviv's town-planning scheme, explaining that, despite government assurances to the contrary, 'the annexation of the *vakıf* land ... involves the government's support to the realisation of the ambitions of those who wish to acquire the land to serve their interests by means for which they have become very skillful in creating justifications and paving the way'.[147]

Conclusion

The evidence presented in this chapter demonstrates the benefits of a diachronic and dialogic approach to the problematic of property rights and land tenure, that is one that examines transformations over time and between different regimes and that brings to the fore the voice and agency of groups whose interpretations of, negotiations with, and often resistance to government policies and legal reforms exerted a determinative influence on the evolution of property regimes on the ground. As in other parts of the Ottoman Middle East,[148] in Jaffa and Tel Aviv, changes in the Code were negotiated through local understandings and conditions: it was the interaction of Palestinian Arabs and Zionist Jews as much as the codifications of Ottoman and later British officials that shaped the particular history of the land question in the Jaffa-Tel Aviv region.

This chapter has also demonstrated the utility of expanding the discussion of property rights and land tenure to include the related discourses of development, modernist town planning and security, which, in Palestine at least, were crucial to its evolution.[149] In fact, the practical experience of the discourse of rights – particularly of rights to land – in Mandate-era Palestine helps one understand why it was so difficult for the British to fulfil their obligation, enshrined in both the Balfour Declaration and the Mandate, to 'safeguard the civil and religious rights of the existing non-Jewish communities in Palestine'.

Moreover, it demonstrates that what Ronald Dworkin has termed 'Law's Empire' – which he defines both as having come into being after the dissolution of the European empires and as centred around a discourse of rights – was not only crucial to the functioning of late-imperial rule, but featured a discourse of rights (especially to land – one of the most basic rights of all) that served not to ensure freedoms, but rather to separate people into epistemologically and teleologically defined categories through which their rights under the law would be determined.[150]

Finally, the variety of sources utilised for this research – Islamic Court records, consular reports, town planning and judicial documents, relevant Zionist, British and Arab memos and press reports – has been crucial to the portrait painted here. Yet, it is still an incomplete picture, as one crucial voice is generally absent, that of the Ottoman officials in Jaffa who attempted to institute the reforms inaugurated in Istanbul. If scholars can integrate the still untapped wealth of Ottoman documents relating to the administration of property and other rights in Jaffa during the final decades of their rule into the conversation made possible by these other sources, an even richer and more complex understanding of the problematic of land in late-Ottoman and Mandate Jaffa and Tel Aviv will be possible.[151]

Notes

1 The text of the Geddes Plan can be found in the library of the Tel Aviv Municipal Archive (hereafter TAMA). Geddes further explained that Tel Aviv's 'geographic, social and even fundamental economic situation is determined by its position as Northern Jaffa'.

2 In fact, recognising the 'unique' character of the quarter, the British government had granted Tel Aviv the status of an autonomous township in 1921.

3 As Israel Cohen (1912, p. 26) described it, Palestine was mired in 'indolence and torpor'. For a general critique of the liberal-modernisation perspectives, see Amin, 1989; Gran, 1996 and, most recently, Frank, 1998. For one dealing more specifically with Palestine/Israel, see the introduction to Lockman, 1996.

4 İslamoğlu, 2000.

5 *Yediot Tel Aviv*, 9 September 1925, 2, p. 3, meeting of Town Council.

6 A view which still defines a good proportion of mainstream Israeli scholarship despite the rise of a new generation of 'revisionist' historians. See Metzer, 1998.

7 İslamoğlu, 2000. For a more general critique of the separation of the state from society, see Mitchell, 1991. This understanding of the positive role of the state in the very constitution of private property belies the liberal imagination of a circumscribed state as being the precondition for private property, unfettered markets and thus economic progress (and is, not coincidentally, identical to the current neo-liberal ideology driving globalisation). More specifically, Huri İslamoğlu argues that during the nineteenth century, the Ottoman state, like its counterparts in London or Paris, was a 'modern centralizing state' whose need for greater and more regularised sources of revenue had initiated a radical transformation in property relations – in particular the spread of absolute ownership of land (by the state or by private parties). The arena for this development was law, specifically, the myriad land laws enunciated in the 1858 Land Code, the 1869 Mecelle, the 1876 Constitution and later administrative rulings.

8 For the Palestinian context and the larger regional and world economies through which these reforms were experienced, see Kana'an, 1998; Wilkins, unpublished manuscript; Schölch, 1993; Doumani, 1995.

9 For a critique of the liberal analysis of the dynamics and meanings of reform in the late-Ottoman state as a whole, see İslamoğlu, 2000; for information regarding the economic development of Palestine, and in particular Jaffa, see note 8 and LeVine, 1999, Chapters 1 and 2. Specifically, continuity was possible because the body of laws and administrative practices inherited by the British was based on a vocabulary common to all modern centralising states. This vocabulary defined the spaces of rule, negotiation and resistance. In defining actual property claims or rights of individuals, groups or the state, 'law is constitutive of the relations it defines': İslamoğlu, 2000, p.8.

10 More specifically, the two alternative receptions and implementations of the Geddes Plan presented here are meant to highlight the importance of both the shared Eurocentric understanding among Zionist leaders and British authorities of Arab Jaffa and its population as backward and incapable of independent development, and the belief in the centrality and power of planning for the 'development' of the country. Because of these common sentiments, the leadership of Tel Aviv was able to plan for the interests of a 'greater Tel Aviv' that was increasingly built on land annexed (via the planning authorities) from surrounding villages, as well as construct a hydroelectric station and, later on, a port

that directly contradicted the interests of Jaffa and its Arab population.

11 As I explain below, officials at the local and central levels of government well understood that the interests of the European and indigenous populations were often in conflict and knew that the process of centralisation and 'privatisation' often worked to the disadvantage of the latter.

12 In fact, the complex political economy of Jaffa, and especially its property market, during the last half-century of Ottoman rule was an arena where law, money and numerous and often competing actors interacted in ways that defy any account of property relations purely in the vocabulary of 'private property' or 'traditional land tenure' that defined both post-Tanzimat Ottoman land law and the liberal critique of it: İslamoğlu, 2000.

13 Particularly the opposition between a 'backward stagnant' East and a 'modern progressive' Europe in which it was framed, and which did not frame planning in Ottoman Jaffa.

14 İslamoğlu, 2000. That is, while both Ottoman and British were modern or, better, modernising states, they did not represent the same modernity. Indeed, I argue that the combined power of the ideologies and discourses of colonialism and nationalism shared by the British and Zionists, but in many ways absent in the Ottoman case (although, as I explore elsewhere, the Ottoman state also saw itself as an imperial/colonial and modernising power vis-à-vis its territories and other Muslim lands, a sentiment which helped lay the groundwork for British rule [see LeVine, 2004 – details p.xiii – Introduction and Chapter 1]), produced a modernity that was much more exclusivist than that experienced under Ottoman rule (precisely because that was not a colonial modernity). To paraphrase Huri İslamoğlu (2000), viewed thus, the exclusionary nature of absolute individual ownership introduced by the Code threatened to undermine the subsistence claims of cultivators in the form of hereditary usufruct rights and collective grazing rights. This was even truer under British rule.

15 Again, referring to Huri İslamoğlu (2000), in doing so, it nuances our understanding of private property as an ordering of centralised states that took place through the practices of the state by emphasising the role of non-state actors (whether the Zionist leadership or local bedouins) in the specificities of this ordering.

16 LeVine, 1995.

17 Just as important, it also showed how Palestinian peasant agriculture and logic of economic life differed from the Zionist

and British notions of modernisation, planning, development and progress.

18 Interview with Huri İslamoğlu, March 1999.

19 Eisenman, 1978, p. 57.

20 Stein, 1984, p. 11.

21 Eisenman, 1978, pp. 28, 64.

22 Eisenman, 1978, p. 139.

23 Eisenman, 1978, p.58. Generally, *mevat* lands were hilly, scrub, woodland or grazing grounds.

24 Stein, 1984, p. 13. It should be pointed out that, going back to the tenth century, there had been debate even within schools of Islamic law as to whether permission from the political authorities was needed to revivify *mevat* land (Eisenman, 1978, p. 58, footnote 29.

25 For a discussion of the centrality of the discourse of the sands to the etiology of Tel Aviv and its development, see LeVine, 1998.

26 Survey of Palestine, vol. I, 1947, p. 233.

27 Survey of Palestine, vol. I, 1947, p. 226.

28 Usually due to negligence by its owners or because the owner died and left no heirs.

29 This was subject to the 'right of *tapu* by any claimants to the land', but in order for someone to have such a right, the land had to be surveyed and registered, which was impossible for many residents of the villages (Eisenman, 1978, p. 94).

30 TAMA, 1/282a, Protocols of Tel Aviv Council, Meeting no 118, 30 September 1917 (14 Tishri).

31 As explained by Mayor Dizengoff (quoted in *Yediot Tel Aviv*, 1936, no 5–6, p. 43).

32 In Ottoman times, land was designated as *matruke* by an imperial rescript (*firman*). While Stein believes that 'possibly the *matruke* category did not exist in Palestine' (Stein, 1984, p. 14), in fact it played a prominent role in several disputes between Jews, Arabs and the British government during the Mandate period.

33 Eisenman, 1978, pp. 146–47. This was one year, it is worth noting, before Tel Aviv was officially constituted as a municipality formally independent from Jaffa. A particularly relevant example of this was a discussion in 1935 to change this law, which was considered to 'cause great inconvenience and is an obstruction to the proper development of the country'.

34 While the High Commission's Executive Council noted in September 1935 that 'the proposal to grant a general power to change the category of matruke land would give rise to popular

suspicion as to the use to be made of that power. It was likely to excite fear among Arabs that the power would be employed for the purpose of bringing Arab common land into Jewish hands': Israel State Archives (hereafter ISA), M56/236/D/119 and M34/34/L280/299. Cf. 'Note on Metrouke for Commissioner of Lands and Surveys', p. 3, memo to Chief Secretary, 16/9/35 (NB: the file numbers for the ISA are written right to left in Hebrew and thus I have written them left to right as a mirror image of the original number).

35 In fact, with the 1933 Land Law (Amendment) Ordinance, *matruke*, which heretofore was considered a subset of *miri*, became a new concept of state domain, one 'which was to expand under the unique development conditions of the State of Israel into a vast domain of State of Israel Lands': Eisenman, 1978, p. 146. I argue that the 'unique development conditions' of post-1948 Israel were made possible by the discourse of development shared by Zionists and British during the Mandate era and, in both periods, were used to transfer rights to land from Arabs to Jews.

36 The italics are mine.

37 Goadby and Doukhan, 1935, pp. 48–49; emphasis added.

38 Goadby and Doukhan, 1935, pp. 38–39.

39 By the Palestine (Amendment) Order in Council 1933, article 16A.

40 Himadeh, 1939, p. 79.

41 Bunton, 1997, pp. 26–75. In fact, in 1930 a British colonial legal expert derisively described the land laws of Palestine as 'an unintelligible compost of the original Ottoman laws, provisional laws, judgments of various tribunals, sultanic firmans, administrative orders ... Public Orders, Orders in Council, judgments of various civil and religious courts ...' (quoted in Bunton, 1997, p. 63). Palestinians did not accept the notion that the British administration left the indigenous laws unchanged: Bunton, 1997, p. 32. It should be noted that my reading of the similarities of British and Zionist conceptions of the transformation in the land regime and the complex relationship between the intents and effects of the British and previous Ottoman land regimes provides for a less clear picture of the situation than that of Bunton. I would argue that the inclusion of Hebrew, Arabic and Ottoman perspectives complicates the picture that would emerge from a focus primarily on British sources.

42 Often from Ottoman to French to English.

43 As Ruth Kark describes it, it was through increased European influence that Jaffa was transformed from a conquered and

destroyed town into 'a new city, very different in size, character and layout from the traditional Middle Eastern town of the early nineteenth century': Kark, 1990, pp. 15, 43, 53. This view of the (lack of a) role of the city's Arab population leads directly to the teleological assertion, common to most mainstream Israeli historiography, that it was Jews and Europeans who were responsible for the undeniable development of the city. This perspective sees the 'uninterrupted course of growth and development' during the later nineteenth century to the birth of Tel Aviv – which 'rapidly [became] the nucleus of a city which was Jewish, modern, distinctive, and autonomous': Kark, 1990, p. 108.

44 Map by M. Jacotin (1810) in Kark, 1990, p. 17.

45 Cf. report on Jaffa in the *PEF Quarterly*, 7/1872, p. 77. Consular reports from the British Vice-Consul in Jaffa during the years 1880–1900 paint a similar picture of the 'fairly flourishing condition' of the economy (PRO, Parliamentary Papers, 1892, C. 6550, nn 1023, Trade of Palestine for 1890–1891, 2; Graham-Brown, 1982, p. 55; Schölch, 1993, p. 142; Kark, 1990, p. 189. For example, the value of Jaffa's exports doubled between 1856 and 1882. As one Jewish source described it, by the turn of the twentieth century it was obvious to all interested parties that 'in the last twenty years Jaffa has progressed, expanded, and grown greatly': Luach Eretz Yisrael, 1899, nos 4, 8.

46 That is, they wanted to use their increasing wealth either to build homes for themselves or for rental purposes or to establish orchards: David Smilansky (from 1907) quoted in Kark, 1990, pp. 125, 142. Cf. Jaffa Islamic Court Records (hereafter JICR), book 80 (1899–1901), no 9, which discusses the sale of an orchard. Arabs came from other parts of Palestine, Egypt, Syria, Lebanon as well as North Africa and Afghanistan. The Shari'a Court records, in particular, document a great increase in locals and foreigners seeking to register the sale of land outside the walls (Abu-Bakr, 1996, p. 370), while Egyptians who came to Jaffa with Ibrahim Pasha in the 1830s founded neighbourhoods such as Abu Kabir and Rashid that clearly referred to their hometowns in the Nile delta (Wilkins, unpublished manuscript, p. 7 for Egyptian immigration in the Shari'a Court records. See JICR, book 17, (1845–48), no 213; book 48 (1888–90), no 88. The growing economic importance of and increased security around Jaffa led to an increased sedentarisation of bedouins in many of the surrounding villages (Biger, 1987). For the close ties between Jaffa and Beirut and Amman, especially among Christians residents, see Malak, 1993;

ibid., 1996. The most important reason for intensified European interest was economic: oranges replaced cotton as the most important export crop to Europe (particularly to Great Britain), which led to the expansion of groves in the area surrounding the town, while a similar rise in demand for grain and sesame led to their increased cultivation in Jaffa's hinterland: Kark, 1988, p. 47; Wilkins, unpublished manuscript, p. 8; Schölch, 1993, pp. 47–48, 86–87; Doumani, 1995, pp. 103–5). Tourism was also becoming a major industry: DAMFAF, Jaffa CCC (Consular and Commercial Correspondence) 30/vi/96 report to Foreign Ministry from Jaffa Vice-Consul. Given these dynamics, it is not surprising that the Jaffa *sijjil* (Islamic court records) contain more descriptions of the development of neighbourhoods outside the city walls than do the court records of other cities such as Haifa: Agmon, 1994, p. 19 (English summary), pp. 41–42 (Hebrew text). For examples of the participation of women in the economic and spatial expansion of the city, see JICR, book 80 (1900), case no 9, 7–8 and book 83 (1900–5), which contains at least a dozen cases.

47 Tarawnah, 1997; Wilkins, unpublished manuscript.

48 DAMFAF, Jaffa CCC, 2/7/87 letter to Foreign Ministry from Jaffa Vice-Consul, where he wrote of his feeling of 'profound lassitude' caused by the 'constant mischief' of the 'highly corrupt' local authorities (especially the judges). Another perspective is that the merchants of Jaffa, like those of Haifa and Beirut, succeeded in establishing themselves as indispensable go-betweens for the import–export trade with Europe, in this way shielding the city from more direct political influence: Doumani, 1995, p. 74.

49 Thus, far from being stagnant, the changing patterns of land ownership in late-nineteenth-century Palestine present 'the clearest example of how Islamic patterns are intimately woven into the fabric of communal society... [they] smoothed its adjustment to final absorption into the world market centered on Western capitalism, [and were] an adaptation to deal with poor public security, benefits of scale operation, equalize economic opportunities... [all of which is] only natural in economies like the Middle East, where production is subject to such uncertainties': Firestone, 1975.

50 Wilkins, unpublished manuscript, p. 507.

51 Though it was not as determinant as some scholars have claimed: Kark, 1990, p. 302.

52 For example, Yusef Moyal appears in an 1898 case as a partner with Muslims and Christians in the purchase of land around the old

city, where he is described as owning 'much land'. What is interesting about the case is both that it served to confirm the sale after a third party had contested the seller's (one Shakr Bey) right to the land and that it contains a rich description of its topography, which included different kinds of fruit trees, a well with a spring and a pool for bathing, an irrigation wheel and two houses, one of which was owned by one of the leading families of Jaffa, the Siksik family. Also cf. JICR, book 87 (1900–5), no 1029 for another instance of Moyal purchasing property, this time from the Chialdi family of Jerusalem. For examples of Christian–Muslim purchases, see JICR, book 129 (1911), no 66–84, which contains a case involving several Muslim families and the wealthy Rok family, a leading Christian family in Jaffa.

53 Shloosh, 1931, p. 20. These neighbourhoods included Neve Tzedek, Neve Shalom, Mahane-Yehuda, Mahane-Yosef, Shchunat-Aharon and Kerem Hateimanim. What is important about this description of the land is that it clearly demonstrates that what would become the Tel Aviv region was both sand and vineyards at the same time (in spite of his later description that there were some 'withered vines planted here and there, abandoned and left'), a point of fact whose importance for understanding the history of Tel Aviv will be discussed below: Shloosh, 1931, p. 143.

54 In fact, the development of neighbourhoods by immigrants from the surrounding Arab countries which paralleled the establishment of Muslim neighbourhoods outside the old city of Jerusalem led to new streets being cut through the existing orange groves, creating new spatial patterns that facilitated the region's ultimate urbanisation, including the villages.

55 As İslamoğlu describes it, 'the central Government perceived individual ownership as closely related to the creation of wealth and therefore of taxable income': İslamoğlu, 2000, p. 38.

56 That is, the extension of state procedures signalled the subjection of other groups to state taxes. In many cases, they resisted the new tax regime, but the terms of resistance were established through the categories of the Land Code. When everyone was part of the same society, resistance and negotiation would have a very different dynamic from when a group outside the society – i.e. the Zionist movement – came onto the scene and pitted one against the other, especially at a time when the title of ownership overrode titles to land use and customary land rights which had protected the population against the greatest injustices of this transformation but were losing their power to do so. Thus, larger

Arab landowners were benefiting from sales while peasant and tenant farmers saw their position threatened.

57 Mandel, 1976, p.1.

58 As recounted in Mandel, 1976, p.39.

59 Ahuzat Bayit was not the only group engaged in land purchases in the Jaffa region. Between 1908 and 1914, numerous land-purchasing societies were established in cities around the world with the express purpose of purchasing land for settlement by Jews in the vicinity of Jaffa because of the general and specific advantages of the region: Katz, 1983, pp.139–48, 140. The increasing influx of people and money led to a dramatic increase in land prices during the latter part of the first decade of the twentieth century.

60 TAMA, 1/20, newspaper clipping entitled 'Ahuzat Bayit' from a 1921 issue of Hatzvi; Droyanov, 1935, p.188; *Yediot Tel Aviv*, 1925, no 2, 3, 9/15/25; meeting of Town Council; *Yediot Tel Aviv*, 1934, no 11–12, 43.

61 The name Tel Aviv means 'hill of spring' in Hebrew, and was the Hebrew title of Theodor Herzl's novel *Altneuland* (*Old–New Land*).

62 Thus, as one Zionist leader explained it, 'the development of a Jewish urban community is without a doubt the most important stage in the bolstering of our position in the country... The process of agricultural colonization is slow and requires large investments and funds, whereas the expansion of a Jewish urban population is quicker and easier' (Chelnov quoted in Katz, 1983, p.11).

63 Arthur Ruppin, quoted in Droyanov et al., 1935, p.77; Dizengoff, 1931, pp.6–7. Elsewhere, the verb used by Ruppin is given as 'rule over' Jaffa's economy; Ruppin, 1969, p.38. Not surprisingly, then, while there are numerous examples of Jews and Arabs working together right up to the end of Ottoman rule, on the whole opposition to Zionism increased in the years following the establishment of Tel Aviv: *Falastin*, 16 September 1911; Mandel, 1976, pp.121–22.

64 1909 was the year that the first proposal for the comprehensive town-planning bill for London was put forth, while only months before the ground-breaking of Ahuzat Bayit, the journal *Architectural Record* explained that 'the best opportunities for effective work were in the undeveloped parts of cities, and here there should be a plan to which the city should gradually adapt itself': *Architectural Record*, June 1909, Notes and Comments, on lecture by N.P. Lewis on city planning, p.449.

65 It is clear that the Zionists were thoroughly familiar with Islamic land categories and knew how to manipulate them to their

advantage. Thus we see that the Tel Aviv Council in 1917 specifically allocated money to plant trees on the surrounding *mahlul* land in order to claim it and also on *miri* land in order to convert it to *mahlul* which they could then claim: Protocols of the Tel Aviv Council, Meeting no 118, 14 Tishri, 1917, located at TAMA, 1/282a. For an even earlier Zionist analysis of land tenure in Palestine, see CZA, L1/57, 'Der Landeinkauf', undated but likely to be around 1905.

66 And thus to the health of Palestine's Jewish community as a whole. Within this modern perspective, opposition by local Arabs, the Jaffa municipality and the Ottoman government was construed as being the result of 'the government's and the Arabs' hatred of the clean and modern city... [which forced] Tel Aviv to become a city unto itself before the end of the Turkish period': Shloosh, 1931, pp. 146–47.

67 Droyanov, 1935, p. 156; Katz, 1984, p. 161.

68 For a good description of the problems facing European cities during this period, see Hall, 1988, Chapter 2.

69 Such examples include the straightening of streets and larger plots of land in newer neighbourhoods, the opening of wide divided boulevards and eclectic blends of European and Middle Eastern architectural styles. See LeVine, 1998.

70 CZA, L18/105/4, L51/52, L2/578; TAMA, Protocols of Ahuzat Bayit, 6 June and 31 July 1907. Apparently, as Katz points out, in purchasing the land at Karm al-Jabali the members of Ahuzat Bayit felt that they were 'beyond the city limits of Jaffa': Katz, 1994, p. 99. The Jaffan authorities, not surprisingly, considered the area within their jurisdiction.

71 Shloosh, 1931, p. 131.

72 Droyanov, 1935, p. 85.

73 Museum of the History of Tel Aviv (hereafter MHTA), uncatalogued notebook listing the names of the heirs of Karm al-Jabali in Arabic/Ottoman and Hebrew, with dates of birth and death and position within the family.

74 The documents include the original contract, the survey or the resale contract to Ahuzat Bayit. According to the contract of sale to Ahuzat Bayit, the borders of Karm al-Jabali were, on the east, the Nablus Road, on the west, Moyal's land (Nahlat Moyal) and Karm al-Baba (described as *mahlul*: vacant land), on the south, the Ermani-Kapus land (Nahalat Haermani-Kapus) and, on the north, the Shahin land – all for a price of 95 centimes per square metre. It is worth noting that these are not the same borders described in

the original Arabic contract with the Jerusalem landbrokers, in which case, the boundaries are listed as the 'private road' (*al-tariq al-khasusa*) to the south, the vineyard of Sheikh Hassan 'Ali and his partners to the east, Karm al-Mashrawi to the north, and Karm Salibi Shalyan wa-Shahin and the 'general road to which all [the roads] lead' to the west (as certified in the *tapu* in 1877). A copy of this contract is found in Ram, 1996, p. 47 of the Appendix). Nor is it the same as those described in the original official survey drafted by the *tapu* office (or some other official public institution, as there are Ottoman tax stamps affixed to the map), which lists both the north and south regions as being *kerem* (vineyards): the survey map is in Droyanov, 1935, p. 90.

75 Thus, in the Arabic contract, it is listed as 21-and-a-half *qirat*, which is not a unit of measure in itself but refers to a percentage of a larger plot of land (divided into 24 *qirat*) to which the one being sold belongs, sold for 2580 French francs, as compared with the 109 *dunums* described in the Ahuzat Bayit contract.

76 The two were Rabbi David Yellin and Dr Aharon Mezi: Droyanov, 1935, p. 87. Complicating matters further was the fact that most of the land outside the old city, particularly in and around the villages, was *musha'*, or at least not divided into small plots (i.e. *mafruz*), making purchases difficult. When it was *mafruz*, the small shares were divided among numerous people, as was the case with Karm al-Jabali: Katz, 1983, pp. 139–48.

77 Mandel, 1976, p. 26.

78 Shloosh, 1931, p. 143. As such, it is another reason why the local Ottoman authorities would have opposed the foundation of the new suburb.

79 Indeed, an official survey of the land states that its eastern borders were contested, while the plots on the north and south were vineyards. A photo of the survey map appears in Droyanov, 1935, p. 90.

80 JICR, books 105 or 114 (1907–9), copy provided to author by Amin Abu-Bakr without the volume and page numbers.

81 Because, according to Moyal, they were based on a well-known and faulty inscription on the cadastral surveys of the region.

82 MHTA, Dizengoff Archive, MhhD/II1, Hebrew minutes of 12/iii/190 'Consultation donnée à Monsieur Dizengoff en ce qui concerne l'achat de la vigne Djebale sise à Jaffa'.

83 MHTA, Dizengoff Archive, MhhD/II1, Hebrew minutes of 12/iii/190. A memo dated 17 June 1909 to the Anglo-Palestine Company (probably from Ruppin) stressed the importance of

ending the dispute with their 'neighbours' and parcelising the land as soon as possible (CZA, L2/71).

84 The government even sent a detachment of gendarmes to what would become Herzl Street to block the construction (according to Ottoman law, it was forbidden to build close to army/police barracks already set up), while Arabs from Jaffa arrived in a 'festive procession. Between the music of drums and trumpets they announced the riots (*paruot*) against the Jews': Natan, 1987, pp.63–81, 67-68; CZA, J85/27.

85 It is clear that the Arabs took note of the distance of the new neighbourhood from the centre of town as well as its separatist character: while the Shari'a Court records described older Jewish neighbourhoods located near Manshiyyeh as 'Manshiyyeh al-Yahud' (Jewish Manshiyyeh), Tel Aviv was referred to as 'mahallah Tel Abib' (the Tel Aviv quarter): JICR, book 148 (1912–13), no 344; book 166 (1914), no 170; book 196 (1920–21), no 383; Abu-Bakr, 1996, pp.600–1.

86 Although, as a rule, land was purchased only from other Arabs, not from Jews (cf. CZA, L18/68/2, German list of five properties: Kassar, Bamia, Bedrani-Kassar, Bedrani-Moyal and Emin Nassif, purchased for Tel Aviv; CZA, L18/68/2, 22/2/14 memo on land purchases in Jaffa by Barski; private paper collection of Dr Hana Ram; Katz, 1983, p.147).

87 CZA, L18/68/2, contract between Thon and Cassar, dated 13 February 1913.

88 For example, the land of Sheikh 'Ali (TAMA, 1/120, undated memo from the Va'ad of the Society for Supporting the Children of Israel, Odessa). Cf. TAMA 1/114.

89 According to Abu-Bakr, the goals of these land reforms was to gain authority of the lands of the nearby bedouin tribes, but it was ultimately Tel Aviv and not Jaffa that would take advantage of the reforms initiated then: Abu-Bakr, 1996, p.513.

90 This building was undertaken because the sands could support multi-storeyed houses and, perhaps more importantly, because the government wanted to strengthen control over both the main roads between the old city and the villages to the north and over the mouth of the 'Auja River, which it desired to utilise for drinking water, electricity and irrigation: Abu-Bakr, 1996, p.600; JICR, book 98 (1906–11), no 1–162.

91 JICR, book, 128 (1911–12), no 1–2; book 129 (1910–12), no 344; book 166 (1914), no 275. The purchases by Christians (particularly the Rok family), which included lands of the Jerisha and

Summel villages, began around 1904: JICR, book 85 (1901–2), nos 36, 71, 166; book 86 (1901–2), no 126, 130, 292; book 91 (1904–6), no 90; book 139 (1911), no 258; book 148 (1912–13), no 68, 220–326; book 156 (1914), no 153.

92 This section was drawn from LeVine, 1998.

93 In fact Tel Aviv 'had intentions of expanding from the very beginning'; Kark, 1990, p. 124. During the last years of Ottoman rule, it was hoped that further land acquisitions would succeed in bypassing the Arab Jaffan neighbourhood of Manshiyyeh and create a link-up with the sea, an accomplishment that the leaders of Tel Aviv believed was a precondition for the very survival and development of the suburb, because it would block any possibility of Jaffa's northward expansion while allowing Tel Aviv to spread without limits to the north and west: Katz, 1994, p. 287. According to Arthur Ruppin, it was the successful purchase of the land north of Manshiyyeh that constituted the decisive step in the transformation of Tel Aviv from a suburb to a city: CZA: A7/9, L2/615; Katz, 1994, p. 288. By 1914, Tel Aviv had encircled Manshiyyeh and had permanently blocked Jaffa's expansion to the north, although, thanks to the efforts of one of the last Ottoman governors of Jaffa, Hassan Bey, perhaps farther north than its leaders would have liked.

94 Thus, for example, Tel Aviv's municipal engineer explained that the dearth of open spaces in Tel Aviv arose because of 'inadequate municipal town planning area' as well as the 'system of land ownership': Y. Shiffman, 1942, p. 167. See *Falastin*, 27 February 1923, p. 3 for an article on a new land-ownership law enacted by the Jaffa municipality.

95 This began as early as the next year with the Amended Land Transfer Ordinance in 1921: Smith, 1993, p. 92.

96 As Stein points out, the land question in Palestine re-emerged after a decade in which several economic crises, a shortage of funds for land purchases and the focus on immigration had overshadowed the question of land purchases: Stein, 1984, pp. 218–19.

97 PRO, CO733/214/87402; Minute to Secretary of State for the Colonies by High Commissioner Wauchope, 2 January 1932.

98 PRO, CO733/214/97049; 'Development Scheme and Report of Mr. French', by O.G.R. Williams, 14 January 1932.

99 PRO, CO733/214; letter to High Commissioner Wauchope from the Secretary of State for the Colonies, 29 January 1932. Just as significant, in a Minute to senior officials dated 15 January 1932, the High Commissioner explains that while the French Report

offers 'long range and large-scale' suggestions, what was needed immediately were concrete proposals for the resettlement of displaced Arabs and development with a view to Jewish colonisation on the smallest scale politically and financially feasible. The possibility of Arab development is absent from his thinking.

100 Which coincided with six administrative districts created in 1936 to implement the policy of decentralising the Town Planning Commissions.

101 Town Planning Handbook of Palestine, 1930, copy at New York Public Library under call letters: SERA, p.5.

102 Owen, 1991, p.7.

103 The High Commissioner would publish an order in the *Palestine Gazette* constituting a 'settlement area', then the settlement officer would publish two notices and proceed with the actual work of settlement of a given village with claims recorded, posted and adjudicated.

104 Bunton, 1997, p. 9.

105 Survey of Palestine, vol. I, p. 234.

106 'Although the British administration might roundly condemn Zionist 'arrogance', and profess to champion the *fellah*'s 'needs', no official British policy statement or plan ever questioned the necessity for land settlement': Atran, 1989, p. 724.

107 Quoted in Atran, 1989, p. 725.

108 Atran, 1989, p. 737.

109 *Yediot Tel Aviv*, 1928, no 6–7, pp. 21, 24, where one Council member complained with regard to Jewish intermediaries who brokered some of the sales that 'in dealing with land purchases you're not dealing with the "cleanest" people'.

110 *Yediot Tel Aviv*, 1928, no 6–7, pp. 21, 24.

111 PRO, CO733/158/7, Despatch from H.C. Luke, acting Officer Administering the Government, dated 9 August 1928, to the Secretary of State for the Colonies. Tel Aviv had been constituted as a local council in 1921. The latter ordinance came into force one year after a new Municipal Law was enacted which gave municipalities greater powers to expand their borders, a right that till then had been totally lacking and was 'so important that it [wa]s almost a question of the life of Tel Aviv' (*Yediot Tel Aviv*, no 6–7, 1934, p. 252).

112 As Granott described it, 'one of the greatest obstacles to the normal development of Tel Aviv was the absence of the land necessary for its expansion': Granott, 1940, p. 177. Even within the municipal area of the city, much of the sandy lands to the north of

Tel Aviv were still in the hands of Arab owners and were becoming more difficult to purchase because the increase in land prices led owners and landbrokers to sell smaller parcels in order to increase their profits: Graicer, 1982, p. 138.

113 Including the neighbourhood of Manshiyyeh, which had a large Arab majority (TAMA, 4/2667b, Memo on proposed changes of boundaries between Jaffa and Tel Aviv, undated but probably 1934).

114 As the citrus groves of the surrounding villages were frequently the staging ground of attacks on Jews.

115 In fact, the British provided an excellent example of the conflation of security and planning when they destroyed large swaths of the old city of Jaffa in June 1936 in retaliation for the Arab revolt, but justified their actions as an act of town planning, renewal and improvement of the old city: Gavish, 1984.

116 TAMA, 4/2667a, Letter to Registrar of Lands, Jaffa, 24 December 1930.

117 Granott, in his 1940 *Land Policy in Palestine*, helps contextualise the settling of Summel's land when he explains that 'the evolution of prices in Sarona [the German colony located next to Summel] is an instructive example of the effect of the advancing values of urban lots upon the prices of agricultural land. Drawn into the vicinity of the city by the expansion of Tel Aviv, Sarona land could be sold as urban land' (p. 41). This is a clear example of how settling the rights to agricultural land adjacent to a Jewish urban area ultimately meant its urbanisation and incorporation into the city's municipal or town-planning boundaries.

118 Including parts of the German colony of Sarona and the lands of the villages of Montifiore, Summel and Jammasin.

119 TAMA, 4/2662b. Explanatory notes in connection with the proposed skeleton town-planning scheme for the land situated east of Tel Aviv.

120 TAMA, 4/2662b, 3, emphasis added. As if the region had once been constructed but, because of Arab backwardness, fell into disuse or dilapidation.

121 TAMA, 4/2667b, Minutes of meeting dated 13 July 1937.

122 In fact, to buttress their claims to the land, Tel Aviv's leaders began advocating the formation of 'some kind of county authority' during this period that would co-ordinate planning and development for the larger region of Tel Aviv, the surrounding villages and neighbouring Jewish satellite towns such as Ramat Gan, which was located next to Summel: Shiffman, 1942, p. 178.

123 Interview with Y. Shiffman, *Palestine and Near East*, January 1943, p.12. It should be pointed out that the government was not of one mind as to the merits of annexing these lands. While the Attorney General and Solicitor General opposed it, the District Commissioner supported it as he and other officials clearly believed that urban and industrial development would constitute a 'betterment of the situation' (ISA, M/44/89/L/308; unsigned note dated 21 June 1945).

124 During this period, numerous 'workers' neighbourhoods' began to be built in the north of the city: Graicer, 1982.

125 Cf. ISA, M/18/LD8/3411, letters from 1929.

126 The villagers' counsel '[did] not deny that the area is bounded by sand dunes, but they do not cover all the land we claim. It has not been planted with trees but vegetables and there are two wells now covered by sand.'

127 Barbara Smith (1993, p.99) writes that 'Not only did British officials misread the previous land laws, but they failed fully to understand local agricultural practices and appreciate the unusual post-war conditions'.

128 ISA, M/18/LD8/3411, Letter to Department of Agriculture dated 7/2/28.

129 The Survey of Western Palestine of 1878 noted that only a few feet under the sands was very fertile soil, while Kallner and Rosenau noted in their 1939 discussion (Kallner and Rosenau, 1939, p.63) that 'almost everywhere the coastal plain has sufficient underground water at moderate depths'.

130 ISA, M/48/G184/3529, Land Appeal no 171/26, 16 June 1927.

131 Thus in one case, the Director of Lands wrote to the Registrar of Lands in Jaffa that a particular Arab, 'Aly El Moustakeem' (a prominent Jaffan who served as Deputy Mayor), was buying land in Sheikh Muwannis in 1927 which he planned to convert into an orange orchard and that he 'suspected' sand dunes to be included in a part of the *musha'* plot that he was buying because sandy land was by definition *mevat* and, belonging to the government, it could not be cultivated or sold without government permission (ISA, M/18/LD8/3411, Letter from Registrar of Lands, Jaffa, to Director of Lands, Jerusalem, 19 May 1929).

132 This was the language Goadby and Doukhan report that a British judge used in dismissing a claim to *mevat* land (Goadby and Doukhan, 1935, p.49).

133 PRO, CO733/230, 'Jewish Agency Observations on the French Report'. The income, according to the Jewish Agency's statistics,

was invested in improving housing conditions, planting small orange groves, modernising the village's irrigation and ploughing systems and increased vegetable cultivation and marketing to Tel Aviv and other Jewish towns, all of which led to the absence of unemployment, as 'those without land were steadily employed as labourers, and even bedouins and villagers from the neighbourhood were attracted to Sheikh Muwannis for work'.

134 CZA, S25/5936; Meeting of representatives of the Tel Aviv municipality, Va'ad Le'umi, Jewish Agency and residents of Jaffa's Jewish neighbourhoods, dated 16 May 1940.

135 *Yediot Tel Aviv*, 1943, pp. 12, 148. Yet, even after increasing the town-planning area of Tel Aviv by more than 50 per cent (from about 9000 to 14,000 *dunums*), the Municipality was not satisfied and demanded an additional extension. Several months later, the city was awarded another 9000 *dunums*, bringing the new total to approximately 22,000 *dunums* (*Yediot Tel Aviv*, 1943, pp. 12, 151).

136 ISA, M/R.21129/3704. Thus, one resident explained that 'Jammasin did not cultivate any part of the [lands]. It had been a part of our grazing lands. Jammasin improved the rest of the old swamp, we did not do so by lease from Sheikh Muwannis people ... I claim defined lands in the disputed area. I do not give up my claim in favour of any grazing claim. I first claimed land at land settlement some five to six year ago before that Government went out to land. I do not know that certain of our people then claimed it as grazing land, but I have heard that a *matruke* claim was made.'

137 ISA, M/R.21129/3704. Thus, one resident explained that 'drainage of swamp took place fifteen to twenty years ago and work lasted for two to three years. I have cultivated in the lands for some sixteen to seventeen years in my patches, but even before the British came I improved some places.'

138 ISA, M/R.21129/3704. Yet, on at least one occasion, a respondent complained that 'when land was improved we had insufficient grazing land'. This is not surprising, considering the importance of watering places for the residents of the villages, who still depended on grazing buffaloes for their livelihood, but it demonstrates that from their own experience in 'improving' the land villagers had learned that reclaiming land for intensive cultivation was in some cases an ill-advised effort, particularly when residents had used the land for grazing their cattle.

139 In one instance, villagers claimed that because of its proximity to the village and use for pasturage, a particular plot of land would more

appropriately be categorised as *matruke* (ISA, M/R.21129/3704, 15 July 1921? Report no 10) on lands lying in the vicinity of Sheikh Muwannis and Petakh Tikva/Mulebbes.

140 Stein, 1984, p.178. The list included mayors El-Said, Alfred Rok and 'Omar al-Baytar, the latter's brother, 'Abdul Ra'ouf, Abu-Khadra, Yaqub Dallal and others (Stein, 1984, Appendix 3), although, according to Stein, there were no lands in possession of absentee landlords in the Jaffa subdistrict in the early 1930s and the lands that were sold, except for one parcel by El-Said, were not in the Jaffa area. All these men were prominent members of the nationalist parties.

141 It was the economically stronger groups in villages which were more interested in the permanent partition of common lands as a way of both minimising uncertainty and strengthening their economic and political position: Kamen, 1991, p.138.

142 Bunton, 1997, p.33. He continues, 'it is evident that a great deal of discretion was given to the courts to ensure that rules relating to property rights always converged with the administrative necessities of the colonial state': Bunton, 1997, p.62.

143 Thus the Muslim–Christian Association of Jaffa criticised the unlimited authority given to the High Commissioner in the 1920 Land Transfer Ordinance. Interestingly, Stein suggests that it was the small notable landowning and land-benefiting class whose livelihoods were threatened by the British management of the land market that was most vocal during the 1921 revolt: Stein, 1984, p.49.

144 *Al-Jam'ia al-Islamiyya*, 21 December 1937, p.3.

145 *Al-Jam'ia al-Islamiyya*, 21 December 1937, p.3. That is a bypass road, and in fact it is clear from the description of the 11 new roads that would be built that they literally carved up Sheikh Muwannis for the benefit of Tel Aviv residents while also creating an industrial zone in what was, as the residents described it, an agricultural village.

146 *Al-Jam'ia al-Islamiyya*, 21 December 1937, p.3. Similarly, a petition from 26 'Jaffan notables' declared that 'the government have agreed to the annexation of pure Arab villages (Summel, Sheikh Muwannis, Jerisheh, Jammasin) to the Tel Aviv town-planning area in spite of the fact that the land of these villages is purely agricultural and is the main source of sustenance to the people of these villages. The strong fair protest of the villages to this annexation was completely ignored. It is only fair therefore that the government should accede to the request of the Jaffa municipality

in annexing these sand dunes to its area' (Hagana Archive, 105/204, Hagana report, 'Yediot me-Yafo', 5 March 1944).

147 ISA, M/RG2/564/18, Letter to High Commissioner dated 20 March 1947.

148 See Martha Mundy's analysis of land tenure in Syria in the present volume.

149 In fact, the conflict over rights to property was mirrored by a contest over rights to water and related resources of the Jaffa-Tel Aviv region: many of the same Zionist leaders who planned the development of Tel Aviv utilised many of the same arguments described in the previous section with many of the same British officials to achieve a Zionist monopoly over hydroelectricity and irrigation from the 'Auja/Yarkon River and to open a port in Tel Aviv that was understood by all sides as constituting a grave threat to Jaffa port and thus to the socio-economic future of Jaffa as a whole. For an in-depth discussion of the struggles over the Rutenberg Concession on the 'Auja River or the creation of the Tel Aviv port and its effect on Jaffa and its port, see LeVine, 1999, Chapter 3.

150 MacNeil, 1997.

151 Since completing this essay I have been able to examine the Prime Minister's Archives in Istanbul for files related to Palestine, Jaffa and Tel Aviv. The results of this research are available in LeVine, 2004 (see Contributors section, p.xiii), Chapters 1–3.

Bibliography

Abbreviations

CCC	Consular and Commercial Correspondance
CZA	Central Zionist Archives
DAMFAF	Diplomatic Archives, Ministry of Foreign Affairs, France
ISA	Israel State Archives
JICR	Jaffa Islamic Court Records
MHTA	Museum of the History of Tel Aviv
PEF	Palestine Exploration Fund
PRO	Public Record Office
TAMA	Tel Aviv Municipal Archive

Primary sources

France
Paris, Diplomatic Archives, Ministry of Foreign Affairs, France

Great Britain
London, Public Record Office
Parliamentary Papers, 1892
Trade of Palestine, 1890–91

Israel/Palestine
Jerusalem: Israel State Archives
Yediot Tel Aviv (copies available at the Tel Aviv Municipal Archive)
Falastin
al-Jam'ia al-Islamiyya
Jerusalem: Central Zionist Archives
Jaffa Islamic Court Records (microfilm copy at University of Haifa Library), alternative version of Islamic Court records at Research and Documentation, Jordanian University

Secondary sources

Abu-Bakr, Amin, *Land Ownership in the Jerusalem Mutasarrif, 1858–1918* (in Arabic), Amman, Abdul-Hamid Shuman Institute, 1996.
Agmon, Iris, *Women and Society: Muslim Women, the Shari'a Court and the Society of Jaffa and Haifa under Late Ottoman Rule (1900–1914)* (in Hebrew), unpublished PhD dissertation, Hebrew University of Jerusalem, 1994.
Amin, Samir, *Eurocentrism*, trans. Russell Moore, New York, Monthly Review Press, 1989.
Architectural Record (journal).
Atran, Scott, 'The Surrogate Colonization of Palestine, 1917–1939', *American Ethnologist* 161/4, 1989, pp.719–744.
Biger, Gideon, 'Arab Farms in the Region of Tel Aviv' (in Hebrew), *Ariel* 48-49, 1987, pp.53–56.
Bunton, Martin, *The Role of Private Property in the British Administration of Palestine*, unpublished PhD dissertation, Oxford University, 1997.
Cohen, Israel, *The Zionist Movement: Aims and Aspirations*, Berlin, Zionist Central Office, 1912.
Dizengoff, Meir, *Renaissance of Tel Aviv* (in Hebrew), Tel Aviv, Eitan Shashoni Press, n.d.

– *To the Friends of My Youth* (in Hebrew), Tel Aviv, n.p., 1931.

Doumani, Beshara, *Rediscovering Palestine: Merchants and Peasants in Jabal Nablus, 1700–1900*, Berkeley, University of California Press, 1995.

Droyanov, A. et al., *Sefer Tel Aviv* (in Hebrew), Tel Aviv, 1935.

Eisenman, Robert, *Islamic Law in Palestine and Israel*, Leiden, E.J. Brill, 1978.

Firestone, Ya'akov, 'Production and Trade in an Islamic Context', *International Journal of Middle Eastern Studies* 6, 1975, 3, pp. 185–209 and 1975, 4, pp. 308–324.

Frank, Andre Gunder, *ReORIENT: Global Economy in the Asian Age*, Berkeley, University of California Press, 1998.

Gavish, Dov, 'The Old City of Jaffa, 1936: A Colonial Urban Renewal Project' (in Hebrew), *Eretz-Israel* 17, 1984, pp. 66–73, plts 2–6.

Goadby, Frederic and Moses Doukhan, *The Land Law of Palestine*, Jerusalem, 1935.

Graham-Brown, Sarah, 'The Political Economy of the Habal Nablus, 1920–48', in Roger Owen (ed.), *Studies in the Economic and Social History of Palestine in the Nineteenth and Twentieth Centuries*, Oxford, Oxford University Press, 1982, pp. 88–176.

Graicer, Iris, *Workers' Neighborhoods: Attempts at Shaping an Urban Landscape through Social Ideologies in Eretz Israel during the Mandate Period* (in Hebrew), unpublished PhD dissertation, Hebrew University of Jerusalem, 1982.

Gran, Peter, *Beyond Eurocentrism: A New View of Modern World History*, Syracuse, Syracuse University Press, 1996.

Granott, Abraham, *Land Policy in Palestine*, New York, Hyperion Press, 1940.

Granovsky, Abraham, *Land Policy in Palestine*, New York, Hyperion Press, 1940.

Hall, Peter, *Cities of Tomorrow: An Intellectual History of Urban Planning and Design in the Twentieth Century*, New York, Basil Blackwell, 1988.

Himadeh, Said, *The Economic System in Palestine* (in Arabic), Beirut, 1939.

İslamoğlu, Huri, 'Property as a Contested Domain: A Reevaluation of the Ottoman Land Code of 1858', in Roger Owen (ed.), *New Perspectives on Property and Land in the Middle East*, Cambridge, MA, Harvard University Press, 2000, pp. 3–61.

Kallner, D.H. and E. Rosenau, 'The Geographical Regions of Palestine', *The Geographical Review* XXIX, 1939, pp. 61–80.

Kamen, Charles, *Little Common Ground: Arab Agriculture and Jewish Settlement in Palestine, 1920–1948*, Pittsburgh, University of Pittsburgh Press, 1991.

Kana'an, Ruba, *Jaffa and the Vakıf of Muhammad Aga Abu Nabbut (1799–1831): A Study in the Urban History of an East Mediterranean City*, unpublished DPhil. thesis, University of Oxford, 1998.

Kark, Ruth, 'Cartographic Sources for the Study of Jaffa: From the Napoleonic Siege to the British Conquest', *Cartographic Journal* 25, January 1988, pp. 37–49.

– *Jaffa, a City in Evolution, 1799–1917*, Jerusalem, Yad Ben Tzvi Press, 1990.

Katz, Yossi, 'Attempts to Purchase Sheikh Muwannis on the Eve of World War I' (in Hebrew), in David Grossman (ed.), *Between Yarkon and Ayalon: Studies on Gush Dan and the Lod Valley*, Ramat Gan, Bar Illan University Publishing, 1983, pp. 139–48.

– 'The Ahuzat Bayit Company, 1906–09: Founding Suggestions for the Establishment of Tel Aviv' (in Hebrew), *Kethedra* 33, 1984, pp. 160–87.

– *Zionism and Urban Settlement: The Jewish National Funds Contribution to Urban Settlement Prior to World War I*, lecture delivered to the Institute for the Research on the History of the JNF, Land and Settlement, May 1992.

– *The Business of Settlement: Private Entrepreneurship in the Jewish Settlement of Palestine, 1900–1914*, Jerusalem, Magnes Press, 1994.

LeVine, Mark, 'The Discourse of Development in Mandate Palestine', *Arab Studies Quarterly*, Winter 1995, pp. 95–124.

– 'Conquest Through Town-Planning: The Case of Tel Aviv, 1921–48', *Journal of Palestine Studies* 27/4, 1998, pp. 36–52.

– 'A Nation from the Sands? Architecture, Planning and the Evolution of National Identities in Jaffa and Tel Aviv, 1880–1948', *National Identities* 1/1, 1998, pp. 15–38.

– *Overthrowing Geography, Re-Imagining Identity: A History of Jaffa and Tel Aviv, 1880 to the Present*, unpublished PhD dissertation, New York University, 1999b.

Lockman, Zachary, *Comrades and Enemies: Arab and Jewish Workers in Palestine, 1906–48*, Berkeley, University of California Press, 1996.

MacNeil, William P., 'Enjoy Your Rights! Three Cases from the Postcolonial Commonwealth', *Public Culture* 9, 1997, pp. 377–93.

Malak, Hana, *Roots of Jaffa* (in Arabic), Jerusalem, self-published, 1993.

– *Memoirs of Jaffan Families: Between the Past and Present* (in Arabic), Jerusalem, self-published, 1996.

Mandel, Neville, *The Arabs and Zionism Before World War I*, Berkeley, University of California Press, 1976.

Metzer, Jacob, *The Divided Economy of Mandate Palestine*, Cambridge, Cambridge University Press, 1998.

Mitchell, Timothy, 'The Limits of the State: Beyond Statis Approaches and Their Critics', *American Political Science Review* 85/1, March 1991, pp. 77–96.

– 'Origins and Limits of the Modern Idea of the Economy', University of Michigan, Advanced Study Center, Working Papers Series, no 12, Ann Arbor, 1995.

Owen, Roger, 'The Role of Mushaa' (Co-Ownership) in the Politico-Legal History of Mandatory Palestine', SSRC Workshop on Law, Property and State Power, Büyükada, 1991.

Ram, Hana, *The Jewish Community in Jaffa: From Sephardic Community to Zionist Center*, Tel Aviv, Carmel Publishing, 1996.

Ruppin, Arthur, 'The Foundation of Tel Aviv', in Yosef Aricha (ed.), *Sixty Years of the City of Tel Aviv* (in Hebrew), Tel Aviv, Tel Aviv Municipality Education Department, 1969, pp. 37–66.

Schölch, Alexander, *Palestine in Transformation, 1856–1882: Studies in Social, Economic and Political Development*, trans. William C. Young and Michael C. Gerrity, Washington, Institute for Palestine Studies, 1993.

Shiffman, Y., 'Tel Aviv: Today and Tomorrow', *Palestine and Near East* 9/42.

Shloosh, Yosef Eliahu, *Chapters of My Life, 1870–1930* (in Hebrew), Tel Aviv, n.p., 1931.

Shur, Natan, 'The Beginnings of Tel Aviv' (in Hebrew), *Ariel* 48-49, 1987, pp. 63–81.

Smilansky, David, *A Town is Born* (in Hebrew), ed. Yossi Katz, Tel Aviv, Defence Ministry Publications, 1981.

Smith, Barbara, *The Roots of Separatism in Palestine*, Syracuse, Syracuse University Press, 1993.

Stein, Kenneth, *The Land Question in Palestine, 1917–39*, Chapel Hill, University of North Carolina Press, 1984.

Survey of Palestine, vol. I, 1947, reprinted by Institute of Palestine Studies, Washington DC, 1991.

Tarawnah, Muhammad al-, *Qadâ' Jaffa during the Period 1281–1333 A.H./1864–1914* (in Arabic), PhD dissertation, University of Jordan, 1997.

Town Planning Handbook of Palestine, 1930.

Wilkins, Charles, 'Jaffa in the Early Tanzimate Period, 1840–61', in Salim Tamari and Ruba Kana'an (eds), *Jaffa: The Modernity of an East Mediterranean City*, unpublished manuscript.

Part Two

CHAPTER 5

Mapping Landed Property: A Necessary Technology of Imperial Rule?

Richard Saumarez Smith

The question mark of my subtitle marks the contrast that I wish to draw in the use of mapping as an instrument of rule by two imperial governments in the nineteenth century, that of British rule in India on the one hand, and that of Ottoman rule in what is today northern Jordan and southern Syria on the other.[1] Stated bluntly, the contrast is of presence to absence. Maps were not unknown in nineteenth-century Ottoman rule either in civil planning or in the military. But mapping does not appear to have been a technology generally applied in administration, at least not to the registration of agricultural land;[2] nor perhaps was Ottoman rule or Ottoman society typically represented on a map in the way that British India was, both as a place and as an idea. The connection between not using maps in land registration and not using them more generally may not be very tangible. But the contrast with another imperial system where maps were part of the culture of rule raises interesting questions concerning the use of maps to represent society and the relation between forms of knowledge and the apparatus of rule. The absence of a practice may be as significant in relation to forms of rule as a presence. A minimal system of local registration may do the job of creating property just as well as, and with less dislocation than, an excessively elaborate one.

Mapping and the culture of rule

I am concerned mainly with cadastral maps, maps of fields (taxable property in agricultural land) at the scale of 16 inches or more to the mile (1:3960, one inch to 110 yards).[3] But I shall approach the question of what such mapping did for imperial government by working downwards from maps at a smaller scale concerning much larger territories. Small-scale maps could show at a glance not only major lines of communication across the subcontinent or which territory belonged to whom, but also the regional distribution of a selected feature or fact, whether material or social. This kind of mapping paralleled the tabulation of population distributions in the decennial census which, from 1871, became a focus of informed knowledge – later, even of political agitation – concerning social groups throughout India.[4] There is thus a link between the use of maps at this broader level and the development of a particular kind of embryonic sociology. The sociology was morphological. The population of India was enumerated under different headings, including caste and religion, and these were then totalled and tabulated by district (an administrative unit containing 1000 villages or so).[5] Every feature tabulated in the censuses was mappable. A picture of Indian society as a whole, immediate in its miniaturised simplicity, could be constructed from the bottom upwards. That was one step. But a second step could also be made. The immediacy of the picture disguised the process by which a selected feature had been made global fact. Miniaturisation could be reversed. The picture of the whole could be turned upside down so that the bottom became an illustration of the top, as if there had been no act of translation, no classification of groups by the census or aggregation into grosser categories – as if the meaning of Brahman or Rajput in one locality were the same as in any other.[6] The mind's eye could turn from a view of the natural features of the subcontinent, at the scale of one to five million, to an enlarged view of any chosen locality at the scale of one inch to one mile (1:63,360), the largest scale of the Survey of India series begun in 1878; why not also of sociological features? In Benedict Anderson's phrase, the power of a map is to say 'it is here not there' that a particular feature, custom, monument or social group is found. But there is more to it than that.[7] It is a power to scale down and up, miniaturising and magnifying, that endorses a corresponding movement in sociology of constructing a global picture from local features and of then turning the picture upside down and applying its gross, not to say artificial, categories like a model to a locality, all in the idiom of fact.

The parallel between cartographic and sociological scaling up and down is associated particularly with the decennial census, for it was the Census Reports written by people like Ibbetson, Crooke, Ridley and Rose that became the foundation for discussions of caste, tribe and race from the 1870s which, in turn, fed into journals like *Man* (founded 1901). But, in an earlier generation, before the decennial census had been thought of, caste had not been the central notion in official understanding of Indian society. Rather, the central notion had been that of village community: as a 'little republic', a phrase made famous at the beginning of the nineteenth century; as a system of rights and duties between different occupational groups; and as a coparcenary of farmers sharing responsibility for cultivation, access to common agricultural resources and the burden of demands from the state for revenue or labour. This moment corresponded to what might be considered an earlier embryonic sociology of India, pre-museum, pre-census and almost pre-map, in the second quarter of the nineteenth century rather than the last, when the principal instrument for gathering information was the collection of local revenue statistics rather than the all-India decennial census, and when discussion was framed in the context of practical application in law and administration rather than of general, not particularly practical, knowledge. This sociology was not morphological but was tied more to political economy. It did not have time, however, to get off the ground before the sociology of caste, tribe and race started to develop, with its glossaries and more appealing visual representation in maps.

The decision to publish Settlement Reports and other government publications 'for general information' was taken only in 1844.[8] Nevertheless, it remains a puzzle why one form of sociology developed in nineteenth-century India instead of another.[9] The policy of upholding local law and custom had been formulated at the very beginning of British rule in India in the

1760s and 1770s, initially concerning 'Hindu' or Muslim law but, later on, more particularly *lex loci*.[10] But there was a tension, almost a contradiction, between governing uniformly and preserving local custom, between defining categories of tenancy in law for a whole province and allowing scope for local variation. This tension between global and local application in administration and law resembles that of an assumed reversibility between miniaturisation and magnification: provincial law was, in part, constructed from the bottom up, yet stereotype headings framed the collection of information regarding local variations and stereotype language informed the writing of each village's supposedly unique constitution. In effect, procedures of science (generalisation) were applied to procedures of gathering information (standardised headings) and procedures of government (standardised measures, uniform application of law, uniform rules of procedure). One might say that this developed as a ruling paradigm in imperial administration in India during the first half of the nineteenth century and became rigid in the second half.[11]

Scaling up and down did extend to the level of field maps in the case of land tenure. During the second half of the nineteenth century, land tenure touched the public imagination, since it was thought to reflect the evolution of social institutions, especially the village community.[12] But, curiously, the power of a field map to represent a sociological feature does not appear to have been recognised at the lowest level in local administration, for instance to illustrate the constitution of a village from the pattern of allotment of fields on shares. Such representation could have been used as evidence of who was a member of a shareholding community – evidence of a special right – but apparently was not. This is a remarkable omission for a government that assigned so much importance to the idea of village community.[13] It was as if officials were unable to exploit the heuristic potential of field maps once these had been drawn, inspected and placed in the custody of a local revenue accountant (*patwari*) or filed safely away in the drawers of a district records room. Field maps were indeed used to show a farmer or local official where plots lay, 'here not there' in Anderson's phrase, and as an index to the record of rights of a village, but not to go from the pattern of plots to an understanding of something about the local society.[14] On the other hand, District Settlement Reports, the reports describing the assessment and registration of land in a district, would come to include small-scale maps representing distributions within the district, for instance of principal castes, but nothing more detailed. In short, the cartographic imagination, even in this map-minded empire, seems to have been structurally constrained and to have taken time to develop.[15] Locally, maps were a useful tool to designate location but not patterns, whereas at higher levels they were an important device for representing how Indian society fitted together; both uses, however, were within an overarching idiom of facticity. In the culture of Britain's imperial rule in India, maps were thus important at all levels of government, although their use varied with the level.

For Ottoman Syria, on the other hand, this was not obviously the case: the link between maps and a form of sociology is less certain, and maps seem to have been used hardly at all at the local level in connection with land registration. This is the first query and contrast. Was there something about the historical continuity of Ottoman rule in Arab lands, as opposed to the discontinuity of British rule in India, that led to a different kind of conceptualisation of subject or society and a different kind of relation at this gross level between sociological knowledge and power? Is the colonialism of British rule in India sufficient answer? Or is the relevant contrast the form and scale of local administration? For someone doing research at the micro level of village revenue or *tapu* registers in today's northern Jordan, there is certainly nothing like the extent of secondary published documentation that exists for the higher levels of district and province in British India (where it exists in English as opposed to the vernacular of the village records). District and provincial reports of all departments of government were the foundation of what I have called the embryonic sociology of India, and they remain the principal source of information for the writing of Indian social and economic history during the colonial period. They are so authoritative that it is hard to reach below the level of district to the primary documents on which the secondary reports were largely based, and hard to question the units in terms of which the information was built up. This, incidentally, is one reason for studying the relation between government and society in such detail at the level of individual villages. Where attention to local detail has been lacking in historical writing, there is one kind of need. But where knowledge of society was constructed in a particular way as a conjunct of imperial rule, colonising the minds of both ruler and ruled, there is a double need first to deconstruct the official structures of knowledge and then to propose alternatives derived perhaps from a rereading of the very local records that formed the base of the official pyramid.

Field mapping and local administration

A different and more difficult query is raised by the contrast in techniques of registering property. What *is* the power of mapping land as property? What does it do to those whose property is mapped and what does mapping enable a government to do that a descriptive list of borders and measurements does not? Here the contrast is between a map and a list. However, it may not be easy to distinguish the effect of mapping fields from the general effect of all the other registers that made up a village's record of rights in northwestern India of which the field map was part. In its historical dimension, the question concerns why British governments in India chose to map fields rather than to employ the more time-honoured practice of listing people and their liabilities, the practice of the Mughals as well as of the Ottomans (though in a different way). This is the question that I shall take up in greater detail below. There is no clear answer. What model did they have in mind: Roman colonies? Field maps had not been a feature of medieval European surveys; no maps were drawn for the 1086 'Domesday' survey that was prepared after the Normans conquered England, a precedent which officials of British India were fond of citing in regard to the land-revenue settlements of northwestern India. I shall suggest that the practice of mapping landed property in northwestern India has several strands in its genealogy. One strand was surely the early-nineteenth-century enthusiasm with which vast sweeps of territory were being newly mapped and conquered. But another strand concerns the way that local administration developed: the articulation between village and district, district and province. As British rule extended to the northwest, reaching its limit in 1849, there was experimentation in the form and apparatus of rule. The district became the keystone in the imperial arch. New applications or procedures could be introduced by an enterprising official in charge of a district and adopted for the province as a whole. Knowledge of local customs was thought essential for efficient government. In the development of district administration during this period, a contrast becomes evident between British and Ottoman rule, a development reflected in the use of maps. I shall now sketch this process.

The first Surveyor-General, James Rennell, had been appointed in 1767 soon after the acquisition of Bengal by the East India Company. Rennell's 1783 *Memoir of a Map of Hindoostan* was the prototype for many subsequent editions. The Great Trigonometrical Survey of India was formally established in 1817, its first Superintendent, Lambton, having actually begun the triangulation of the southern peninsula some 15 years earlier. (Everest, a name with which everyone is familiar, joined the Survey in 1818 and became its Superintendent in 1823 on Lambton's death.) The purpose had been scientific and technical, both to lay out a grid of triangulated reference points and to measure a portion of a great arc from south to north for comparison with measurements in the Arctic Circle in order to determine the amount that the earth was flattened at the poles.

The Revenue Survey

The relation of mapping to land revenue was formally recognised in northwestern India by the establishment of the Revenue Survey in 1823 to complement the basic procedures of land administration laid down in Regulation VII of 1822.[16] For the rich country of the northern Indian plains, more detailed maps were desired than those which had been produced by the Topographical Survey under Colin Mackenzie in southern India from 1799. But the Revenue Survey was not yet cadastral, not even in the broader sense of field mapping that I am using (not formally tied into a precise global grid): no field maps were prescribed. The purpose of the Revenue Survey was to provide the government with an adequate basis for conducting settlement operations: to delineate the boundaries of villages and estates on maps at the scale of four inches to the mile (1:15,840), to calculate the superficial area of these units of revenue administration, to sketch some internal detail such as the extent of uncultivated land or the position of roads and the village site, and to gather some quantifiable general information ('statistics') such as the number of houses, ploughs and wells or the approximate number of the population. The Revenue Survey was for administrative use as a preliminary to the detailed revenue settlements; its maps were never published, nor were they considered part of the local record available for consultation by the local populace.[17] It bridged the higher scientific aims of the Great Trigonometrical Survey to establish a reference grid and the more detailed aims of land-revenue settlements to assess the productivity of the land and to determine who should pay the revenue (the person made owner of the land in question). The position of a village's boundary was drawn on a map by the Revenue Survey as boundary posts were fixed in the ground, while the village's economic assets and legal right-holders were recorded in registers prepared during settlement operations. At the beginning, in the 1820s, that was the division of labour: general external boundary maps prepared by the Revenue Survey and detailed lists of internal matters prepared at settlement; no field maps had to be prepared either by the Revenue Survey or at settlement. A third form of document prepared at settlement was the contract between the government and the village specifying how the village might manage its internal affairs, provided it maintained revenue payments, but for the moment the relevant contrast is between map and list. Quite soon afterwards, in the 1830s and 1840s, field maps did become a routine part of settlement operations and the dual role of local records started to take shape:[18] at the local level, as the interface between government and people, the basis of village administration and of rights to land; and for higher levels as the source of statistical abstracts as well as information on agricultural custom and customary law. Although the legal terms in which details were recorded were stereotype, village records were considered a 'photograph of society', a true representation of the constitution and state of a village at a particular time, hence true even when viewed at a smaller scale in abstract.

Revenue Surveys in northwestern India eventually merged into the Survey of India after they had done their preliminary work of informing government and after the first settlements had been completed. The present status of the early four-inch-to-the-mile village Revenue Survey maps in the Punjab reflects their erstwhile intermediate position between local instrument and general scaleable information, between the 16- or 32-inch field maps preserved in district revenue records rooms, which can still be inspected for specific local purposes with government permission, and the published one-inch topographical maps for the whole of India. The village Revenue Survey maps of the 1840s and 1850s are also preserved in district revenue records rooms, but in the village abstract notebooks of a later revised settlement that gave background information on each village for officials to use when they toured the district, and whose hand-written observations are sometimes appended to the tables of statistics. Their present use is confined to people like myself, who stumble across them in their search for the key to British imperial rule.

Revenue policy

Since one major branch of mapping in India was tied to revenue, a word is necessary here on government policy. The framework of land-revenue policy for northwestern India was laid down by Regulation VII of 1822 and given final shape by the revision of this regulation in 1833. This brought into effect an alternative both to the permanent settlements of land revenue in Bengal, whereby revenue liability had been fixed in perpetuity on individual owners of estates (*zamindari* settlements), and to the annually fluctuating settlements with individual cultivators in Madras (*ryotwari* settlements). In northwestern India, the village became the unit of revenue administration, and settlements were designed to last twenty or thirty years before revision. Within a village, those who were responsible for cultivation – those deemed proprietors – were held liable for revenue relating to their plots. But, at the same time, they were jointly liable for the revenue of the whole village. If one person defaulted on his revenue payments, liability fell first on his co-sharers, then on others within his section of the village and ultimately on the village as a whole. This required a formal constitution to be written, in the form of the contract mentioned above, setting out the village's internal divisions and the share of each proprietary unit within its section. Other provisions were also written determining how the village would administer its affairs. A dual policy was thus instituted both to create individual property in land and to preserve the corporateness of the village community. To effect this balancing act, a great deal of information was required, not only concerning the village customs that were to be preserved, especially those relating to coparcenary shareholding, but also concerning the productivity of land in order to fix the revenue rate at a level intended to be low enough to afford cultivators a reasonable profit on their cultivation and thereby to stimulate the market in land. This is the origin of the wealth of information – though much of it stereotype information – contained in the revenue records of each and every village in northwestern India, which correspondingly formed the base of the pyramid of knowledge about Indian society.

Field maps

Regulation VII did not prescribe the drawing of field maps. But it did prescribe a full internal measurement of fields as a basis both for the registration of holdings and for assessment. The theory was that an appropriate revenue demand could be set at a certain proportion of the profits of cultivation, which in turn could be calculated if sufficient data were known on crop yields, soils, market prices and rents as well as on general agricultural assets. A uniform and scientific basis of assessment would be independent of local opinion, the practice of past governments and the different forms of tenure.

Once a revenue demand had been set for the whole of a village, it could be left to the village to distribute internally among the proprietors as they wished, whether on shares, on a summary rate, or on soil rates per unit area of cultivation. The register of fields contained the basic data of the dimensions of each field and its area, whether it was irrigated, who owned it and who cultivated it. It also recorded the crops grown in each field during the season of the survey. With such detail, a field map was hardly necessary as a record, except as an index to the field registers. As a check on the completeness and accuracy of the register, on the other hand, field maps were seen to be important.[19]

Standardisation of measures

Several strands of influence may be detected behind this elaborate system of registration and assessment, among which utilitarianism may be considered paramount. In 1819, James Mill had become assistant examiner at the East India Company's offices in London with responsibility for revenue affairs. Ricardo's theory of rent was applied to the problem of fixing a rate of assessment that did not impoverish farmers. Bentham's remedy of social engineering through government and law underlay much of British policy in India at the time. A second strand, not unconnected with utilitarianism and the desire to make law accessible to the public, was the policy to give proprietary title to peasant farmers rather than to a superior class of tax-farmer or local lord (if there were any), in order that government deal directly with peasant farmers organised collectively in strong 'little republics' rather than through intermediaries. And a third strand could be said to be empirical, following observation by officials that existing measures varied not only from village to village, but sometimes even within a village. From the 1820s, district officials were encouraged to leave their offices and tour the country, getting to know it for themselves. According to the first strand, measures of area had to be standardised if assessments were to be fair and the country were to prosper, an essential goal where the land revenue was by far the greatest part of government income. The fact that a local measure like a 'plough' of land might be an adequate measure of productivity within a village was discounted in the desire of government to impose its own standard and to know things for itself.[20] A plough of land signified, in the first instance, how much land could be ploughed by a team of oxen in a certain time; it was therefore the unit in terms of which the members of a cultivating community held shares to village lands commensurate with their resources (the human labour that they commanded, the animal labour and, more generally, their status); and finally, in the allotment of fields on those shares, a plough signified a certain size of holding equalised for quality by the method of allotting a plot in each different location. The measure thus took account of the variables used in government assessment: a community was its own assessor. But, of course, the measure varied with a village's circumstances. In a hard-pressed village, a team of oxen would have less land to plough than in one better off, though in each a plough represented what a household needed.[21] The idiom was of subsistence, whatever the actual yield, rather than of profit. For an outside government to rely on such a measure, then, went against the ethos of uniformity and the desire to know in its own terms. It did not matter that its own assessments involved elaborate measurements and mathematical calculations. Later, after the 1850s, assessments did become less contrived and the qualities of cultivators (for instance their caste) were included among the agricultural assets to be considered in addition to bare quantities. But, in the beginning, quantification ruled. And by the time there was some change of heart, the local idiom of shareholding in terms of 'ploughs', by which productivity was related to resources and resources to shares, had been unalterably changed through the creation of private property.

The notion of property acted against the idiom of ploughs in three ways. Firstly, it distinguished one group of farmers ('proprietors') from others ('tenants' as well as sharecroppers who lacked the resources to manage the cultivation of an individual plot on their own).[22] Although the plough was recognised as a 'customary' – not economic – measure of right by settlement officials, it was applied only to those awarded proprietary rights and not to shareholders who did not belong to the ancestral core. Secondly, property was assumed to have fixed boundaries. Periodic re-allotment of the cultivable land whereby disparities could be adjusted was therefore heavily discouraged.[23] In plains villages, where equalisation of land was synchronic (holdings consisting of seven or eight plots scattered around the village) rather than diachronic (holdings consisting of two large plots re-allotted every second year), such re-allotment may have been infrequent.[24] But, by comparison with northern Jordan under Ottoman rule, where re-allotment continued until the British Mandate even in villages of the plains, the insistence on fixed boundaries to property in the Punjab may be seen to have undermined an important mechanism for a community to re-assert the principle of fair shares and to adjust to change. The third point of difference between the notion of property and the idiom of ploughs was that the latter was an idiom of subsistence, not of profit.

Government intrusiveness

In any case, whether or not a field map was originally prescribed for Revenue Surveys and settlements, the degree of penetration into a village by the British government in India was altogether different from that of the Ottoman government in Greater Syria at roughly the same time, to the extent that one should ask whether different conceptions of government were at work. In both the regions under discussion, agricultural production had been characterised by communal land management. However, the policy adopted by each government in the registration of rights in such systems differed. In brief, leaving aside the manner of measurement, the Ottoman practice permitted holdings to be registered in shares rather than as individual plots, at least for *musha'* (collectively held) land which in the plains villages of the Hauran covered almost all of what was cultivable, and thus did nothing to prevent a village from managing its common resources in the way that it wanted, for instance by periodic re-allotment.[25] This can be said to have upheld the institution of shareholding, while at the same time introducing a form of private property in land as effectively as and with less government interference than the elaborate system introduced in north-western British India. There, through written constitutions, a form of shareholding was upheld that was subservient to private property rather than the other way round. Firstly, a distinction was made between proprietors and tenants: registration was in two columns rather than in the undifferentiated one of the *tapu* registers, an elaboration that incidentally was to lead to extraordinarily complex registration by the end of British rule ninety years later, so involuted that the metaphor of a photograph could no longer apply. Secondly, when rights were awarded at revenue settlements the first consideration was to identify those in a cultivating community to whom might be awarded proprietary title and then to record their shares and write a constitution, rather than the other way round: first identifying the shareholders in the community, and then assigning proprietary title. In the latter case, the chief evidence for the shareholding system might well have come from the layout of fields on the ground, for this showed concretely how holdings had been allotted to shareholders and was thus a complete representation – or map in another sense – of the shareholding community, the very institution that the government was committed to uphold. But, in practice, proprietors were identified not from the field pattern upwards, despite the swarm of surveyors who trod the land, but outwards from the village headmen on such criteria as who had occupied the land first and who was of superior social status. Entries in the column of the field register for the owner of a plot were filled not actually from the ground up, but by reference to a pre-existing preliminary list of landowners and tenants that had been prepared at the start of settlement proceedings.[26]

The two basic registers of a village's settlement record from which other registers were prepared were both lists: the field register and the preliminary register of landholders. If a field map was not originally prescribed, and when it was prescribed was not used as evidence of right, what was its particular use to government? Why was it ever introduced?

Development of local, district administration

The answer historically, unsatisfactory though this may be, is that the preparation of field maps seemed to be a good idea: good, that is, to procedurally minded men intent on systematising their part of the bureaucratic empire being developed at the time and who were wedded to the idea that village records should have maximum utility. Maps of one sort were already being prepared (those of the Revenue Survey); with so much measurement prescribed as part of the procedure of settlement, it was a short step to include field maps – not much more than a decade of administrative trial and error. Moreover, field maps could be prepared with far less cost by village revenue accountants (*patwaris*), after a little training, than by professional surveyors. This is a point that I wish to emphasise, that some of the form of early administration in northwestern India was determined organically, even non-intentionally (in Foucault's terms), while local district administration, the heart of the British imperial system, found its feet. This includes some of those instruments of rule that we now look back upon as characteristic of the peculiar relation between knowledge and power that developed during British rule in India. The complementarity between rule by local record and rule by higher-level report was not invented in a day. Relations between knowledge and power have their own historical condition.

In two senses, the approach to assessment was already cartographic, even without a field map. First, the business of settlement followed that of determining village boundaries. To the bird's-eye view of government, every square inch of territory was already demarcated into separate units called villages, and this same way of thinking was easily extended to the notion of landed property: all the land in a village had to belong to somebody, individually or in common. Property was in discrete parcels of land, levelled as on a map, not in the heap of harvested grain on a threshing floor. Secondly, assessment covered the totality of that land, it was not confined to land that was actually cultivated. This was a significant departure from the practice of previous governments. Government's right to land revenue, according to theorists of the time, was to a share of the produce from every square inch of cultivation. This had been the Mughal practice to which the British government considered itself heir. But the British extended the practice to include cultivable wasteland; rates of assessment were applied to wasteland as well as to land that was actually cultivated, albeit lower rates. Land that was uncultivable, including the village site, was not assessable: literally, it was 'deducted' (*minhai*). The principle of deduction from a notional whole was then applied to exemptions (*mu'af*) from paying the revenue on plots held by religious bodies, especially the village mosque or shrine. In other words, the bird's-eye view was that all land within village boundaries was subject to government assessment, although some land would not in fact be assessed ('deducted'), and some assessed land would be exempt from revenue payment. Assessment proceeded inwards from the village boundaries, so to speak, rather than outwards from the village site and from village leaders standing on that site negotiating with government officials about which plots of land were held by whom. This latter procedure seems to have been that of *tapu* registration of the post-Tanzimat Ottoman government, for which there was no independent survey of fields, and plots were identified by describing their borders in the four cardinal directions. Village boundaries were not fully determined, at least initially, by *tapu* authorities whose mandate was to identify immovable sources of wealth: plots, houses and plantings of trees or vines.[27] Sheep and goats were also taxed, but that did not affect *tapu* registration. By contrast, the British in northwestern India reduced the taxation base to land alone while extending the definition of taxable land to the whole territory. In this sense, the approach was cartographic. No more head counts for revenue purposes, no more censuses of ploughs, no levies on wood or wool or cattle; the latter were customary privileges which villages might be permitted to levy for their own internal administration, if custom could be proved, after the overall government tax on land had been determined.

The organic development of local district administration in northwestern India from the 1820s is reflected in the use of maps. As with any organic growth, some branches adapted to the new environment while others became extinct. The four-inch Revenue Survey maps are an example of the latter. As the process of settlement developed and field maps became routine, so the more general Revenue Surveys became otiose. Field maps gave internal details within a village more fully and on a larger scale, while settlement statistics were more detailed than those of the Revenue Survey. On the other hand, the one-inch topographical Survey of India maps gave all the necessary features of the landscape although on a smaller scale and without delineating village boundaries.

Household censuses and maps of village sites

A second illustration of this organic development is the maps of village sites that were prepared in some districts of the Punjab for a very brief period in the 1850s. These were related to improved household censuses in much the same way as field maps were related to field registers, although without any kind of legal engagement to pay tax. In some form, household censuses had been taken at the time of revenue settlements since the 1820s, before the idea of a single synchronic census for the whole of British India had been conceived.[28] A more elaborate household census, listing each household head, exploited one niche in the new environment of local administration while the village site maps exploited another. Household censuses have an ancient genealogy in the technology of government as an instrument of taxation more than as a means to construct a picture of the whole population of a society. During the Mughal period, revenue assessment had sometimes been based on a census of ploughs, while a household census or enumeration (*khana shumari*) had provided the basis for a tax on the population, separate from the land revenue. Where this latter function was continued under British rule, the tax on houses became a strictly local affair as income for a village to pay its watchmen (the kind of tax that was regulated in a village's constitutional paper) or as part of municipal income of towns to pay for public works.[29] Another function of the household census was to provide information on the size and specialisation of the labour force and on the holdings of animals. As with all facets of land registration, the procedure and content of a household census was progressively improved between the 1820s and the 1850s to give fuller information subject to more thorough supervision. But so long as censuses remained part of settlement operations, there was no systematic summation for units above a district, and the census registers remained part of the local revenue record. The first census for the whole of the Punjab was made on 1 January 1855 from a combination of new enumerations (in districts where settlements had not been completed) and updated figures of household censuses taken at the time of settlements. Thereafter, household censuses as part of the local record were superseded by the synchronic all-India census, whose function was to generate a statistical representation of the whole of India in which the smallest tabulated unit was the district.

The village site map was a child of what I call 'rule-by-records' in local administration. But severed from its connection with a household census, it was still-born. As local administration developed after the 1820s, the function of village settlement records broadened from being the main source of information for government to being the main interface between government and people, where rights and customs were recorded on the basis of which disputes were settled. The superstructure of law rested on this base. At the same time, 'rule-by-records' became complemented at a higher level of imperial government by a 'rule-by-reports'.[30] Because revenue assessment was confined to agricultural land, the field map that was now prepared as part of the settlement record of a village excluded the village site. There was thus a niche in local government that could usefully be fertilised with the culture of mapping and, in one particular district, this is what happened. It was the brainchild of a settlement officer who did not have the flair of a Lawrence or a Temple, galloping across the countryside settling the revenue contracts of so many villages a day. Or perhaps it was the brainchild of his Indian assistant, Kali Rai, a man who had already shown his talent of interpretation with a vocabulary of agricultural terms published with government backing, and who was being encouraged to develop the genre of local gazetteer in the vernacular.[31] In any case, half way through the settlement operations of this district, maps of village sites began to be prepared, systematically although not to a uniform scale, to complement the household census. Maps of towns were prepared in a similar manner. The map of the town of Ludhiana, with a population in 1854 of 29,000, measures 2.5 by 3 metres; with the accompanying household census register, it took two surveyors one year to complete. I do not know for how many districts village site maps were prepared besides the two or three whose settlements were started under this one man. In Ludhiana district, these maps dating from 1853–54 remain the only documentary source of information concerning the location of houses on the village site consulted by villagers to this day.

Genealogy of proprietors

A third illustration is not of a map so much as of another kind of representation of the village community, a genealogy of proprietors. This, too, had been optional at early settlements. The only genealogy that I have seen in the records of the first settlement of Ludhiana district, that of 1853, was of a family that held both the land and the revenue assignment of a village; it is a bare skeleton of names. But it was another niche that could usefully be developed to make the village records more accessible to the public and to give concrete form to the new more exclusive idea of the village community as a coparcenary of proprietors rather than of farmers generally. In this new formulation, shares derived ideally by inheritance from founding ancestors rather than from a periodically revised reassessment within the community of its common resources and its members' individual assets. The periodic re-allotment of holdings, leading to a new map on the ground, was not compatible with the idea of fixed boundaries for landed property, nor with that of recording those boundaries on a map to be consulted in a district records room. A more comprehensive form of genealogy was devised by a settlement officer in the 1850s that combined three functions:[32] a historical charter for present proprietary rights from a set of founding ancestors, a record of the way that inheritance had actually occurred within living memory, to be continually updated, and an index of the detailed registers of holdings. Underneath the name of each surviving male descendant on the family tree was the number of his proprietary holding, its area and its measure of right or share. The genealogy had a further epistemological function, in that the local history of a village's foundation, written at the bottom of the genealogy, was linked to the supposed history of the region; for instance, tribal or racial migrations from the northwest of the subcontinent several centuries beforehand. It is impossible to assess the effect that this kind of genealogy might have had on the historical consciousness of villagers, or to disentangle its effect from that of the classification of the population by caste, tribe and religion in all departments of administration at the time. One measure of the combined effect is the growth of claims to particular caste identity and status from the 1890s, a tendency that in turn cannot be divorced from the politicisation of the census returns of religion from 1911. Another measure is that after Indian independence in 1947, when the system of land administration began to be modified – the tenancy law was changed, customary law was dropped, the village constitutional papers ceased to be relevant – the identity of ancestors on a genealogy of proprietors was no longer made in terms of caste.

In the 1860s and 1870s, however, as the function of the local revenue records changed to become a continuously updated 'photograph of the actual state of the community' able to be consulted both by government and by the public, so the field map and the genealogy of proprietors became the chief means of access to the more detailed registers of a village's record of rights. The two primary registers of the initial settlement of a district, the preliminary list of landholders and the field register, had done their work and no longer needed to be prepared. Dimensions of fields were now written directly on the field map, while crops were no longer a matter for permanent record. A person wishing to consult the records would typically start either with the name of a person or with the location of a field from which to conduct his search. Genealogy and field map were thus paired for their utility. But if ever they had actually been married – if the holdings of proprietors had ever been plotted on the field map to show the pattern of holdings on paper, as surely the pattern of holdings on the ground was known to the actual members of a village – then the disparity would have been evident to the observer between the two forms of shareholding: that of the proprietary community in which proprietors alone had shares in common resources, and that of the older shareholding community of cultivators defined by economic co-operation and subsistence.

Conclusion

To sum up, field maps were introduced into the routine of settlement operations in northwestern India somewhat haphazardly. Although not originally prescribed, in the prevailing culture of mapping they soon came to be considered a good idea since they added both to the utility of the village records and to the thoroughness of registration. Their preparation allowed a check on whether all fields had in fact been registered, and once prepared they served an important function as index to the detailed registers. But the culture of mapping did not extend to a heuristic use of field maps, for instance the use of the pattern of holdings as evidence of right. After field maps had been filed in the drawers of a records room, their examination was only ever partial, in response to a particular inquiry, which was not conducive to the discovery of holistic patterns. During the formative period of local administration, other kinds of maps and registers were prepared, notably that of the village site to accompany an improved household census. But despite its obvious utility, this did not survive the globalisation of the census into a synchronic all-India affair nor the bonding of local rule-by-records to higher-order rule-by-reports. For a brief period, a form of empire based on local record, but without its suffocating complement of scaled-down knowledge from on top, seems to have been a possibility in British India. Of course this would still very much have been a rule in which the authority of the written record effectively reduced local autonomy under the claim of upholding local institutions. Rights, customs and identities were fitted into a frame of classification and law; the pattern on the ground was transferred to paper, and subjects could only interact with government according to formal rules of procedure in terms of the official categories recorded – unless they resisted, which they did spectacularly in 1857.

If one wants to analyse the use or non-use of maps in administration, one must therefore look at the form of administration rather than at the specific techniques of mapping or the accuracy of measurement achieved. The culture of mapping in India fitted into an ethos where knowledge of Indian society by its rulers was valued for the power that it gave to make effective prescriptions in law and administration. It was essential that this knowledge, at once prudential and factual, be available not just to the official on the ground, but in the form of selections or abstracts to all higher levels in the imperial hierarchy. India, however, was large and the elite civil service, trained in Britain, could not be allowed to become unwieldy. The size of a district, the smallest administrative unit under the direct charge of this elite and the heart of the imperial system, could therefore not fall under a thousand villages or so. Knowledge of a district consequently took a certain form: personal and paternalistic as far as dealings of the official in charge of the district were concerned, who had to believe not only that he knew his charges but knew what was best for them; remote when the knowledge was translated into official stereotype categories, the only way of dealing uniformly throughout the province with so many villages. Of course, there was an arrogance in such a system, reflected most obviously in the degree of intrusiveness into the inner workings of a village, an arrogance that one associates with colonialism. But I am trying to put the case in terms that allow comparison of imperialisms without reducing their distinctive histories. The administration of a thousand villages has to take a different shape from that of a hundred. Local notables cannot be inducted into the administration in the same way; negotiation will be different over what statistics may be collected and how intrusive investigations can be.[33] The knowledge that oils an administration must take a different form too.

The representation of a village community in the village revenue records of northwestern India through field map, genealogy of proprietors and constitutional paper reflected developments in local government. The accuracy or faithfulness of this representation is not a point at issue. What matters is that in subjecting local rights and customs to legal record, the site of settling disputes was transferred to the record room and courthouse, and the rights and customs themselves could only be challenged according to official procedures. The schema that people carried in their heads of who was related to whom and how this related to the pattern of fields on the ground was translated into formal terms and preserved on paper in the records room, subject to formal procedures of inspection and alterable only after due process of law. Even to know their rights, farmers had to consult the records, for no title deeds such as *tapu* were given them.

This stands in contrast to what happened in post-1858 Ottoman rule in what is today northern Jordan. There, property was usually expressed as shares in common land (*musha'*) and transactions were in shares. The strips of land that were actually cultivated by shareholders were periodically re-allotted: in some villages as frequently as every two years, in others after fifteen or twenty years, depending on the form of allotment and the degree to which it equalised different qualities of land. The schema that people carried in their heads of who was related to whom or of the relative standing of each person in the community was forever being re-drawn on the ground by the community itself without the intervention of government. No field maps were drawn – in any case, how could a map of plots be useful if plots were regularly changing position when the land was repartitioned? In other words, one of the key mechanisms of shareholding, the periodic re-allotment of land, was left intact under Ottoman rule, whereas in British India, despite the policy to conserve village coparcenaries, it was actively discouraged as property was established in individually held plots of land within fixed boundaries. Yet a form of property in land was created by the Ottoman form of registration. Shares became property, to be gifted, sold or transmitted through inheritance in part or as a whole according to law. Although the location of a person's holding would change when land was re-allotted or re-partitioned, the size of his share was not changed, in order, perhaps, to bring it into conformity with his actual resources; that would have been to go back to a still older form of shareholding in which a 'plough' of land (*feddan* or *çift*) really did correspond to the agricultural resources of the cultivator (family labour, animal labour and farming implement), or in which a married man was really allotted twice that of a bachelor, as some older farmers in the Kura district of northern Jordan told us had been the custom before *tapu* registration.

About higher levels of administrative practice under late-Ottoman rule and their relation to forms of knowledge about Ottoman subject and society, I can only say that it seems quite different from the situation in British India during the same period, but more investigation is needed. What a limited comparison with mapping and registration in India shows is that the absence of a practice may be as significant as a presence, when seen in the context of local government. Where was the need to develop an embryonic sociology of Arab society when local notables with their own knowledge of the country were the officials in charge of a district at a scale more intimate and in a society less differentiated than in British India? In any case, the existence of a technology does not guarantee its use; and only with use does technology acquire value or function in a system. Some applications of mapping in India had but a brief presence, no use for them being found either as part of the local record or to illustrate a feature of Indian society. Others, successfully combining local fact with panoptic or pannomial distance, are with us still.

Notes

1 A preliminary version of this study was presented at the seminar on Property Rights, sponsored by the European Science Foundation, at the Middle East Technical University, Ankara on 25 December 1996. I am grateful to Professor Huri İslamoğlu for inviting me to participate. The fieldwork on which the study is based was undertaken in India from 1973 to 1977 and in Jordan jointly with Martha Mundy between 1990 and 1992. In a way, the study presents a comparative context for observations concerning the limited use of maps in late-Ottoman land administration made by Mundy, 1992, p. 224; Mundy, 1994, pp. 62–63; Mundy, 1996, p. 78. But I alone am responsible for what follows!

2 Maps are known to have been prepared for *sultani çiftliks* in Palestine, but are not known for land registration generally: see Kark and Gerber, 1984, pp. 30–32.

3 The field maps of the Punjab and North Western Provinces were not strictly cadastral in the sense of being fitted into a precise triangulated grid, unlike those prepared in the provinces of Bengal and Madras after 1870 and those prepared from the 1830s, though idiosyncratically, in Bombay. There was continuing tension between surveyors-general, wedded to a 'scientific' view of cartography, and land administrators, who claimed that the field maps of village revenue records were accurate enough for their purposes. See Markham, 1871 and, more generally on the relation between science and empire, Edney, 1997.

4 Compare Anderson, 1991, Chapter 10, pp. 163–85.

5 One of the first measures undertaken in 1839 by the British government in Ludhiana district (Punjab), where I did research, was to consolidate the territory – make it more mappable – by exchanging shared (*chuharmi*) villages with the Sikh government

of Lahore. See Oriental and India Office Collections, British Library, Board's Collections 80499, Draft 543 of 1841, no 6–7.

6 Compare Winichakul, 1988, quoted in Anderson, 1991, p. 173, regarding the delineation of international boundaries: 'In other words, a map was a model for, rather than a model of, what it purported to represent'.

7 'Interlinked with one another, then, the census, the map and the museum illuminate the late colonial state's style of thinking about its domain. The "warp" of this thinking was a totalizing classificatory grid, which could be applied with endless flexibility to anything under the state's real or contemplated control: peoples, regions, religions, languages, products, monuments, and so forth. The effect of the grid was always to be able to say of anything that it was this, not that; it belonged here, not there ... The "weft" was what one could call serialization: the assumption that the world was made up of replicable plurals ... For the colonial state did not merely aspire to create, under its control, a human landscape of perfect visibility; the condition of this "visibility" was that everyone, everything, had (as it were) a serial number.' Anderson, 1991, pp. 184–85.

8 See Saumarez Smith, 1985. 'Settlement' was the term used for the operation of assessing the revenue of a village or district and registering rights to land. 'Survey' initially covered both maps and statistics: when the Revenue Survey was set up in North West Provinces in 1823, it was contrasted with, though complementing, settlement operations. Field maps and the collection of village statistics in the Punjab were undertaken initially at settlements, but subsequently by village revenue accountants in the normal course of keeping village records up to date.

9 For a recent look at the sociology of caste, see Bayly, 1995. But there is no comprehensive overview for the whole of the nineteenth century: sociological analysis retreats into history for the first part of the century.

10 Stokes, 1959, pp. 1–3.

11 Edney draws a connection between mapping and uniform administration: of the parliamentary committees concerned with the renewal of the East India Company's charter in 1833, he says, 'A uniform, detailed map of India was touted as a key element in the establishment of a single, India-wide administration of the revenue and civil justice systems' (Edney, 1997, p. 322). But unfortunately his analysis does not consider field surveys, nor hardly the Revenue Survey, his focus being on the higher order Great Trigonometrical

Survey. The following paragraph shows his reasons, which I quote in full to provide incidental background to the idea of cadastral surveys in nineteenth-century Europe: 'Perhaps the best indicator of the practical infeasibility of the cartographic ideal is the failure by almost every state before 1880 to incorporate a cadastre into their systematic topographic surveys. Conceptually, cadastral surveys were important contributors to the imagined ability to make a map at a scale of 1:1. The various reconsiderations of cadastral surveys in British India as well as in Europe all proceeded from the expectation that they ought to be based on territory-wide triangulations and that they ought to be the primary surveys from which all smaller-scale maps should be derived. But in reality, the survey of each individual village remained unique and separate on its own geometric basis. Cadastral surveys were accordingly significant for the development of cartographic literacy among Europeans in the eighteenth and nineteenth centuries, both in terms of pointing toward the possibility of fulfilling the ideal and in promoting map use. Nonetheless, the cadastral surveys were, in practice, too large-scale, too detailed, and too unwieldy for comprehensive mapping. Their role in this study is accordingly ambiguous. Ideologically influential, they contributed little to the comprehensive mapping of India.' Edney, 1997, pp. 27–28.

12 The great reference work is Baden-Powell, 1892, a work of synthesis written a generation or more after the actual work of settlement had been completed. Maine's seminal *Village Communities*, 1871, had drawn on the first published Settlement Reports from the 1850s.

13 'The Governor General would wish to uphold Native institutions and practices as far as they are consistent with the distribution of justice to all classes ... With the knowledge now generally prevalent respecting village coparcenary there is no apprehension that our officers will not exert themselves to maintain these important bodies in all their integrity' (Governor General's Despatch of 31 March 1849 constituting the Board of Administration for the Punjab, quoted in Tupper, 1881, vol. 1, p. 2.)

14 Hirst, 1912, p. 46: 'The early *khasra* [field-register] maps ... are very inaccurate; these maps were only supposed to act as indices to the *khasra* records. In other cases it was not considered necessary to make a map as an index to the *khasra* records.' Implicitly, Hirst was contrasting here the earlier field surveys with the more recent properly cadastral surveys of Bengal.

15 Markham, writing in 1871, says (p. 272): 'Few attempts have hitherto been made to produce really good maps to illustrate the

physical geography and statistics of India'. He then compliments a particular Settlement Officer of the Punjab, E.A. Prinsep, for the 'best series of illustrative maps' of Sialkot district in west Punjab, saying that 'similar maps should be prepared in the rest of India'. The 16 maps, drawn at the scale of 6 miles to the inch, show distributions of various sociological features such as 'agricultural tribe' and tenure as well as various administrative subdivisions. They were published in 1865, along with corresponding statistical tables, as vol. 2 of the Settlement Report, although they were given a separate name: *Statistical Account of the Sealkote District.* Prinsep was responsible for introducing several other new features into the form of village settlement records, including the Genealogy of Proprietors (see below).

16 See Markham, 1871, pp. 82ff and *Selections from Revenue Records, North-West Provinces* (hereafter *SRR*), 1872. Part I of the latter (pp. 1–83) is entitled 'Resolution of the Government of India, 1st August, 1822', of which paragraphs 320–78 concern the revenue survey and its relation to settlement. For Revenue Surveys in South India, see Edney, 1997, pp. 171ff.

17 The four-inch village maps of the Revenue Survey which were prepared for the entire Punjab plains up to the Indus were used to compile one-inch district maps before the three departments of Trigonometrical, Topographical and Revenue Surveys were merged in the Survey of India in 1878: *Report of the Indian Survey Committee 1904–05*, 1905, part I, p. 10 and part II, p. 14. If the development of a comprehensive strategy of mapping at different scales and for different purposes in India seems irregular, I can only quote Edney (1997, pp. 28–29), citing Andrew S. Cook, the keeper of maps at the Oriental and India Office Collections, 'as being more the result of accident than of design'.

18 An inquiry in 1831 into whether field maps were prepared in the North West Provinces (part of a general investigation into the progress of settlement operations and surveys under Regulation VII, 1822) revealed that in only three divisions of the province were they prepared (SRR, pp. 362, also 267, 336, 347). As a result, the Governor-General directed a 'modified system of conducting the surveys and settlements', in which a field map was to be prepared 'in all cases of *byachara* tenures' (where there was some form of communal allotment). This was embodied in Regulation IX, 1833, revising Regulation VII, 1822.

19 'Minute by Mr. Bird, 25 September 1832', SRR, pp. 452–63, paragraph 29: 'The advantage of the field-map is not, I think,

generally understood, except by those who have been accustomed to prepare and make use of it. But the fact is, that without it there is no security that the whole area has been measured. An European officer may go into a *mouzah* [village] with his *khusrah* [field register], and measure all the fields he can readily find, compare them with the *khusrah*, and find all right; he might even measure every field in a *khusrah*, and yet he would have no measure of knowing that the area of the *mouzah* was correct, because he would have no means of knowing what land belonging to the *mouzah* might have been omitted out of the *khusrah* altogether.'

20 The Court of Directors of the East India Company specifically objected to assessment on ploughs in a despatch of 1830. See the discussion of this point in Saumarez Smith, 1996, pp. 282–83, footnote 14.

21 My analysis of the absolute size of a 'plough' in 54 contiguous villages in Ludhiana district of the Punjab at the time of the first settlement in 1853, however, shows that the range of variation was small within neighbourhoods having similar soils. Saumarez Smith, 1996, Tables 8.2, 8.3.

22 The official categories of tenancy throughout the Punjab were 'hereditary tenant', whose right of occupancy could be inherited, and 'tenant-at-will'. In a few districts, other categories were also given legal recognition and registered. Sharecroppers were generally not registered unless they took responsibility for the revenue or rent of a particular plot, nor was the labour commanded within a household (sons, wives, servants), nor was the bottom 10–15 per cent of the rural population – whose labour was, in a sense, common to the dominant farming community – excluded from living in the main residential site of the village. Rural society in the Punjab was altogether more stratified than in Jordan. Saumarez Smith, 1996, Chapters 3, 5.

23 'The most curious custom, regarding the division of *biswah* [used here in the sense of responsibility], which I have met with in the Delhi territory was found at Kaundla, a *Khadir* village [subject to flooding in the rainy season], possessing wells sufficient to irrigate its whole cultivation. Here the lands of each *Panna* [subdivision] were redistributed either every year, or every few years, each holder possessing a different field, with every fresh distribution. As however the continuance of such a custom would in a great degree render nugatory the present records of settlement, they have now made a permanent division, which is not to be disturbed in future.' Gubbins, 1852, paragraph 69.

24 In one or two villages of the block of 84 whose settlement records I have examined, the action of settlement induced a full reallotment. Saumarez Smith, 1996, pp. 141–42, footnote 16. But, in most villages, holdings were registered as they existed at the time.
25 See Mundy, 1992, pp. 217–38.
26 In Ludhiana district, this loose-leaf preliminary register of 1852 is unofficially called 'Gokul Kumar' after the official in charge. It does not survive for every village, but where it does it is of special value because it shows how the size of holdings was conceptualised before the field survey had begun, usually in terms of 'ploughs'.
27 On boundaries, see Mundy, 1996, p. 78.
28 In Holt Mackenzie's report of 1826 on the progress of settlements undertaken in the North West Provinces under Regulation VII, 1822 (SRR, pp. 84–202), he notes (paragraph 657): 'As to the population, I am not aware that in any quarter any dissatisfaction has been created by the inquiry as to the number of the people; and though probably the returns are not very accurate, they must still be nearer the truth than any calculation that could be formed from the mere specification of the houses. Possibly, to take a census of the people as a distinct measure, and on a general system, might excite alarm (though the alarm of the people is sometimes merely the laziness of our officers) and might give occasion to abuse. But combined with the settlement of the land revenue, which is of course the matter of paramount interest, and conducted village by village, the operation seems to be unobjectionable; and the opportunity of so conducting it ought not assuredly to be lost.'
29 See, for example, Ahmed, 1980, pp. 129–65.
30 Saumarez Smith, 1985.
31 Wynyard, 1850; Rai, 1846; Rai, 1849; Rai, 1850, a chapter of which is identical to Wynyard, 1850.
32 Saumarez Smith, 1985, p. 166, footnote 34, referring to Prinsep, 1865, Appendix 22, 'Specimen Pedigree Table of Mehal Durgapoor'.
33 See Martha Mundy's chapter in the present volume and Huri İslamoğlu's discussion of the relation between *temettuat* and *tapu* in her paper, 1997.

Bibliography

Abbreviations

SRR: Selections from Revenue Records, North-West Provinces

Unpublished primary sources

Great Britain
London, British Library, Oriental and India Office Collections
Board's Collections 80499, Draft 543 of 1841

Published primary sources

Report of the Indian Survey Committee 1904-05, Simla, Government Central Printing Office, 1905.

Selections from Revenue Records, North-West Provinces: AD 1822–1833, Allahabad, North-Western Provinces Government Press, 1872.

Secondary sources

Ahmed, S.U., 'Urban Problems and Government Policies: A Case Study of the City of Dacca, 1810–1830', in Kenneth Ballhatchet and John Harrison (eds), *The City in South Asia*, London, Curzon Press, 1980, pp. 129–64.

Anderson, Benedict, *Imagined Communities: Reflections on the Origin and Spread of Nationalism*, revised and extended edition, London, Verso, 1991.

Baden-Powell, B.H., *The Land Systems of British India*, 3 vols, London, Oxford University Press, 1892.

Bayly, Susan, 'Caste and "Race" in the Colonial Ethnography of India', in Peter Robb (ed.), *The Concept of Race in South Asia*, Delhi, Oxford University Press, 1995, pp. 165–218.

Edney, Matthew H., *Mapping an Empire: the Geographical Construction of British India, 1765–1843*, Chicago, University of Chicago Press, 1997.

Gubbins, C., 'Settlement of Pergunnah Kurnaul, Zillah Paneeput', *Selections from Public Correspondence, North-West Provinces*, vol. 2, no XXXI, Agra, Secundra Orphan Press, 1852, pp. 27–64.

Hirst, F.C., *Notes on the Old Revenue Surveys of Bengal, Bihar, Orissa and Assam*, Calcutta, Thacker, Spink and Co., 1912.

İslamoğlu, Huri, 'Temettu Registers as a System of Classification of the Ottoman Modern State', paper presented at the workshop on Statistics and State Formation, Johns Hopkins University, 12–13 April 1997.

Kark, Ruth and Haim Gerber, 'Land Registry Maps in Ottoman Palestine', *The Cartographic Journal* 21, 1984, pp. 30–32.

Maine, H.S., *Village Communities in the East and the West*, London, 1871.

Markham, Clements R., *A Memoir on the Indian Surveys*, London, Allen & Co., 1871.

Mundy, Martha, 'Shareholders and the State: Representing the Village in the Late Nineteenth Century Land Registers of the Southern Hawran', in Thomas Philipp (ed.), *The Syrian Land in the Eighteenth and Nineteenth Century*, Stuttgart, Franz Steiner Verlag, 1992, pp. 217–38.

– 'Village Land and Individual Title: *Musha*ʿ and Ottoman Land Registration in the 'Ajlun District', in Eugene L. Rogan and Tariq Tell (eds), *Village, Steppe and State: the Social Origins of Modern Jordan*, London, British Academic Press, 1994, pp. 58–79.

– '*Qada*' 'Ajlun in the Late Nineteenth Century: Interpreting a Region from the Ottoman Land Registers', *Levant* 28, 1996, pp. 77–95.

Prinsep, E.A., *Report on the Revised Settlement of Sealkote District*, vol. 1, Lahore, Chronicle Press, 1865.

Rai, Kali, *Khet karm*, Delhi, n.p., 1846.

– *Fatehgarhnama: tawarikh-i zila*ʿ*-i Farukhabad*, Delhi, Urdu Akhbar Press, 1849.

– *Hidayat-nama kam-i paima'ish kishtwar*, Delhi, Urdu Akhbar Press, 1850.

Saumarez Smith, Richard, 'Rule-by-records and Rule-by-reports: Complementary Aspects of the British Imperial Rule of Law', *Contributions to Indian Sociology* (n.s.) 19/1, 1985, pp. 153–76.

– *Rule by Records: Land Registration and Village Custom in Early British Panjab*, Delhi, Oxford University Press, 1996.

Stokes, Eric, *The English Utilitarians and India*, Oxford, Clarendon Press, 1959.

Tupper, C.L., *Punjab Customary Law*, vol. 1, Calcutta, Superintendent of Government Printing, 1881.

Winichakul, Thongchai, 'Siam Mapped: a History of the Geo-body of Siam', PhD dissertation, University of Sydney, 1988; subsequently published as *Siam Mapped: A History of the Geo-body of a Nation*, Honolulu, University of Hawaii Press, 1994.

Wynyard, W., *Dastur-ul-*ʿ*amal tartib-i naqsha wa khasra abadi wa tartib-i khana shumari*, Lahore, Koh-i Noor Press, 1850.

CHAPTER 6

The Cadastral Metaphor: Intersections of Property and Topography

Alain Pottage

Enacting a simple but expressive political ritual, Chinese emperors periodically had themselves borne to a mountain summit, from which they would undertake a sovereign survey of their domain. Territorial mastery was asserted or reaffirmed by the imperial eye's appropriational sweep.[1] This performative metaphor for the power of perspective expresses a well-established theme in the theory of cartography. Critical accounts of cartographic knowledge argue that maps, whether administrative or private, constitute a specific technology of power. Hence the suggestion that maps are linked with what Foucault called the exercise of 'juridical power' and that, through the use of maps, 'the world is disciplined. The world is normalised. We are prisoners in its spatial matrix.'[2] This theme, which is something of an orthodoxy in studies of cartography, colours many accounts of cadastral mapping and land registration. The emergence and deployment of cadastral maps is explained in terms of the exercise of governmental power.

To what extent does the theme of perspectival mastery illuminate the nature of the specific bureaucratic techniques involved in cadastral mapping? Are these techniques best understood in terms of some model of juridical or governmental ambition? This chapter suggests that it is more interesting and more productive to understand the function and character of cadastral maps not in terms of these metaphors of mastery, but as a specific technique based upon the on-going adaptation of administrative norms to changes in social expectations. This general approach is developed in the context of one specific example of cadastral mapping drawn from the English experience, that is, the movement towards land registration which spanned a remarkably 'long' nineteenth century. Perhaps the observations derived from this example are largely confined to that context. England or English law was already destined to be Weber's difficult exception,[3] and land registration brought with it a form of bureaucracy which, because it associated private law facilitation with various forms of fiscal or administrative *bricolage*, was so peculiar as to defy any kind of ideal-typical classification. Yet, although English peculiarities may resist generalisation, the example of registration of title in England does support some observations about the role and function of cadastral mapping. The suggestion is that this form of mapping consists in a specific technique of indexation which requires administrative modesty rather than juridical mastery.

Of course maps have long served as the instruments of various administrative programmes. The theme of perspectival mastery, which informs what might be called the cadastral metaphor, might take as its warrant a more familiar imperial precedent. Well before the reign of Augustus, the Romans had developed an administrative technique of registration: '[they] organised their territory and especially newly acquired territory with a view to its agricultural exploitation; they did so not only by measuring it and by fixing the boundaries of private and public property, but by actually "constructing" it on the ground'.[4] In this case, to construct meant to inscribe the territory itself with the traces of an administrative topography, carving rectilinear paths into the ground, sub-dividing these large oblongs into plots with different fiscal and legal qualities, and then embedding into them the markers of their administrative status. Legal and administrative criteria were pressed into the physical landscape. This finely tuned bureaucratic mechanism might be identified as the prototypical form of the cadastral survey; it turned surveying techniques to fiscal purposes and, in so doing, found a way of making cartographic representations commensurate with bureaucratic notations. However, in this chapter it is suggested that the operation of modern forms of cadastral mapping differs quite significantly from the Roman model of territorial mastery. Indeed, the modern form of the cadastral map is characterised by the comparative modesty of its ambitions. Instead of attempting to press social life into a topography, the modern cadastre seeks to accommodate itself to the demands made by various overlapping social practices. It confines itself to the role of offering a minimal, flexible, common denominator for transactions which cut across these differentiated practices, rather than attempting to constrain them within a rigid, pre-determined, normative framework. It is true that the cadastral metaphor is often part of the self-description of cadastral maps and land registration programmes, but the actual operation of these programmes is not explicable in terms of this description. For that reason, one might say that the 'imperial' example of cadastral mapping is indeed only a metaphorical formula; it describes an ambition rather than a practical reality, and the ambition tells us little about the practice.[5]

The cadastre as metaphor

The first step is to detach the term 'cadastral' from a somewhat narrow usage. My references to cadastral mapping will probably irritate those historians of cartography who identify some form of fiscal application as the defining hallmark of the cadastral map. And indeed, if one fastens the term to its dictionary definition[6] it seems right to draw a distinction between a properly 'cadastral' map in which topographical techniques are deployed in the service of taxation policies, and a mere property map which supports the more focused task of registering land transactions. Yet to restrict the definition of cadastral mapping in this way is to miss the implications of the fact that modern ('multipurpose') cadastral applications are shaped by a much more extensive and pervasive bureaucratic rationality, one which is not confined to fiscal policy. On the other hand, the less restrictive view that cadastral maps represent a particular species of property map does not suffice to make the distinction between 'simple' property maps and 'cadastral' property maps. The argument in this chapter is that cadastral mapping is distinguished by a factor that is often implicit in fiscal operations, but which, because it is not reducible to fiscality, also characterises what are sometimes distinguished as mere 'property maps'. It consists in what might be called the bureaucratic reconstruction – or the bureaucratic 'appropriation' – of planimetric representations. And although some might prefer a less encumbered term – 'administrative mapping', for example – to describe this administrative process, the point of using the more specific term is simply to emphasise that the modern multipurpose cadastre is the ultimate extrapolation of a logic that was also at work in the past in a range of different administrative applications of maps. Indeed, in the last part of this chapter, I suggest how this general 'cadastral logic' was adapted to the specific problems of proof of title in English law.

In describing this process of constructive appropriation, it is important to notice the heterogeneity of 'fiscal' operations. Alain Guery's study of the *capitation* exacted by Louis XIV in 1695 draws an important distinction between an older model of taxation which implied the use of juridical criteria (such as status) to make economic judgements, and a newer mode of governmental rationality which sought to understand and exploit the forces of economic production. The programme adopted by the *capitation* of 1695 was a somewhat unstable compound of these two forms of taxation. To the extent that it was a graduated tax which applied to all men, irrespective of the traditional privileges of *noblesse*, and to the extent that it broke with the traditional code of sovereign largesse and feudal aids by attributing a novel and specific fiscal 'interest' to the state, it participated in the emergent technique of governmentality. On the other hand, it also persisted with the use of criteria and categories of status to identify wealth:

> Louis XIV's administrators and advisors did not have available to them the conceptual tools which we now have. Before the Physiocrats, they were unable to conceive of taxation in terms which enabled them to identify which stage of a single economic process was tapped by the particular tax which they had in mind. Instead, they believed that taxes tapped quite distinct sources of wealth, each quite unrelated to the other. Society was conceived of neither economically nor sociologically, but legally, in terms of status and hierarchically-ordered entities. It was assumed that there was some correspondence between wealth or fortune and social status.[7]

For that reason, the distinctions which were later made by physiocrats or economists between direct and indirect taxes or real and personal taxes were, in this period, based upon the classically juridical distinctions between real and personal, corporeal and incorporeal, or moveable and immoveable property. Physiocratic themes informed a transformation of cadastral programmes in France. Specifically, under the influence of Turgot and Trudaine there was a movement in the latter part of the eighteenth century towards a system which attempted to calibrate some proportional measure between the liability of each taxpayer and their share of a particular economic process.[8] And even though this eighteenth-century model consisted in nothing more than a set of simple surveys or inventories, it instantiated a fiscal programme based on the adjustment of normative prescriptions to cognitive evaluations.

Why emphasise this distinction in a study of the bureaucratic technique of mapping? To begin with, it makes the point that to adopt a reductive identification of cadastral maps with fiscal programmes is to reduce these complex variations to a common denominator and, in so doing, to close off those aspects of the technique which are most interesting and problematic. The result is 'an approach which implicitly assumes that because in its techniques of registration as much as its quality, the object is always the same, a cadastral map always occupies more or less the same position in social space: a cadastre is always a cadastre'.[9] Indeed, the denominator is neither common nor coherent. There is always a discrepancy between a given fiscal programme and the practical negotiations, compromises and diversions which effectively (re-)materialise it. Given this discrepancy, it is more productive to describe cadastral mapping in terms of an administrative programme which binds together a particular set of administrative techniques (forms of thematic topographical notation, statistical aggregations, techniques of recording and updating and so on), and organises them by reference to a planimetric map, whether or not the programme is fiscal in character. In these terms, a cadastre is a bureaucratic or governmental gloss on a planimetric map, the accuracy of the map being only a secondary virtue.

This distinction between planimetric maps and their bureaucratic glosses might seem strange, not least because many cadastral operations seem entirely dependent on the planimetric accuracy of maps. In France, for example, in the reforms of 1807 which introduced the model of a cadastre based on *plans parcellaires* (individual land parcels) in place of the existing assessment *par masses de cultures*,[10] the impartial geometric precision of the surveyor was the guarantee of fiscal equity. One of the administrators of this process, answering the objection that the new assessment produced only a rough and inequitable 'mosaic' of land parcels, pointed out that the precision of new surveying methods was such that the maps of each commune fitted together seamlessly, 'with no gaps or overlaps', and recommended that the critic should familiarise himself with the impartial art of surveying, 'which, of all the exact sciences, has perhaps made the most progress'.[11] Yet, although the rhetoric tied fiscal equity to geometric exactitude, there was an unbridgeable difference between the mapped surface and administrative features that the cadastre impressed upon it. Cadastral programmes presuppose planimetric topographies, but they are not identical with them: the essential unit is the cadastral land parcel, and accuracy is one of its accidental features. The nature of this relation between the map and its administrative gloss is clearer in the case of registration of title than it is in the case of taxation. Registration presupposes a simple distinction between property and topography:

> Property boundaries in the nature of things cannot be shown on a map. For property boundaries exist only in the mind. Property is a legal concept; its boundaries are notional only. The imaginary line which in law separates one man's land from another's is a mathematical two-dimensional line. It has notional length and depth, but no breadth. It cannot, therefore, be represented on a map.[12]

Although the claim that property boundaries cannot be shown on a map is something of an overstatement, the distinction itself is unquestionable. Plainly, property boundaries are not themselves cast as features of the physical landscape, but they are identified and attributed by reference to features such as hedges, walls, pavements, rivers and so on. Indeed, traditional practices invested the physical landscape with social expectations, making of it a sort of hybrid medium in which 'physical', 'economic' and 'legal' representations of land were confused. So, for example, certain physical features of the landscape – hedges, streams, copses or ditches – were the common reference points for various overlapping activities, not because each of these referred to the same points in abstract (cartographic) space, but because together they produced a local experience of space, generated by units of measure adapted to local technologies and bounded by 'monuments' that were identifiable and were usable as such only by someone within the locality. Cadastral maps, in their modern form, are one answer to the practical problems occasioned by the dissolution of this sort of 'hybridised' knowledge of land. The modern cadastral map offers a formal scheme or code for differentiating topographical, legal and economic representations of land. From this perspective, the defining innovation of a 'cadastral' property map consists in the process of translating topographical representations into administrative data and, more specifically, in the elaboration of a bureaucratic scheme of indexation.

Indexing entitlements

The nature of cadastral indexation is quite clearly revealed in the modern applications of cadastral techniques. Contemporary theories of cartography suggest that 'the basic components of mapped thematic data are theme, location, and time. Cartographic displays and other information products typically measure one of these, use another as a control and hold the third as fixed or constant.'[13] If one treats ownership as a particular kind of 'thematic code', one can adapt this scheme to a description of how cadastral indexation 'abstracts' from topographical information. First, the spatial information displayed in a planimetric map is converted into a set of indexing criteria which typically unfold down through county, town, district and street to a particular land holding. The ultimate product is a 'cadastral polygon' or 'land parcel'[14] which is distinguishable from adjacent polygons and which may be sub-'divided', or aggregated with its neighbours, without changing the co-ordinates of the indexing scheme. In the process of being translated into this form, spatial information is stripped of the significance which it has 'on the ground', becoming instead the supporting framework of an administrative unit which, in turn, serves as a constant reference point for the observation of changes in the configuration of tenure. The role of this 'thematic code' of ownership is to identify and incorporate valid transactions and to allow changes in the configuration of the land parcel to be monitored (changes in owner or ownership or modifications in the indexation of rights). The point is that the effective topology in this process is not the layer of 'lived landscape' which would be recognisable to an inhabitant of the mapped territory; rather, topographical data is used to construct a syntactical framework for the differentiation and articulation of property rights.

The innovation of the modern 'multipurpose cadastre' is that it adds other layers of administrative topology to the basic cadastral map, ideally in a form which allows users to move seamlessly from one layer to another or to aggregate information across different layers according to the modern paradigm of a geographic-information system (or land-information system).[15] Whether the objective is the valuation of properties, the maintenance of utility pipes or the development of zoning policy, what is required in each case is a method which allows data drawn from different topological layers to be associated by plotting a temporal relation between them. Again, the raw topography of the land is irrelevant; indeed, the creation of a base map which can sustain these largely incommensurable applications reduces the shared topographic base to an even more abstract common denominator. The creation of a multipurpose cadastre would involve a decision as to whether to begin with a planimetric map mapping physical features or a cadastral map which selects only some of those features as the co-ordinates of a property index. Each map would have different characteristics, and the differences are interesting for two reasons.[16] First, a problem arises precisely because cadastral indexation is an abstraction from planimetric topography; a cadastral map is likely to suffer from a degree of planimetric inaccuracy thanks to variations in the nature and accuracy of surveying techniques or perhaps even the different rates of shrinkage of paper maps.[17] Second, a multipurpose cadastre would be based on a hybrid planimetric-cadastral map whose co-ordinates would be derived not from recognisable features or 'monuments' of the local landscape, but upon a 'geocode' generated by satellite geometry. This highly abstract grid of geocodes would accommodate various forms of topological information, and planimetric detail would 're-enter' the cadastre only as a way of making topological relationships between various bits of administrative data or as just another contingent topological resource. These operations carry the process of abstraction much further than does the nineteenth-century scheme of land registration, and they remain somewhat more 'ideal' than practical,[18] yet they do reveal the sense in which cadastral maps supplant the planimetric surfaces from which they were created, and they begin to suggest how ownership is reconstructed within a cadastral index.

Indeed, to introduce the particular context of this inquiry, the story of land registration in nineteenth-century England shows how this model of indexation was already latent in the way that the issues were constructed. In the English context, the administrative virtue of property maps had less to do with the familiar problem of identifying land than with the fact that they promised to resolve the newer and more complex problem of indexing interests in land. The difficulty of the indexation question is exemplified in a complicated proposal advanced in 1830 by Lewis Duval, a member of the elite group of conveyancing counsel, and one of the Real Property Commissioners who considered the question of registration in that year:[19]

> In 1830, the [Real Property Commissioners] had reluctantly concluded that the optimal scheme, a map-based index, was unobtainable because of the cost of conducting the national survey necessary to produce the maps. A simple index by grantor's name would have been hopelessly unmanageable, even if subdivided by geographical region, so Duval combined both these elements with a novelty of his own: indexation by root of title. That is to say, that document would be identified which conveyancers would accept as the oldest necessary, in any particular case, to investigate as part of the proof of title; it would be allocated a reference number, and then all other subsequent documents deriving from it would be indexed by the same number. It was good, but it was complicated.[20]

Duval's problem, and indeed the problem for any reform scheme, was that registration required an efficient and simple scheme of indexing. Minimally, this required the provision of a stable reference point which would, on the one hand, enable purchasers to detect any existing interests adverse to the estate they were buying while, on the other hand, allowing the owners of those adverse interests to advertise their presence to purchasers. Simply to have used an owner's name as an index would have been disastrous because as the ownership of the land changed, many of the adverse interests which concerned buyers would have remained attached to the names of previous owners and might therefore have been undiscoverable.[21] Indeed, even if the names of previous owners had been recoverable, to have required purchasers to trawl through the list of past owners in search of 'live' property rights would have been to reintroduce the very complexities and uncertainties which registration was supposed to resolve. What was needed was an abstract, fixed 'ownership office' which would be occupied and exercised by each successive owner and which would remain throughout as a constant and common target for all searches and registrations. Duval's scheme of indexation by root of title was an attempt to construct such an abstraction by taking an antique document and treating it as the source of all subsequent entitlements and therefore as a reference point which remained constant throughout or despite changes in ownership.

The defect of this scheme was that it preserved the traditional 'genealogical' model of property rights in which to establish the validity of a particular entitlement it was necessary to trace its pedigree back to some mythical founding document. Even if the deposition of all intermediate documentation could make the process secure, the scheme would have been inefficient and overly complex because it would have meant preserving a good deal of documentary dead wood, and because the genealogical proof of actual and effective rights made conveyancing expensive. The corresponding virtue of property mapping was that, in replacing historical indexation with spatial indexation, it provided a record of ownership which immediately disclosed only those entitlements which were active and effective. Each given parcel of land delineated the ownership office to which each owner acceded and against which adverse interests were registrable and discoverable.

Maps had for some time been used to describe and identify the lands transferred by property transactions. Also, they had found some favour with owners of landed estates, or rather their stewards, as valuable accessories to financial administration. However, although maps were familiar implements, and although by the end of the eighteenth century maps had become relatively accurate, the nature of proof of title in English law was such that their only use in conveyancing was as convenient aids to identification, rather than as elements of a formal proof.[22] Certainly, there was nothing in the older law which resembled the operations of 'cadastral' indexation. The emergence of a distinctively cadastral form of property mapping in England is marked by the moment at which topographical representations no longer answered to the practical expectations of landowners. Indeed, many of the objections to the first scheme of compulsory registration of title were focused on just that point. Lawyers and landowners worried that the location of fences would not be properly shown on maps and that if the line of a boundary fence, hedge or ditch was not drawn properly, an owner might lose a significant sliver of land to his neighbour. Therefore they emphasised that maps should be drawn with such precision as would enable owners and purchasers to identify and, if necessary, agree on the precise line of a boundary. The Registry addressed these anxieties by making two points. The first was that conveyancing had never worked in this way. The Registry had conveniently revived the old conveyancing practice of leaving the exact boundaries of a plot of land undefined so that the map merely indicated the location of the plot rather than seeking to offer an accurate and conclusive delimitation of its area.[23] The second point, facilitated by the first, was that what mattered were the techniques for indexing rights in relation to land, rather than the planimetric accuracy of the map. So, for example, in response to the suggestion that the new 25-inch-to-the-mile Ordnance Survey map could not be taken as a basis for identifying ownership, not least because the map itself disclaimed any sort of legal, evidentiary authority, the response of the Registrar was clear as to the role of the map: 'I regard the way in which we use the Ordnance map as absolutely controlled by the words we put upon the register. The map is the servant of the register.'[24] So although the theme of accuracy was undoubtedly useful in convincing lawyers of the benefits of registration,[25] the administrative value of the map lay in its ability to generate an abstract index. Indeed, only 10 years after the introduction of the first phase of compulsory titles registration,[26] and one year before the inquiry in which these anxieties were aired, the Registry had formalised the practice of processing transactions without reference to the base maps, relying instead on a numerical code which had been generated from the map.[27]

Lawyers were even more concerned about the abstract nature of these processes. In failing to insist on accuracy, the Registry betrayed its reliance on an invisible and fallible form of administrative discretion. Indeed, the officials themselves recognised this sensitivity. In presenting the Royal Commission of 1909 with an account of his educational tour of Germany and the Austro-Hungarian Empire, Brickdale, the first holder of the office of Chief Land Registrar, balanced his admiration for the efficiency and accuracy of the German cadastre against his concern that it might have been somewhat too efficient for the English landowner: 'in European States officialism is not so much objected to as it is here, and consequently an official system which works very well in Continental countries may be unsuitable for English communities'.[28] The irony was that 'officialism' was precisely the defect attributed to registration by its adversaries. The complaint was that the process of abstraction from the situation as it was 'on the ground' left landowners dependent upon the administrative competence of officials and the proper exercise of the quasi-judicial authority of the Registrar.[29] The process of bureaucratic indexation was incomprehensible to conveyancers, who could not understand how the security of private-property rights could be entrusted to an administrative body, and their difficulties in making sense of this new form of 'bureaucratic property' became the occasion or pretext for an argument in defence of their economic monopoly.[30] Here, I am concerned with the somewhat more abstract question of how this model of cadastral indexation functioned – that is, the character of the specific technique of cadastral mapping. The answer is complicated by the fact that the Registry was such a peculiar form of bureaucracy; land registration was a *sui generis* operation, coupled to the private practice of lawyers and the expectations of landowners, the workings of communications technology and the demands of governmental agencies.

Terrain and territory

Although the construction of a cadastral index was the real achievement of title registration, the arguments made in favour of compulsory registration emphasised the benefits of attaching property rights to a mapped terrain. In that sense, the theme cadastral mastery was an important component of the self-description and justification of land registration in England. The idea that registration would finally achieve a correspondence between 'rights in land' and 'the land itself' was very well established by the time that the process of legislative reform had succeeded. In an account of the virtues of the emerging scheme of compulsory registration, Brickdale focused on two central reasons for attaching property interests to a cadastral map. First, in restoring titles to their material, spatial foundation, the register prevented the possibility of any (fraudulent) duplication or overlapping of rights; the map 'renders it practically impossible to register the same piece of land twice over [and] it enables the boundaries of each property registered to be readily compared and made consistent with those of adjoining estates'. In other words, land was a fixed, finite substance, which could now be clothed in a closely tailored framework of rights, thanks to the availability of accurate Ordnance Survey maps and their bureaucratic glosses. Secondly, Brickdale observed that

> the adoption of as high a standard of accuracy as possible would appear desirable for obvious reasons [and] the ordnance map, which forms the basis of every land registry plan, is so precise and accurate that vagueness is impossible, and error... is brought out into immediate prominence.[31]

These conceptions of 'accuracy' implicitly invoked the 'cadastral metaphor' for property mapping – that is the ambition to inscribe the legal framework of rights into the land itself, not by means of the imperial Roman process of physical inscription, but by taking the Ordnance Survey map as a faithful and utterly accurate medium of transcription. To refer the legal foundation of rights to a mapped representation was as good as inscribing it in the land itself.

The question is whether the map was indeed such a faithful or selfless medium of translation, whether, that is, the terrain that it made available to the Registry was indeed a mirror of the 'external' territory. This, in turn, raises the question of how maps refer to the territories of which they are maps. Only if the relation is one in which the map functions as a basic common denominator for all forms of social activity, either because it is quite simply 'accurate' or because it is secured by some form of power, does it make sense to treat the correspondence between map and territory as the basis of cadastral maps. And only then would the self-description of cadastral programmes and the theoretical approach which elaborates this self-description be plausible. However, given the observations made at the start of this chapter, I propose to address these issues not by focusing on the way that (administrative) maps 'discipline' or 'constrain' their target territories through the exercise of some form of juridical or governmental power, but by suggesting how the cognitive limitations of any cartographic or topographic perspective impose a quite different form of relation founded in the model of administrative adaptation that is exemplified in cadastral indexation. The cadastral map is sustained not by a relation of correspondence, but by the on-going adaptation of topographic categories to 'territorial' changes.

The familiar model of cartographic correspondence is exemplified in an article written in 1882 for the *Annuaire du Club Alpin Français* by a certain Colonel Goulier, who explained, in some detail, the best technique for folding a map in advance so as to make it more readily serviceable 'in the field'.[32] In prescribing how the map should be folded, unfolded and then positioned by the walker or climber, Goulier's guide somewhat obsessively codified the assumptions that underlie most practical uses of maps. The user is supposed to translate 'between' the cartographic 'terrain' and the lived 'territory' by reducing and accommodating his visual experience to the representation contained in the map. The perspectival architecture of the map leaves only one place for the user, and a map is usable only on condition that one occupies that position and sees the territory as it should be seen. In that sense, one might indeed say that a map simply *is* the territory that it maps. A map 'covers' a territory only by supplanting or excluding it, replacing its multiple 'topologies' with a simplified selective topography: 'a map is *in situ* to the extent that the site itself is absent'.[33] Yet this too is a cartographic ideal which is effective only so long as the map is put to a highly specialised and highly codified use. Not all uses can be codified in this way, or even if they are the code itself becomes subject to various forms of reconstruction. Even if the map 'covers' the territory, the territory nonetheless exceeds any representation: 'there is an important sense in which the map is the territory, even though paradoxically the territory is not the map'.[34] This poses problems for both property and cartography as they were traditionally conceived, and it ultimately undoes the 'imperial' model of cadastral mapping.

To explain how it does so, I adopt and develop a distinction drawn by Bernard Lepetit between 'terrain' (a cartographic or topographic surface) and 'territory' (the fabric of society). The distinction is based on an opposition drawn by Viollet-le-Duc's *Dictionnaire de l'architecture française du XIe au XVIe siècle*, between 'proportion' and 'scale':

> Proportion does not establish a correspondence [*rapport*] between different domains, but is situated entirely on the side of the given object: 'proportion should be taken to refer to the relations between the whole and its parts'...Architectural scale is a more complex function. It refers to a relation [*relation*] (rather than a correspondence [*rapport*]) between a building and that which forms no part of it (rather than between its various parts).[35]

Viollet-le-Duc's conception of 'proportion' expresses an arithmetical or geometrical relation between the whole of an object and its constituent parts. It refers to what is more conventionally called 'scale'; it establishes a measure of harmony or commensurability within a single field. Viollet-le-Duc's conception of scale is distinguished from his conception of proportion in that the former establishes a relation between two fields, or more specifically between objects and people. In these terms, Greek architecture is said to have been concerned with proportion, with, for example, the relationship between the diameter of columns and the gradient of the stepped plinth upon which they rest. It was not concerned with scale, or the ratio between the height of those steps and the length of the Greek citizens' legs. Bernard Lepetit's account adopts this as a template for the distinction between 'terrain' and 'territory'. A terrain is the topographical surface revealed by the cartographer, for whom even the most complex configuration of topographical features can be accommodated and ordered within the homogeneous dimension of proportion. A territory, on the other hand, presents a problem of scale; it is 'a spatial formation which is not produced by the organisation of a spatial field, but by practices which develop according to largely incommensurable logics [*des pratiques d'acteurs qui se développent selon des logiques peu commensurables*]'.[36] That is why the territory always exceeds any terrain. A (mapped) terrain is only a selective 'interruption' of the complexity of a territory; it attempts to impose a linear spatialised order upon the discontinuous dimensions of a territory.

For the purposes of this chapter, what is interesting is less the distinction itself or the easy inference that a terrain does some sort of violence to its corresponding territory, but rather the question of how the 'excess' of territory over terrain is (re-)introduced into each terrain. To begin with, a mapped terrain exists only within the territory that it represents. The assumptions exemplified in the scheme of Colonel Goulier's guide and implicit in the cadastral metaphor take it that a map or terrain 'exists' within a territory by corresponding to all or part of it. The 'existence' of a map is warranted by its ability to represent or supplant the territory by means of a relation of correspondence which from the perspective of the cartographer can be described as scientific or objective, while for the enlightened critic of cartography it is partial and secured only by a form of power. Either way, cartographic 'proportion' is a schema that functions in such a way as to reconcile (or discipline) the differences of 'scale' that characterise a territory. That assumption is undone by the fact that cartographic proportion and, by implication, the perspective of the (empowered) cartographer itself constitutes one of those 'incommensurable logics' that creates the problem of scale in the first place. Far from affording a view of the 'whole', or being a basis for imposing a partial view of the whole, the 'whole' that is reconstructed by and within cartographic proportion is merely a local or specific version of an inconceivable 'whole', and the difficulties of scale come about precisely because none of these local representations of the 'whole' is commensurable with those projected within co-existing terrains. Terrains are therefore selective in a way that is not explicable as mere partiality.

Here, it is important to emphasise that maps are not the only form of terrain; the category includes any sort of selective patterning of the social fabric whether by means of statistical propositions, political programmes, scientific facts or legal rights. Indeed, as the case of the multipurpose cadastre suggests, the more differentiated these territorial experiences are, the less likely it is that a single terrain might answer all needs or accommodate all perspectives; ultimately, one reaches the point at which planimetric information is (re-)introduced into the index of the multipurpose cadastre as just another set of contingent inputs (see above). The various terrains that compose a territory are produced as ways of sustaining a particular perspective or experience, whether it be that of the cartographer, the economic strategist or the urban planner, and these enterprises are sustainable only if they can accommodate the disruptions caused by the incalculable excess of 'territory' over 'terrain'. What is at issue is the 'coupling' of terrains to one another or the resolution of the difficulties that arise when each terrain recognises the peculiar boundedness of its representations (in terms of its operations if not its self-definition), and therefore has to cope with the fact that territorial 'excess' will inevitably confront it in the shape of incompatible representations formed within other terrains. The 'existence' of maps and other forms of terrain is therefore sustained by a process of on-going adaptation in which each terrain distinguishes its own particular representational scheme from those which emerge from the territory, continuously 'testing' that scheme by way of a sort of learning process. In this way, territorial complexity finds its way into each terrain, and this process is considerably more complicated than any notion of correspondence might suggest. Thus by extrapolating the terms of Lepetit's distinction, one reaches a somewhat different account of how cartographic schemes and other terrains exist 'within' a territory.

This has obvious implications for the understanding of cadastral mapping in general, and land registration in particular. The administrative art of cadastral mapping consists in making topographical notations sensitive to the expectations modelled in other terrains. Focusing on the specific context of English property maps, the point is therefore not to impose a particular topographical scheme upon the world, using it to 'freeze' the framework of rights, but rather to create a set of responsive criteria that are adjusted so as to sustain expectations formed in a set of differentiated terrains. In the case of property, the peculiar form of the relation of 'terrain' to 'territory' can be drawn out of Bentham's model of property rights as the bases of expectations:

> The conduct of Justice in deciding the right to an article of property in dispute between two parties is governed by two considerations ... 1. To consider the parties themselves, it ought to bestow the article in question upon the one of them whose expectation of having it is the strongest. 2. To consider the public, it ought to bestow... it upon that one of the parties on whom the public ... expects most strongly to see it bestowed.[37]

In other words, the function of property rights was to ensure that things remained with those who had invested them with the 'greatest' expectations. However, those expectations had, in some sense, to be warranted. Bentham introduces the proviso that the juridical calibration of expectations should take place against a consideration of the publicity of the rules which, in the first place, allowed parties' expectations to be formed. Given Bentham's view that documentary formalities could never be conclusive of the issue,[38] legislators and adjudicators were set a difficult task. Having once publicised rules and thus offered them as the bases of expectations, having thus modelled the 'terrain', legislators or adjudicators were then expected to observe the way in which these property criteria were appropriated within the territory, making whatever adjustments were necessary to advance the programme of utility. This is a particular formulation of a general problem. Legal criteria or, more specifically, documents of ownership are appropriated within diverse social practices and, even if participants deviate from the publicised rules, the law may have to adjust its formal expectations in the light of their 'fairness' in a particular case. In other words, the 'terrain' staked out by property criteria cannot be imposed brutally upon the world. More to the point, no modern register of title could take the Roman colonial cadastre as its model. Rather, the task of law's administrators is to monitor the discrepancy between publicised property criteria and the world in which they are used. The point is not to crystallise property rules into topographical shapes but, again, to use the mapped surface as a grid against which to observe changes in the configuration of ownership.

Lepetit's distinction between terrain and territory is a particularly apt model for the description of this process. It offers one suggestion as to why the cadastral metaphor should be so obvious and yet so unworkable. Its obviousness springs from the basic parallel between property and topography: these are 'parallel' forms of knowledge in the sense that each stakes out its own particular 'terrain' within the larger 'territory'. They are similar, too, in the respect that each (in different ways and subject to different qualifications) supposes that the 'land' to which it refers is a stable, immovable and immediately accessible substance. The trouble is that each offers only a particular perspective on land (or, more precisely, social uses and interpretations of land). The virtue of the 'imperial' cadastre is that it stabilises these somewhat precarious terrains. It binds one to the other, thereby forging a common representation of land. However, in modern contexts, this model is unworkable because the 'territory' of modern society is diffracted into what Lepetit calls a set of 'incommensurable logics'. Thus any attempt to express property criteria directly in the form of topographical notation would soon be undone by the fact that property categories and topographical figures instantiate quite different ways of 'knowing' land. In contrast to the imperial ideal,[39] a modern cadastre can function only if it keeps its distance from the map which it uses to register rights.

The modern cadastre does not seek to fix rights, once and for all, by reference to a rigid topographical 'terrain'; rather, it works by differentiating its administrative or normative programme – whether it be registration of title, town planning or environmental regulation – from the particular topographical terrain which it uses as the basis for its operations. In other words, the topographical terrain becomes a surface against which changes in the configuration of ownership are observed and interpreted, rather than a grid of rigid prescriptions to which ownership practices would have to conform. As a result, by adapting its use of topographical criteria to its observation of changes in ownership, the modern cadastre holds out a set of denominators that can accommodate various 'terrains' without losing their legal or administrative specificity. Adapting Bentham's notion of expectations, one might say that the business of modern property law is to 'expect expectations'; it monitors the expectations of the various participants and adjusts its own normative expectations – that is, its rules as to the formalities and consequences of transactions – accordingly. The technique is based upon administrative modesty rather than 'imperial' mastery. Even the comparatively simple nineteenth-century scheme of title registration might be seen as an example of this kind of administrative adaptability. The nineteenth-century scheme of registration offers an example of just this 'distancing' manoeuvre; the bureaucratic processes worked only because they gradually freed themselves from the strictures of the map by translating topographical figures into an abstract index. And, as with the more recent model of a 'multipurpose cadastre', the nineteenth-century scheme achieved flexibility by reducing its topographical base to a minimal index or denominator which could be taken up and fleshed out by different forms of transaction. The register itself is only one element of this process. Whereas the register facilitated transactions by maintaining an abstract common denominator, the judges adjusted the legal consequences of those transactions according to their interpretation of social expectations. Indeed, many adaptations took the form of anticipatory measures built into the structure of the index. This form of 'responsive administration' reached its most refined accomplishment in the model of the multipurpose cadastre. Whereas the nineteenth-century scheme of registration still held some residual elements of the supposition that land was a fixed common surface, contemporary land-information systems are linked by an abstract geocode. As a result, each topographical representation of land is treated as a partial or selective interpretation, or as one particular 'terrain' within the territory.

'The sinewes of the land'

Although the process of registration did not accord with the advertised image of cadastral inscription, it nevertheless secured rights to land in a way that its advocates could not have recognised. The register may not have bound property rights to their material referent, but the new index did solve a particular problem with the proof of title to land. Whereas the advocates of registration saw the problem as a difficulty in binding paper titles to the 'land itself', the fact was that English land law had long been concerned with the circulation of paper titles rather than the situation 'on the ground'. The difficulty addressed by the register was that early-modern routines for stabilising paper titles had been eroded by changes in land ownership and land-use patterns, and the register's index was successful because it offered a basis for continuing to deal in 'paper' rather than 'land'.

Even before the advent of geographical information systems, cadastral indexing had transformed the nature of ownership. Indexation was not just a more efficient way of processing the traditional elements of ownership; it thoroughly reconstituted the structure of legal ownership as a basis for economic and social expectations. Of course the semantic components of property law remained much the same; the division of tenure into an array of estates and interests was not substantially affected by the introduction of registration of title. However, because these semantic elements were articulated by a different social or discursive technique, land became a different sort of juridical commodity. In property law, 'land' is a mere figure of speech. The thing transferred by the making of a deed or an administrative entry in a register is ownership, an abstract quality which is suspended between land and paper and which constitutes the essential but insubstantial bond between land and the expectations that are formed in relation to it. Yet despite the apparent fragility of ownership, the description of property as 'the great delegaliser'[40] remains entirely apt; tokens of ownership manage to bind expectations to material things in such a way that expectations can be delimited and understood without constant recourse to the courts. Nonetheless, in relation to land ownership, paper has an importance that it does not have in relation to personal property; paper title enables one to distinguish lawful ownership from mere factual occupation or to construct increasingly complicated transactions in relation to a slice of land.

In this context, 'paper' is also a mere figure of speech. In traditional practices of land transfer, paper documents were saturated with a particular kind of practical knowledge. The validity or tenor of each document was dependent upon the consistency of this medium of practical knowledge and upon the various techniques which were used to give it stability. The traditional characterisation of documents is nicely expressed in Coke's specification of what a purchaser could expect his seller to deliver to him as proofs of title: 'The purchaser shall have all the charters, deeds, and evidences, as incident to the lands, *et ratione terra*, to the end he may the better defend the land himself, having no warrantie to recover in value; for the evidences are, as it were, the sinewes of the land ...'[41]

Figuratively, the notion that written proofs were the organic 'sinewes' of the land expresses the sense in which expectations were bound to land not by the propositional content of a paper document but by the human techniques of record and recollection which sustained the reproduction of documents and the practical stability of their propositional content. On the one hand, a document 'materialised' the land in question; it was a palimpsest upon which local knowledge wrote and re-wrote the defining features of the land, referring them to co-ordinates which were layered in a local memory. This was another context in which 'the landscape was its own map'.[42] On the other hand, the document identified owners, recounting the story of the transmission of the land, which usually followed the descent of kinship. Documentary sinews were 'organic' in the sense that they were spun out of a fabric of social memory which was accessible either through the medium of particular witnesses or in the more diffuse knowledge of the community. So, for example, Coke goes on to note that 'if all the witnesses to the deed be dead (as no man can keep his witnesses alive, and time weareth out all men)', then the best proof of the deed came from the 'violent presumption' of 'continuall and quiet possession'.[43] More specifically, the metaphor focuses on the adversarial nature of proof or the idea that documentary proofs would successfully enable the purchaser to defend an action for possession. This, in turn, touches on the peculiarly English concept of relativity of title, a residue of the twelfth-century division of labour between the seigneurial courts and the royal courts, which produced the curious situation in which the latter, more popular, form of justice could be invoked only by those who renounced any claim to an absolute property right and were content to prove only that they had a better right than their adversary.[44] The upshot was that ownership as it was asserted or defended, either actually or in anticipation, was effectively detached from the land itself; instead, it became an abstracted interest in the land. This was the quality articulated by documentary sinews.

Lawyers soon fashioned a more meticulous form of documentary fetish. After some preliminary hesitations about the ability of paper documents to carry 'land' from one owner to the next,[45] English land-transfer law became committed to the idea that ownership could be reduced to paper and the evolution of professional conveyancing practice gave organic knowledge an appearance of rigidity by casting it in formal criteria. The conveyancer's idea of how ownership could be insulated from the vicissitudes of social memory is somewhat metaphorically expressed in the idea that documentary proof resembled proof by logical demonstration:

> if the question be, whether certain Land be the Land of *J.S.* or *J.N.* and a Record be produced whereby the Land appears to be transferred from *J.S.* to *J.N.* now when we shew any such third Perception, that doth necessarily infer the Relation in Question, this is call'd Knowledge by Demonstration.[46]

This peculiar 'third perception' consisted in an intuitive apprehension of the relation between truth and each of the points in the development of a proof. Even if the ownership of 'J.N.' was not self-evident, the relation of each document to its successor was so. This attempt to equiparate property proofs to demonstration as the unfolding of intuited self-evident relations abrogated the impure temporality of historical transmission. Paper was more than just a fallible representation of a past event; it was, in a somewhat archaic sense, a witness to the transaction. In archaic legal systems, witnesses had two seemingly distinct roles. In their first capacity, as 'maieutic witnesses', they validated a particular transaction or event by observing its performance. In their second role, as 'probative witnesses', they testified to this performance. In effect, these two roles were identical. Even when they testified in court, witnesses were not retrieving or recollecting a past event: 'before the judge, they *continued* in their role as observer-participants [*les témoins restent des assistants*], one might say that they bore with them a self-evident truth [*une certitude qui s'impose*]. As even their designation suggests, they were those who "knew", but this knowledge was sealed within them.'[47] The point is that the truth that they bore with them was the same as that which they had gathered in affirming the 'original' transaction. Their original apprehension remained alive and active, ever-present rather than recollected. Likewise, the early-modern use of documents as proofs imagined that the truth relayed by a formal deed had not journeyed through social-historical time only to arrive as a fallible and enfeebled truth. The paper document unfolded ownership in and of itself; there was no evidential interval. The fantasy was that a paper document might become ownership itself – that is that it might forge the bond between persons and land so securely that it would remain uncorrupted by practical social knowledge.

Yet this was only an abstract ideal, and 'demonstration' fought a losing battle against 'history'. It was impossible to create or sustain the sort of social vacuum within which a demonstration would work as such. And, although conveyancing theory came to concede that the highest standard of proof that was available in practice was 'moral certainty', even that looser standard of proof was unrealistic. People were suspicious of documents, and they did not rely on official conveyancing criteria as measures of certainty. In part this was because the official criteria of validation were unattainable, and in part it was because there was, in any case, a much better and cheaper basis for confidence, namely the 'reputation', longevity or plausibility of a title or its vendor. These were practical rather than legal presumptions which helped to answer the question whether the declared provenance of a title was probable or whether the 'voice' of the document was plausible. Of course, there was a form of 'conversation' between practical proof and formal proof. Because the ultimate measure of validity or marketability was set by conveyancing criteria, the process of formal proof raised the questions to which practical proofs offered the readier answer. As in a relation of verisimilitude, formal criteria traced the image of the ideal conveyance and practical proofs determined how closely a particular candidate approximated to that ideal. The relation was one of external resemblance rather than one of internal demonstration. In this curious relation between the formal and the practical, conveyancing abstractions turn out to be parasitic upon the very resources of practical knowledge that they attempted to overcome. The practical complicity between formal ideals and practical realities worked only because 'landed' expectations were gathered around the relatively stable inheritance and management practices of the aristocracy. Only when the fabric of economic and social expectations became more diverse did this arrangement become problematic. In that sense, because it removed property in land from the early-modern fabric of inheritance genealogies, cadastral indexation marked the somewhat belated modernisation of English land ownership.

Cadastral indexation released formal property criteria from their dependence on practical knowledge. Documents of title were no longer saturated with organic expectations. Rather, the register or index became the foundation or presupposition of proprietary expectations. The very artificiality of the index and its ability to observe and record complex shifts in the configuration of ownership is essential to this function. Rather than attempt to fix a configuration of ownership by inscribing it on a map, the object is to condense the index into a set of criteria which can be appropriated within diverse property practices while remaining recognisable to and manipulable by the bureaucracy. The process is made easier by the fact that the criteria have evolved in parallel with the evolution of land use and by the fact that the deficiencies of the scheme can be compensated or justified by judicial decisions. Yet in place of the older forms of 'traditional truth', registration offers a codified basis for expectations. The practical knowledge upon which the scheme depends is not that of its consumers, but that of its producers; it consists in the established routines and discretionary interventions of the administration. The nature of this administrative process is precisely what is represented above in terms of the distinction between 'terrain' and 'territory'.

Conclusion

Doubtless, cadastral indexation as I have defined it could be described as just another form of perspectival mastery. The argument might be that as a hybrid structure of geometry and writing, the cadastral index makes the world available in a novel and more tractable form:

> space on paper can be made continuous with three-dimensional space. The result is that we can work on paper with rulers and numbers, but still manipulate three-dimensional objects 'out there'. Better still, because of this optical consistency, everything, no matter where it comes from, can be converted into diagrams and numbers, and combinations of numbers and tables can be used which are still easier to handle than words or silhouettes.[48]

> Power is given to an average mind just by looking at files: domains which are far apart become literally inches apart; domains which are convoluted and hidden become flat; thousands of occurrences can be looked at synoptically. More importantly, once files start being gathered they can be arrayed in cascade: files of files can be generated and this process can be continued until a few men consider millions as if they were in the palms of their hands.[49]

In these terms, cadastral indexation, because it depends on just such a configuration of maps and files, affords a form of mastery. Indeed, the index itself, because it compresses the complexity of the lived landscape into a dimension which can be moulded and manipulated administratively, seems to grant an even more effective form of perspectival mastery. Yet this overlooks the necessary modesty of any administrative process. The idea that spatial compression affords mastery is true only if, rather like cartography's modern critics, one sees space as the principal dimension of social life. The trouble with this notion is that it overlooks the temporal differentiation of the social fabric. Time, more than space, is what differentiates a territory into discontinuous 'terrains'; the latter have 'incommensurable logics' because they set up different temporal (and spatial) horizons. They occupy different 'presents' and project different pasts and futures.[50] These domains are observable only through schemata which are flexible or modest enough to account for their own fallibility and for the fact that observed domains will adapt themselves in response to their awareness of being observed. In other words, the spatial categories or forms that constitute 'optical consistency' are used to track time and changes in events that emerge from different terrains motivated by processes that can never be fully understood precisely because they belong to radically differentiated temporal horizons. Again, optical consistency can do no more than model a terrain; it cannot master a territory. A terrain may be more or less successfully modelled, and, as with the modern multipurpose cadastre, the price of 'success' is the acceptance of limitation. The informative and sustainable scheme is that which is pre-adapted and on-goingly responsive to the complex dynamic relations between terrains. This is far removed from perspectival mastery.

Notes

1 Berque, 1995, p. 42.
2 Harley, 1989, p. 1.
3 For an acute analysis, see Murphy, 1997, Chapter 3.
4 Nicolet, 1988, p. 159.
5 This approach does have one problematic consequence; the term 'cadastral' appears in two senses throughout this chapter, to indicate the metaphor of cadastral inscription or construction and also to describe schemes of indexing. Hopefully the context of each reference allows the distinction to be made.
6 *Oxford English Dictionary*, s.v. 'cadastral': 'Of, pertaining to, or according to a cadastre; having reference to the extent, value, and ownership of landed property (strictly as a basis of distributing taxation)'.
7 Guery, 1986, p. 1050.
8 See Kain and Baiggent, 1992, p. 218.

9 Lepetit, 1996, p. 919.

10 This mode is described in Kain and Baiggent, 1992, pp. 227–28: 'A map at 1:5000 was produced on which were plotted from two to eight categories of land use, such as arable, grass, vines, and chestnuts, distinguished by color tints. The area of each land-use zone was calculated from the map, as was the total extent of the whole commune. Proprietors then declared the content of the fields and land parcels they owned in each of the land-use zones. Comparison between the total declared area and that calculated from the maps produced a weighting factor which could be applied to increase declared areas in other, unmapped, communes in each arrondissement, thereby establishing the total tax liability for apportionment. The problem was that, as the maps did not show field boundaries, it was not possible to take any account of variations in yields, and therefore revenue, between fields in the same land-use zone. Complaints came from all sides – the government, municipal councils, mayors of communes, and landowners – all agreeing that a parcel-by-parcel survey was the only solution.'

11 Hennet, 1817, pp. 11, 13, respectively.

12 Stewart-Wallace, 1931, p. 45; Stewart-Wallace, 1932, p. 85.

13 Vrana, 1989, p. 34.

14 See Huxhold, 1991; Rugg, 1995, p. 195.

15 'The typical functions of a GIS [geographic information system] involve the following operations on spatial data: topological operations which transform and generalize two-dimensional spatial data, thus producing maps at various levels of aggregation, overlay analysis techniques which combine maps as layers and enable various visual, statistical and logical operations on the resulting coverages, buffering and related spatial subdivision methods which identify areas conforming to various criteria, elementary statistical operations involved in describing, smoothing, and developing methods of error and bias in data': Batty, 1990, pp. 54–55.

16 '[A] planimetric database contains information that is similar to that contained in a cadastral database (streets, intersections, rivers, etc.); however, it is missing the information necessary to map parcel boundaries. On the other hand, planimetric databases contain other information not recorded in cadastral databases such as: curb lines (defining pavement width), building locations, and utility facilities on the ground (manholes, fire hydrants, transformers, street lights, and power, telephone, and cable TV poles': Huxhold, 1991, pp. 188–89.

17 See, for example, Hvidegard, 1991, p. 606.

18 Critics observe that 'GIS produces an illusion of autonomy which transcends social contexts': Aitken and Michel, 1995, p. 17.

19 *Second Report of the Real Property Commissioners* (1830), MCP xi, p.1.

20 Anderson, 1992, p. 59. See also p. 82.

21 This problem had been anticipated in one of the first polemics contra compulsory registration: Hale, 1694, p. 8: 'if only [the conveyance] from the last Seller [is registered], then is the Purchaser in the Dark still, what Estates were in the antecedent Owners, and how Derived, and so the Design ineffectual to the end proposed'.

22 This is discussed more fully in Pottage, 1994, p. 361.

23 This was a complex question, which was only obliquely addressed by the Registry: 'Under Lord Westbury's Act, 1862, the boundaries were very carefully defined, and were considered to be guaranteed as accurate under the Act. Before any property could be registered there was always what was called at the time a perambulation of the boundaries, and the exact position of the property boundary was noted on the map in the presence, wherever possible, of the adjoining owner. That led to a great deal of... unnecessary expense. [A]ccordingly, [it was] recommended that in any future Act boundaries should not be accurately defined, but that they should be treated in the same sort of way as boundaries are treated in ordinary conveyancing; that is to say, there should be something in the Act corresponding to the expression which is put into most conveyances 'little more or less'. [T]he boundaries of a registered property are not exactly defined, and that enables properties to be registered without notice to adjoining owners': Brickdale, Chief Land Registrar, Minutes of Evidence, Royal Commission on the Land Transfer Acts, 1909, PP, p. 20. The matter was not quite so simple, as the following exchange (p. 22) reveals: 'q. 370: "Is it always easy to draw a line between a boundary question and a question of title?" – "I cannot say it is easy"; q. 371: "Because according as the boundary is in one place or another a tract of land, which may be large or small, is or is not in the title?" – "I think it would depend, for one thing, upon the nature of the property and its position, and the uses to which it is likely to be put".' Of course the process of property mapping could be combined with the process of development, rather than simply following on from it. Brickdale was cautious about this: '[W]e get a great deal of help from the surveyors of the estates; they always give us their development maps, but it is not quite safe to go

entirely by those, because they do not always follow them out': ibid., q. 588, p. 32.

24 Minutes of Evidence, Royal Commission on the Land Transfer Acts, 1909, PP, p. 22.

25 '[T]here is the substitution of clear and well-made plans, founded on the ordnance map, checked by competent surveyors, for the loose verbal descriptions, and sometimes inaccurate and misleading plans, to be found in many conveyances': Minutes of Evidence, Royal Commission on the Land Transfer Acts, 1909, PP, q. 165, p. 12.

26 Compulsory registration of title was introduced first to certain areas of London by means of an Order in Council made in 1898 under the terms of section 20 of the Land Transfer Act 1897.

27 Notice the objections of the conveyancers: 'To convey large interests by a mere number, or by reference to a deed with scarcely any particulars of the same, is almost incomprehensible to a careful conveyancer who is not on the Registry staff' (observations of a witness giving evidence to the Royal Commission of 1909, q. 8807, p. 297).

28 Minutes of Evidence, Royal Commission on the Land Transfer Acts, 1909, q. 8807, p. 297.

29 This objection is made, admittedly in rather cruder terms, in Hale, 1694, p. 9: 'Men in a little while, may lose their Estates, by the Countenance that a forged Deed shall receive, by being Inrolled among the publick Records of the Office; for the Officer can never examine the Truth or Reality of the Deed, or if he could, it would not be reasonable that Mens Estates should depend upon the Judgment of any ignorant Clerk, or Officer'.

30 See Pottage, 1995, p. 371.

31 Report of the Registrar of the Land Registry for the Years 1902, 1903, 1904 and 1905, PP, 1906, Cmnd. 3132, paragraphs 23, 31.

32 Jacob, 1992, pp. 117–18.

33 Buci-Glucksmann, 1996, p. 23.

34 Turnbull, 1989, p. 61.

35 Lepetit, 1993, pp. 118, 129, citing Viollet-le-Duc.

36 Lepetit, 1993, p. 128.

37 Bentham manuscript, cited in Postema, 1986, p. 153.

38 Postema, 1986, p. 446.

39 The cadastral schemes of later-republican and early-imperial Rome attempted to bind the condition of the land more or less permanently, by identifying plots of land in terms of an authorised agrarian use, by attributing it to owners who were qualified (in

terms of status) for that use and, at least in some cases, by making the land inalienable. Indeed, few variations on this method, if any, allowed administrators to keep track of changes in tenure (Nicolet, 1988, pp. 176–77).

40 'The only great delegalizer with a minimum of rules and a maximum of effects that has been invented in legal history is the institution of property because of its clear and simple way of pre-deciding conflicts': Luhmann, 1988, p. 121.

41 Coke, 1724, book I, s 1 6b (a commentary on a late-fifteenth-century text, *Littleton's Tenures*).

42 Verran-Watson, 1989.

43 Coke, 1724, 7a.

44 See generally Milsom, 1969, esp. Chapter 6.

45 See, for example, Clanchy, 1993, p. 260: '[In the thirteenth century] the drafting rule became general that the past tense should be used in charters for the act of giving: "Know that I, A of B, have given", not simply "I give". This emphasized that the ceremonial conveyance was the crucial transaction, whereas the charter was merely a subsequent confirmation of it.'

46 Gilbert, 1754, p. 3.

47 Gernet, 1985, p. 136. The translation is made more awkward by the fact that there is no simple way of rendering the connotations of the French phrase 'assister à'. Clanchy raises the question why 'early drafters of [medieval] charters are often reluctant to state the time and place of writing and why they invoke the aid of God and his saints so frequently': Clanchy, 1993, p. 295. The practice might have been an echo or survival of this archaic mode of witnessing not testimonially but so as to constitute the deed or transaction. The problem of 'forgery' arose because witnesses could not remain in that eternally still time from which they saw and spoke as witnesses; when they rejoined the flux of social time, their 'original' knowledge was modified.

48 Latour, 1986, pp. 1, 22.

49 Latour, 1986, p. 28.

50 See Luhmann, 1998.

Bibliography
Primary sources

Second Report of the Real Property Commissioners (1830) MCP.

Minutes of Evidence, Royal Commission on the Land Transfer Acts (1909) PP.

Report of the Registrar of the Land Registry for the Years 1902, 1903, 1904 and 1905, PP (1906) Cmnd. 3132.

Secondary sources

Aitken, Stuart and Suzanne Michel, 'Who Contrives the "Real" in GIS? Geographic Information, Planning and Critical Theory', *Cartography and Geographic Information Systems* 22/1, 1995, pp. 17–29.

Anderson, J. Stuart, *Lawyers and the Making of English Land Law, 1832–1940*, Oxford, Clarendon Press, 1992.

Batty, M., 'Using Geographic Information Systems in Urban Planning and Policy-making', in Fischer, Manfred and Nijkamp (eds), *Geographic Information Systems, Spatial Modelling and Policy Evaluation*, Berlin, Springer Verlag, 1990.

Berque, Augustin, *Les Raisons du Paysage*, Paris, Hazan, 1995.

Buci-Glucksmann, Christine, *L'Oeil Cartographique de l'Art*, Paris, Galilée, 1996.

Clanchy, M., *From Memory to Written Record*, Oxford, Basil Blackwell, 1993.

Coke, Edward, *Coke upon Littleton*, London, 1724.

Gernet, Louis, 'Le Temps Dans les Formes Archaïques du Droit', reprinted in Louis Gernet, *Droit et Institutions en Grèce Antique*, Paris, Gallimard, 1985,

Gilbert, Geoffrey, *The Law of Evidence*, London, 1754.

Guery, Alain, 'État, Classification Sociale et Compromis sous Louis XIV: La Capitation de 1695', *Annales ESC (Economies, Sociétés, Civilisations)* 1986, pp. 1241–69.

Hale, Sir Matthew, *Treatise on the Inrolling and Registering of all Conveyances of Lands*, London, 1694.

Harley, J.B., 'Deconstructing the Map', *Cartographica* 26, 1989, pp. 1–28.

Hennet, Alphonse, *Du Cadastre. Réponse à l'Ouvrage Intitulé : La Vérité sur le Cadastre*, Paris, 1817.

Huxhold, W.E., *An Introduction to Urban Geographic Information Systems*, Oxford, Oxford University Press, 1991.

Hvidegard, Jonna, 'Conversion of the Danish Cadastral Maps to Digital Form', in Krysia Rybaczuk and Michael Blakemore (eds), *Mapping the Nations: Proceedings of the 15th Conference of the International Cartographic Association*, London, International Cartographic Association, 1991.

Jacob, Christian, *L'Empire des Cartes: Approche Théorique de la Cartographie à Travers l'Histoire*, Paris, Albin Michel, 1992.

Kain, Roger J.P. and Elizabeth Baiggent, *The Cadastral Map in the Service of the State*, Chicago, Chicago University Press, 1992.

Latour, Bruno, 'Visualization and Cognition: Thinking With Hands and Eyes', *Knowledge and Society: Studies in the Sociology of Culture Past and Present* 6, 1986, pp. 1–40.

Lepetit, Bernard, 'Architecture, Géographie, Histoire: Usages de l'Echelle', *Genèses* 13, 1993, pp. 118–38.

– Review of Estado Pro Ruiz, 'Geometría y Propriedad. Los Origines del Catastro en España, 1715–1941', *Annales Histoires, Sciences Sociales*, 1996, pp. 918–20.

Luhmann, Niklas, 'The Self-Reproduction of Law and its Limits', in G. Teubner (ed.), *Dilemmas of Law in the Welfare State*, Berlin, Walter de Gruyter, 1988.

– *Observations on Modernity*, Stanford, Stanford University Press, 1998.

Milsom, S.F.C., *Historical Foundations of the Common Law*, London, Butterworths, 1969.

Murphy, Tim, *The Oldest Social Science. Configurations of Law and Modernity*, Oxford, Clarendon Press, 1997.

Nicolet, Claude, *L'Inventaire du Monde: Géographie et Politique aux Origines de l'Empire Romain*, Paris, Fayard, 1988.

Postema, Gerald, *J. Bentham and the Common Law Tradition*, Oxford, Clarendon Press, 1986.

Pottage, Alain, 'The Measure of Land', *Modern Law Review* 51, 1994, pp. 361–84.

– 'The Originality of Registration', *Oxford Journal of Legal Studies* 15, 1995, pp. 371–401.

Rugg, Robert, 'Defining Standard Features for Land Use Applications', *Cartography and Geographic Information Systems* 22/3, 1995, pp. 195–204.

Stewart-Wallace, J.S., 'Land Registration in England in Relation to Mapping and Surveying', *Conveyancer* XVII, 1931, *Conveyancer* XVIII, 1932.

Turnbull, David (ed.), *Maps are Territories: Science is an Atlas*, Geelong, VA, Deakin University Press, 1989.

Verran-Watson, Helen, 'Maps are Territories: Science is an Atlas', in David Turnbull (ed.), *Maps are Territories: Science is an Atlas*, Geelong, VA, Deakin University Press, 1989.

Vrana, R., 'Historical Data as an Explicit Component of Land Information Systems', *International Journal of Geographical Information Systems* 3/1, 1989.

CHAPTER 7

The State of Property: Late Ottoman Southern Syria, the *Kazâ* of 'Ajlun (1875–1918)[1]

Martha Mundy[2]

Ownership and legal personality

Anthropological analyses have long considered property as a social relation between persons concerning material or immaterial 'things'.[3] In this sense, anthropology has never been dupe to the naturalness of property; on the contrary, anthropologists have generally argued for the social construction of notions of person and thing, legal subject and object. Its engagement in the problem of universals concerns quite another level of the human condition.

But what is striking about these otherwise sophisticated discussions is the degree to which the persons of anthropological analysis remain familiar ones: human gendered individuals or corporations of such individuals associated through kinship or production, 'persons' who can, in one way or another, be seen in the field. Here, anthropologists diverge from jurists, who otherwise share an understanding of the constructed nature of the categories of ownership relations. For jurists, the range of 'moral persons' or 'juridical persons' appears larger. This is no doubt because jurists deal primarily with formal written law and because their law has over centuries developed complex legal instruments documenting property in the service of major economic and political agencies, states and merchants.

Anthropologists, by contrast, have traditionally served to provide documentation of agents with far less economic power

– persons who belong to what once formed less centralised societies incorporated into state systems, or small groups of persons, rarely among the most privileged, in historical state societies. In many an anthropological analysis of property relations, the state thus appears either in the background as a kind of stage-set, or along with other major private economic agencies as a threatening englobing power imposing rules of a peculiar sharpness upon the more gently ambiguous local legal concepts. And it is characteristic of the ethics of post-1960s anthropology, even in its most applied form in the service of development agencies, that anthropological specialists see themselves as documenting the fate and wishes of often very human persons in the face of powerful systemic agencies.

'In the face of...': the phrase may serve as introduction to my argument. Put briefly, I shall argue that we take seriously the anthropomorphism of the image of the face – or, truer to the law, the image of the mask – of powerful systemic agencies. The persons engaged in property relations are not only those individuals engaged in tangible corporeal relations, notably relations of production in agriculture, but also the legal persons (*personae*) of agencies of state. These *personae*, central to the social relations of property today and, as legal creatures, never simply reducible to the sentient human actor, need to be recognised as such.[4] Even jurists do not always do this in the analysis of property law, for they happily focus on doctrine to the exclusion of the administration of entitlement where the *personae* of the state lurk.[5] In this way, moreover, property relations may return to where they belong in a political anthropology.[6]

Legal transformation of ownership

The case to be examined here formed part of a great state system of the early-modern and modern period of European history: the Ottoman Empire. The period in question, the nineteenth century, and particularly the second half of that century, was one of intense inter-state competition. In the Europe of the nineteenth century, states adopted veritable ideologies of private property, especially property in land. Although the Ottoman administration eschewed strident ideological adherence to private property in land, under the pressure of inter-state competition it adopted the central tenets of nineteenth-century policies of government: state prosperity rests on the security of individual wealth, corresponding to individual subjecthood and tax liability.[7] The implementation of this policy required that the state identify its individual subjects, their properties and corresponding tax liabilities and, on this basis, promote the creation of wealth and the assurance of good governance.[8] In this sense, the Ottoman case is not at all exotic or exceptional to the history of the nineteenth century, neither in general terms nor in the particular history of the outlying district to be discussed: southern Syria, contemporary northern Jordan.

The scale at which we shall examine this transformation is, I shall argue, also relevant to our seeing the political *personae* in property relations. At the highest level of state, in Istanbul, one can trace processes of discursive production within the departments of state. Key figures stand out there, individuals who unite in their person several discursive traditions and institutional *personae* over a career; the figure of Cevdet Paşa is exemplary in this regard.[9] Institutional *personae*, whole departments of the state, can be seen to work in contest and collaboration. Moreover, one can examine the flows of documentary correspondence from the provincial administrations to the Porte in the capital. Shifts in administrative idiom, design of forms for recasting and classifying the individual subject of imperial rule, correspondence downwards and upwards from the provinces, so central to generating pressure for change in the procedures of administration – all of this the scholar can observe.

At this level of state, rather as in the jurists' fancy, property appears a matter of documentation. From the perspective of the central administration in Istanbul, however, it is hard to see the *personae* of legal discourse in relation to the sentient persons of anthropology's daily relations and visible landscapes. The award of property title is not meant to occur at the highest level of state, but at a lower level of administration, where persons with a claim to property title and legal persons of the administration meet, not only metaphorically but also quite practically. Thus property relations in more than a purely discursive sense actually appear, both to the ruler and to the subsequent analyst, in the provinces, where local knowledge meets administrative form. It is at this level, from province to province and district to district, that the outcomes of the administrative recognition of title differ one from the next. Here, in a dynamic that moulded subsequent regional political histories, administrative *personae* encountered actors within quite tangible relations of production and exchange. It is thus at the level of such a district that we shall consider the construction of the late-Ottoman state of property.

It is, moreover, this level of administration which was designated by state law as most relevant. The first clause of the 1859 Ottoman Regulation of Title to Land (Tapu Nizâmnâmesi), issued shortly after the 1858 Land Code, states that 'in the provinces, the finance employees, that is the Directors of the Registry and Finance and the Directors of the Districts (*kazâ*), being empowered to devolve and to transfer *miri* land, have the legal status of the "land-captain" (*sâhib-i arz*)'.[10] In this clause, several legal *personae* supplant an existing legal *persona* with regard to the right to grant legal title rights to *miri* land.

What is at issue here? In this phrase lies condensed the promise of a transformation of both government and property. The major European translation of this regulation renders '*sâhib-i arz*' as '*le propriétaire de la terre*' – the landowner.[11] This is misleading, and so I shall here translate the term by 'land-captain' so as to avoid the misunderstanding that the translation 'landowner' would otherwise produce.[12] In the legal language of eighteenth- and early-nineteenth-century *fiqh*, the *sâhib-i arz* was the person who held the right to manage revenue and grant cultivation rights on behalf of the fisc.[13] In practice, this intermediary figure headed a household with fields of action simultaneously public and private, fiscal and commercial.[14] The regulation promised his replacement by figures of an administration self-consciously defined as the *personae* of the formal administration of state. This said, the phrasing of the clause suggests an unfinished quality to the elaboration of the administrative division of labour; award of title is here within the purview of the finance administration, with the respective roles of finance, registry and district directors as yet left unspecified.

The administrative construction of title which the 1859 regulation heralds was to extend throughout the second half of the nineteenth century. Given the older order of ownership right which this development was to replace, it is not surprising that the first administrative person designated as replacing the *sâhib-i arz* is a revenue official. The older order of right was, in good part, understood in revenue terms, in terms of the flow of produce upwards from processes of cultivation and distribution. The *sâhib-i arz* possessed the right of management of land and of collection of revenue, that is he held a title (*berât*) to what we may term 'an estate of administration'.[15] In return for this, the holder owed part of the revenue to the state treasury, the ultimate owner in the chain of owners. Below the *sâhib-i arz* in the chain of the movement of the fruits of production, of fiscal dues and claims, stood other owners of right.

In practice, below the 'estate of administration' of the *sâhib-i arz* stood not only the layered estates of production, but also a subordinate estate of administration, that of the village. This entailed practically important rights vested in village leadership for the management of common land (threshing grounds, forests and pastures in different combinations, according to regions), of provisions for village servants and of the allocation of any collective taxation imposed on the village. Unlike the superior estate of administration of the *sâhib-i arz* assimilated to the category of ownership of state administrative offices more generally, the rights of this subordinate estate of administration appear relegated to the category of custom, and without jurisprudential treatment in the literature of late Hanafite *fiqh*. This ambiguity also marked the treatment of such rights under early Tanzimat legislation.

By contrast, *fiqh* of the sixteenth to early-nineteenth centuries did elaborate legal categories for rights in the 'estates of production'. Here, categories of ownership applied, on the one hand, to agricultural capital, such as plantings, walls, manured or transported soil and an associated right of cultivation, and, on the other hand, to the very right to plough grain land, termed *mashadd al-maska*, in the *fiqh* of Syrian jurists.[16] The enjoyment of each such right of ownership was subject to conditions. In the chain of fiscal relations built upon grain production, alienation or sale of rights by an owner was subject to the consent of the owner of the superior right. Thus jurists who accepted the logic of this order were wary of employing the classical term for property, *mülk*, since according to classical doctrine this described ownership free from hierarchical supervision of the terms of the transaction and use of said property.[17] Accordingly, when describing transactions in such rights, late-Hanafite *fiqh* adopted terms derived in part from administrative law that differed from those employed for devolution and exchange in rights of *mülk* ownership.

In the Tanzimat reforms, then, the officers first designated as granting title to the new forms of ownership belonged to the revenue administration. As we shall see, however, this was only the first step in a long process of administrative development. The new order, as stated in the Land Code (Arâzi Kanûnnâmesi) to which the Regulation of Title (Tapu Nizâmnâmesi) was tied, replaced the superior person, the *sâhib-i arz*, with figures in administrative departments, and recast the nature of ownership and its object. The new laws accepted super-ordinate ownership in the name of the state, but otherwise admitted no hierarchical levels of ownership. Thus, with regard to the practically existent but legally untheorised village 'estate of administration', this appears only obliquely in the founding legislation (1858 Land Code and 1859 Regulation of Title) as a restricted category of village commons tied to vital services.[18] Given the practical importance of the village estate of administration in many rural parts of the empire, the 'Instructions Concerning the Correct Procedures for Title [*tapu*]', published in volume 2 of the *Düstur*, do stipulate that the registration of land in a village should classify all lands – both cultivated lands to be registered as individual property and other categories, notably forests and pastures which may be held as village commons. The *tapu* scribe was to consult with the village council and also with other knowledgeable persons ('*ve sâ'ir erbâb-i vukûf ve ma`lûmât*') – a formulation that presumably also permitted figures of regional power (the former 'land-captains') to participate in negotiations concerning the fixing of such rights in the state registers. On the basis of this investigation, the *tapu* scribe was required to list the types of land in the village and to determine whether the village had more pasture or forest land than it required. If so, the scribe was to communicate this fact to the administrative council so that it could initiate the procedure for auctioning such forest or pasture land to the highest bidder. Although there is even here only an implicit recognition of the *de facto* village administration of commons as various types of land, and village authorities are treated as mere sources of information for the schedules of the administration, it is characteristic of Tanzimat reforms of local government and property that the village elected council is privileged here as interlocutor over the former land-captains who administered more than one village. In practice, at this time state administration did not challenge this *de facto* village administration of commons. It was only somewhat later, as we shall see, that the state was to establish an administration to deal with 'forest' common lands, and was to set about curtailing further the legally untheorised estate of administration managed by the village elected council.[19]

The Tanzimat reforms differed markedly here from Russian reforms of village administration in the same period. Both sought to strengthen village political institutions, and so to replace the former intermediaries – the land-captains – with more direct links between formal state administration and cultivators. The Tanzimat reforms recast regional leaders into janus-faced officers elected for two-year terms onto formal judicial and administrative bodies, and simultaneously institutionalised village authority in the form of an elected council of elders (*ihtiyâr heyeti*) with primary decision-making powers and a headman (*muhtar*) burdened with notary and administrative duties. *Tapu* registration itself worked to transfer knowledge of the persons holding rights and of the objects of rights to the registers of the government, in return for which each holder of right received his/her own title document, each with the Imperial cypher (*tuğralı*) drawn up by the *tapu* scribes in the next higher administrative level, the *lîvâ*, and sent to the provincial registry office for checking before being distributed by the district *tapu* scribe to the owners themselves.[20]

But, unlike the Russian assignment of agricultural land to the village, Ottoman reforms admitted no village common property in ploughing or horticultural lands. In the primary form of ownership of *miri* agricultural land, as defined in the 1858 Land Code, the owner of right held not some part of the objects of an estate of production but a more general right of economic use and disposal (*hakk-ı tasarruf*) of land.[21] This right became perpetual, subject only to continuing cultivation and payment of tax. The object of right in grain farming, as in other forms of agriculture or land use, was now defined as an area of land, measurable in like manner from one end of the empire to the other.[22] And the *persona* who might hold this right was resolutely an individual human person. In time, moreover, recognition of title to types of land other than state land became subject to this same relationship and administrative practice of registration: *mülk* and *vakıf* property, be it buildings, plantings or land, had to be registered through the formal administration in like manner to *miri* land.[23] The *personae* of formal administration alluded to in the programmatic first clause of the Title Regulation became central to property relations in all manner of ownership of what is called today real estate.

Administration

Clause 1 of the Title Regulation supplants one legal *persona* with another: the former 'land-captain' with the agent(s) of formal administration. In the law, this occurred at the stroke of a pen; in administrative practice, it was inevitably more complex. The knowledge to be inscribed in the grids of the formal administration lay, so to speak, in the heads of the land-captains; their status as intermediaries could be legally annulled, but practically some of them at least had to serve as agents, donning the mask of other legal *personae* within the new administrative order.

In Ottoman Tanzimat administration, the *kazâ* was the first level at which administrative officers belonging uniquely to the central bureaucracy were appointed; later, in the nineteenth century, certain sub-districts (*nâhiye*) were to acquire rudimentary administrative staffs, but until the end of the empire in September 1918 primary administrative development remained at the level of the *kazâ*. It is at this level that professional administrators, appointed from the top, were joined by figures possessing local knowledge, the first-level notionally elected figures of a formal, not household, administration. Here, figures with local knowledge, elected from below into formal offices defined by the centre, provided information required to fill the grids of the new printed forms with the details of the property and corresponding tax liability of individual subjects. These figures of local authority were simultaneously being schooled in the terms of the new laws.[24] Elected officials subject to recognition by the administration are also characteristic of Tanzimat reform institutions at the village and later sub-district levels of administration. The village elected council and the headman were cast as the lowest rung in the formal administrative hierarchy,[25] but it was only from the levels of the district to the province that such elected figures presided together with professional administrators on governing councils: administrative, judicial and later municipal. It was, moreover, the district council of administration (*meclis-i idâre*) which, as we shall see, legally certified the declarations concerning title to property made by village authorities to the *tapu* scribe.

In the rest of this study, the focus will remain at the district level, where we shall explore the administrative construction of the new state of property in two dimensions: first, change over time in the administration of title certification and, second, the integration of figures of regional importance into the elected offices of the formal administration. It is the objective of this study to demonstrate the intertwining nature of these two processes central to the political administration of the district.

The region: the *kazâ* of 'Ajlun

The *kazâ* of 'Ajlun of the *lîvâ* of Hauran formed the southernmost part of the nineteenth-century province of Syria (*vilayet-i Suriye*). The district was one of settled agriculture, and comprised mountains, rolling hills and the southernmost extension of the great Haurani plain. It contained just over a hundred villages.[26] From the 1830s, supported by both the administration of the state and the demand for grain on the European market (only undercut from the 1870s by cheaper grain in Mediterranean markets imported from India and the Americas), population and fixed settlement of the plains villages had grown steadily, with cultivators also migrating into the area from Palestine and the central Hauran. To the east and, to a lesser extent, the west in the Jordan valley and Galilee, were semi-nomadic and nomadic populations: to the northeast, the largely nomadic Bani Sakhr, who also in part wintered in the Jordan valley, and to the southeast, the Bani Hasan, who practised mixed systems of semi-nomadic pastoralism and cultivation on lands which they registered formally in the mid-1880s.[27] The plains produced primarily grain (wheat, barley and sorghum) and pulses; the hills also had important areas of olive cultivation and lesser areas of vines and fruit. The area thus comprised several different sub-regions, each of which possessed its distinct leadership, although in earlier eras a single figure had been sometimes designated as responsible to the central government.

Beginning in 1876, Ottoman administrators in the *kazâ* headquarters of Irbid began to deliver titles to property in land and other real estate to owners in villages of the area. There are two points concerning property registration in the district which need to be borne in mind.

First, although no common village property in agricultural land was permitted under the Land Code, in this region, where open-field systems of crop agriculture were commonplace, owners were allowed to register their individually owned shares of agricultural land in a village as shares under the legal category of 'ownership by association'.[28] This form of the representation of right permitted considerable continuity in agricultural practice at the same time as it satisfied the requirement of individual ownership. Such forms of agricultural production inevitably entailed an ambiguous continuity of village administration of land – ambiguous in that the practical importance of village management of shareholding, re-distributional systems of agriculture was accompanied by no formal legal status for this village 'estate of administration' in agriculture.

Second, the region was one in which ownership right was largely awarded to the cultivators and not, as in a number of areas of the Empire, primarily to those who under earlier law owned superior rights to revenue administration, i.e. those of the former category of *sâhib-i arz*. Furthermore, since the timing of land registration in good part coincided with a recession in the international price of grain, the new property right was to remain largely with the cultivators; urban merchant capital did not find the purchase of rain-fed land in the region sufficiently attractive to face the local political opposition such acquisition entailed.[29]

This fact is critical to the nature of political administration in the district over the period. In other areas of the Empire, where former land-captains acquired title to *tasarruf* rights in the lands of whole villages to which they had formerly held rights of revenue and administration, and where they presumably also came to occupy elected posts on the district councils, the effective character of political administration may well have appeared more oppressive and less legitimate to the cultivators.[30] In the *kazâ* of 'Ajlun, by contrast, these figures did not monopolise rights to title in this manner. Hence the several levels of administration defined by Tanzimat legislation were to come into play politically and not just formally.

Narrative history

The narrative account given below is bounded by the documentation from which it is abstracted. It begins with the first registration of title under the new forms of *tapu* administration in 1876, a few years after the first of the series of *Yearbooks of the Province of Syria* (*Salnâme-i Suriye*) published lists of district administrators for 1868–69; it ends with the last Ottoman *tapu* registers of 1918, preceded by many years by the last *Yearbook of the Province* published in 1900–1 detailing administrative cadres. This account is evidently constrained by its evidence: if earlier documents had been available, the 'beginning' of the narrative could have been more continuous with emerging practice; if lists of the local administration had continued to be published in the early twentieth century, then it would have been possible to correlate, in greater detail, changes in the form of certification of title and continuing administrative development for the years 1901–18. As it stands, the narrative inevitably cannot go beyond the documentation available.

There are a few documents which give some insight into the administration of revenue and right in the district just before *tapu* registration. It appears that a few leaders of sub-districts (*nâhiye*) sought to register villages where they held rights in the early years of *tapu* registration in the district. While such documents provide information required to prepare for registration under the new regulations, they appear to reflect earlier modes of representation of right in a manner not true of the schedules of holdings drawn up by the *tapu* scribe, according to instructions issued from above. Of these more local documents, let us briefly consider three produced for the village of Makhraba in January 1882.[31] Bound into the registers of the *tapu*, the three documents include a statement concerning the village drawn up by the local authorities, a note from the *tapu* scribe to the Finance Director of the *kazâ* of 'Ajlun, and the response to this by the Finance Director.

As can be seen from the reproduction of the first document (Figure 1), undated and in Arabic, it is inscribed within a rectangle.[32] In the middle of each side is a description of a landmark or name of the adjoining village at the respective point of the compass. This information is certified by the headman of the village, Ahmad Efendi al-'Azzam, of the leading family in the sub-district of al-Wustiyya, by the headman of the neighbouring

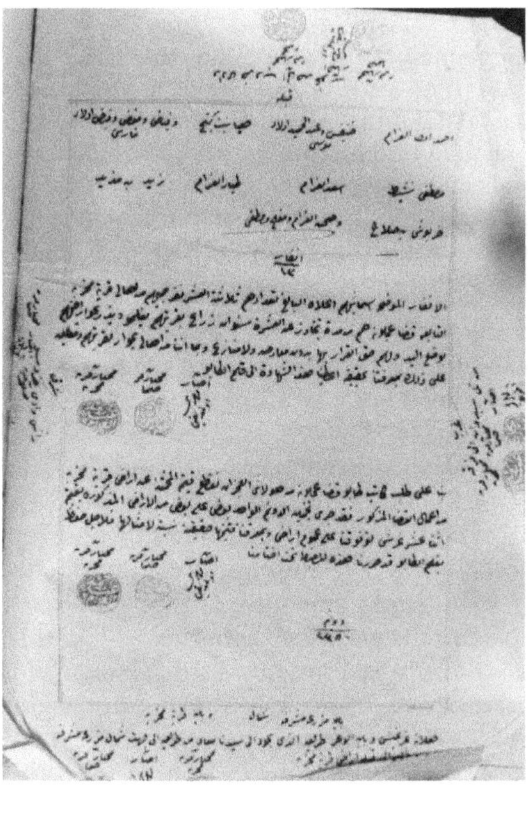

Figure 1
Document drawn up by local authorities for the village of Makhraba, bound into *tapu* register of January 1882.

village and by another elder of the village. The text within the triangle starts with a list of the 14 names (13 men, 1 woman) arranged into 10 clusters, beginning with the *efendi*. It ends with the words '13 persons [*anfar*]'. Following this are two statements, each stamped by the same three authorities, who attest the landmarks of the village borders in the mid-point of each of the four sides of the rectangle. The first reads:

> The persons whose names appear above number 13, persons, all people of the village of Makhraba of the *qada'* 'Ajlun. For more than ten years, they have been farmers in their village, ploughing and sowing the lands which they hold in occupancy possession [*bi-wad' al-yad*] and for which they hold rights by *haqq al-qarar*, without any opposition or contest. As people of the vicinity of their village who know the truth of these things, we have given this testimony to the *tabu* official.

The second statement concerns the value and area of the village lands:

> In accordance with the request of the *qada'* 'Ajlun *tabu* scribe to those humble souls [i.e. those listed above], we fix (*naqta'*) the estimated value of the lands of the village of Makhraba which belongs to the financial administration of the above mentioned *qada'*. The *dunum* is evaluated at 12 *ghurush* on average. We toured all the land and on the basis of our knowledge of its true value, in line with similar [land], we drew up this document under our seals to be kept in the *tabu* registry.

This second statement is again attested by Ahmad 'Abduh al-'Azzam, *mukhtar* of Makhraba, by the *mukhtar* of the neighbouring village of Samma and by a third notable. Lastly, the total number of *dunums* is given: 2350.

The next document, in Ottoman Turkish, is from the *tapu* scribe to the Director of Finance. He notes that the village is with Ahmad Efendi al-'Azzam, along with 12 other persons who enjoy actual possession; that the testimony from the vicinity grants them rights by *hakk-ı karâr*; that since all previous taxes appear to have been paid, he is granting them provisional title documents on the basis of right acquired by *hakk-ı karâr*.

The Director of Finance writes back in Arabic noting that he finds the annual sum of fixed tax (*mal wirku*) for the village to be 500 piastres (*ghurush*) and the sum paid in lieu of the tithe (*badal a'shar*) to be 800 *ghurush*, as fixed in 1879–80; that the village has paid its fixed taxes (*mal*) every year since 1871–72, together with its tithe (*a'shar*) since 1879–80, and that there are no back taxes due.

The following aspects of this correspondence appear relevant to anterior tradition: the documents concern the village as a whole, the fiscal evaluation of land and the identification of right-holders rests with regional leaders rather than the elected village council of elders, the village contains both persons and lands described separately to the state official but without definition of the internal allocation of land to these persons,[33] the fiscal value of land is fixed according to an average across all lands of the village, and the term *hakk-ı karâr*, describing the legal basis of the new title (*tapu*) is simultaneously one long used to denote the right to cultivation. This representation of due and right belongs to the preliminary stages of land registration, when a number of villages around the *kazâ* headquarters, several of which, such as Makhraba, were closely associated with a regional leader, proceeded to register title.

Ahmad Efendi al-'Azzam, who here provides information for the registration of title in Makhraba, served at this time (1878–80) as one of four elected members on the judicial council (*meclis-i de'âvî*) of the district, which in 1879–80 became the Court of First Instance (*bidâyet mahkemesi*).[34] This Council was one of two bodies at the *kazâ* level where elected regional leaders worked together with appointed officials. In the Tanzimat reforms, the judicial council, recast as the Court of First Instance in the first regulation of 1879 governing civil courts, had jurisdiction over all cases concerning *miri* land, criminal issues and most commercial matters.[35] The jurisdiction of the Islamic court, by contrast, was gradually restricted to issues of personal status (marriage, divorce, custody, inheritance, care of orphans), although its power to register agency (*vekâlet*) allowed it to give legal form to a promise to effect the transfer of land at the *tapu* offices. The judicial council was thus a body that had wide jurisdiction over property and criminal matters, becoming increasingly professionalised over the years, and that, by the incorporation of locally elected members, served as a place of education in the new legislation for the regional leaders successively elected to it.

As we have seen, the Tanzimat reforms invited regional leaders to serve as elected officers for two-year terms on formal juridical and administrative bodies, and recast village government in the form of an elected council of elders (*ihtiyâr heyeti*) with powers of decision and of a headman (*muhtar*) burdened with notary and administrative responsibilities. All of these legal *personae*, collectively the political administration of right, appear in the statements which certify the award of *tapu* directly in the registers of title kept in the district headquarters. The attestations to title provide a chart of the legal *personae* whose relations construct property.[36]

In the early lists of the subjects and objects of this new form of title, an element of contract can still be felt in the sequence of attestation to *tapu* right. The first attestation is signed by the village headman, the members of the village elected council and the title scribe for new property declaration (*kâtib-i yoklama*); the second is signed by all the principal figures of the administration and the members of the administrative council of the *kazâ*, that is by all the officials of the *kazâ* administration except the treasurer, i.e. the district governor (*kaymakam*), assistant governor (*nâip kaymakam*), director of finance (*mal müdürü*), scribal official (*kâtib-i tahrîrât*), prefect of the descendants of the Prophet (*nakibü'l-eşrâf*) and the members of the administrative council elected from the locality. In these early years, it was not only the cumulative run of property titles in a village which received the attestation of the administrative council, but also any subsequent transactions of right entered by individuals in the *tapu* registers.

The administrative council, like its sister the judicial council, which from 1879–80 became the Court of First Instance, was a body on which figures elected from the locality joined appointed members of the central administration in local government.[37] The course of this marriage did not run entirely smoothly during these early years of registration: a *kaymakam* was sued by a number of the figures of authority in the *kazâ* for demanding bribes to ensure their appointment. The evidently negotiated character of the practice of administration in these early years comes through the long pages of deposition in this prosecution, but so too does the formal, indeed arrogant, legalism of the responses of the *kaymakam*, in which he denounces the prosecution as contrary to regulation and provoked primarily by rivalries internal to the higher administration of the *lîvâ* and province. But, perhaps in part as a reaction to this important case – which as a prosecution of an official under administrative law was communicated to the Office of the Council of State (Şurâ-yi Devlet) in the capital – or simply as part of common procedures of administration in these years, a Special Commission for the Lands of Hauran was formed, and began work on registering land in 'Ajlun in early 1882. In the *tapu* registers of these years, the members of the commission (composed of a head, an employee of the property registry of *lîvâ* Hauran, the *kazâ tapu* scribe and two members) signed a second paragraph of attestation between the first, signed by the village authorities, and the third, signed by the administrative council of the district. But by the end of the second year of work of the commission, the first attestation of the village authorities simply disappears from the register, and the registration of several villages at a time may be jointly attested by the commission and the administrative council. Thus, by the middle of the 1880s, the element of contract between village authority (with its implicit estate of administration) and state administration, evident in the attestations of the first eight years of land registration, disappears from the registers.

This shift coincides with the institutional development of district administrative structures of some effectiveness and complexity by the mid-1880s. When in the late 1850s direct administration was established in 'Ajlun, this entailed little more than a governor and a few troops. This official cannot have governed, save through the regional leaders of the district. By the end of the 1860s, district administration had evolved only a little, comprising five civilian posts: a *kaymakam*, his deputy, a *mufti*, a finance director and a treasurer. These few officials clearly continued to work closely with regional leaders on the two major district councils. In 1869, the civil members of the administrative council, the body with responsibility for tax matters in the district, were two major rural leaders, Yusuf al-Sharaida of Tibna of the Kura sub-district and Hasan Barakat Fraihat of Kufrinja, figures previously responsible for tax collection in their respective *nâhiyes* who had long played a part in the government of the district as a whole.[38] Alongside them appears as Christian member, Khulaif al-Ghanma of the large plains village of al-Husn, a man who seems prominent in the finance of local-government transactions.[39] And serving on the judicial council were members of other major regional leading families: Ibrahim Sa'd al-Din of the 'Ubaidat of the Kafarat sub-district, Kulaib al-'Azzam of the Wustiyya sub-district, and Mahmud al-Musa, perhaps of al-Husn.[40] The early 1870s saw the appointment of two scribes, one who served on the administrative, the other on the judicial council, and of a first *tapu* scribe in 1876, but little else.[41]

It is in the 1880s that we find extensive development of formal administrative institutions throughout the Province of Syria. In the *kazâ* of 'Ajlun, it was in 1880–81 that a separate tax office with three employees was established; in 1882 that the Special Commission for the Lands of Hauran began work in the area; in 1882–83 that the area became linked by a telegraph office with one employee, and the first professional assistant prosecutor was appointed to the Court of First Instance.[42] The year 1883–84, when the small but symbolically important shift in the form of the attestation to title, discussed above, was introduced, proved a turning-point in administrative institutionalisation. It witnessed the appointment of a supervisor for an institutionally distinct office of correspondence and the formation of a third council, the municipal council of the town of Irbid.[43] From the outset, the members elected to the municipal council, which had general issues of social welfare and economic development as part of its brief, cut a different figure from the regional rural leaders, notably the leaders of the three primary political clusters of the Fraihat of Kufrinja, the Sharaidah of al-Kura and the 'Ubaidat of al-Kafarat, who, during these years, served continuously as members on the two major councils, particularly the administrative council with responsibility for both tax matters and attestation of property titles in the district. By contrast, the men elected to the municipal council came from Irbid and its surroundings, most belonging to leading families of what was still a very small town. The distinction of these men appears in good part to be a product, or through the service, of the new complex of government in Irbid.[44]

The year 1884 also proved to be the last in which the two great rural leaders, 'Abd al-Qadir Yusuf al-Sharaida and Husain Barakat Fraihat, served simultaneously on the administrative council.[45] This did not prove the end of the election of a Sharaida or a Fraihat to this council or to the Court of First Instance, but it did mark the end of the absolute centrality of the leaders of the Kura and Kufrinja on such councils.[46] By contrast, men from each of the major families of the 'Ubaidat of al-Kafarat, from the villages of Harta, Kufr Saum and al-Rafid, present on the councils from the earliest years, became ever more prominent on the councils in the years after 1885. Geographically close to Irbid, the leaders of the 'Ubaidat proved extraordinarily engaged with the Ottoman administration in Irbid. But alongside the rural leaders, in 1885 AD, the Civil Court admitted to its elected ranks a member from the leading families of Irbid, Qasim Hijazi, who only the previous year had been elected to the newly established municipal council.[47] In subsequent years other such men from Irbid and its vicinity were regularly elected to one or other of the two major councils.[48]

Administrative development continued in the second part of the 1880s. In 1886, Kufrinja became the first *nâhiye* to have a formal administrative director;[49] in 1887–88, two of the members on the civil court became *mülâzim* (supernumerary official) members, a scribe for public works joined the administration and, more notably, a tax-collection commission (*tahsîlât komisyonu*) was formed composed of the *kaymakam*, the head of finance, the head of correspondence, the *tapu* scribe and a soldier.[50] The year 1888–89 saw the appointment of a formally appointed scribe to the Islamic court and of a second scribe for new registration of property (*kâtib-i yoklama*) beside the *tapu* scribe and the opening of a department of forest administration with three employees.[51] This department marked the beginning of state administration of what previously had *de facto* belonged to the village 'estate of administration'.

If we turn back to the *tapu* registers and the form of attestation to title during these years of administrative development, we find that from 1888 the second *tapu* scribe for new registration of property (*kâtib-i yoklama*) began touring the villages of the area. The aim of his tours was to ensure that the village council and headman inform him of the deaths of any owners since the first *tapu* registration, as well as of any properties that may have remained undeclared to the authorities. This campaign was to continue for more than a decade (1889–99). The attestations to the lists drawn up in this period have a markedly different tone, however, from those in the registers of the Special Commission for the Lands of Hauran in earlier years. Now the state should possess all information concerning the lands and their owners in the villages: the village authorities, themselves the lowest rung of the administration, were threatened with prosecution should they hide any such information from the eyes of the *tapu* administration. Below these undertakings, drawn up and signed by the *tapu* scribe, follow the signatures of the headman and the village council. And, once returned to the district headquarters, the register was signed by all members of the administrative council. During these years, individuals also came to the *tapu* office in Irbid to register transfers of rights, and these individual entries likewise were attested by all the members of the administrative council. But the entries resulting from the tours of the scribe in the villages form by far the larger part of the entries in the registers. These cover a number of persons in a given village, and appear to reflect the concern of the administration to bring into line the lists of ownership title with those of tax obligations. Thus in certain *tapu* registers we find references to fiscal numbering placed in the margin against the objects of ownership; this reflects the development of distinct registers and offices for the administration of the two categories, individual property and individual tax liability, attached to similarly identified and hence occasionally cross-referenced objects of ownership.

As noted above, in 1888–89 the executive, tax and title officials of the district all joined in a newly formed tax-collection commission;[52] in 1892–93, an employee for the collection of *tapu* fees was recruited to the administration,[53] and in 1893–95 the existing administration was reinforced by five registration officials posted short-term to the district, two of whom were surveyors (*messâh*).[54] Although the absence of tax records for the district makes it impossible to determine the exact function of these officials, they appear to have aided the district tax-collection commission by registering individual tax liability in the villages of the area in a manner parallel to the earlier Special Commission for land registration. Once the special officials left, in 1896–97, the finance administration of the district was given separate status as a department, comprising the director of finance, an assistant director of finance and the treasurer.[55]

Following the consolidation of fiscal administration sketched above, the 1890s witnessed administrative developments of four major kinds. The first concerned formal education. If election to the councils served as a form of education for regional and then urban leaders in the law and new regulations, it was in the 1890s that the formal training of an educated elite for this area began locally. In 1893–94, the first state-appointed school teachers were named for Irbid and Jerash.[56] In 1895–96, an education commission was established under the headship of the deputy *kaymakam*, with eight civilian members and a scribe; with the exception of 'Abd al-'Aziz al-Ka'id of Suf, the members were from the more northern part of the district.[57] They represented figures closely engaged with the emerging order of government and hence of education. In 1896–97, school teachers were also appointed by the state to al-Husn and in 1897–98 to Kufrinja.[58]

The second development was the opening of a branch of the Agricultural Credit Bank in 1895–96 with 'Abd al-'Aziz al-Ka'id of Suf as head, he also serving on the education commission with members Sa'd al-'Ali of al-Bariha, a man who also served on the councils of the period and was an increasingly important financier in the Irbid area, Muhammad al-Shara'iri of Irbid, who also served on the district councils and as head of the municipal council, and Mahmud al-'Ali, a figure who often appeared on the municipal council and who may have been a relative of Sa'd al-'Ali.[59] The board of the Agricultural Credit Bank brought together men of financial experience in the orbit of the burgeoning administration of Irbid. The bank marks the state's engagement in the advancement of credit to individual owners of land, but in line with the developing administration of property the local social organisation of credit was itself already changing. Whereas earlier lines of credit appear to have linked regional leaders to capital based in the cities of Nazareth, Tiberias and Damascus, and to established middlemen in the towns of al-Husn and Suf, the town of Irbid gradually welcomed merchants, mainly from Damascus but also from Palestinian towns, who settled and provided credit to individual cultivators on a much smaller scale than the earlier patterns of finance. The development of this economic network appears closely intertwined with the administrative development of the state of property.

The third development was the appointment in 1897–98 of two employees for population registration (*nüfus*).[60] In general, in the province of Syria the putting into effect of population registration had long proved slow.[61] A full census of the population of the district was eventually to be effected only in 1910, when, in a manner parallel to the temporary assignment of specialised employees that we saw for property titles and then for tax, central support was accorded to the carrying out of population counts in the Hauran.[62] These lists were drawn up in collaboration with village *muhtars*. We shall return below to the centrality of this development for the form of government achieved in the district during the last years of the Empire.

The fourth development was the transformation of the civil court into a more professional institution. As we have seen, the court began as a council in which professional administrators, not necessarily professional jurists, joined with leaders of the region who served as elected members. The year 1882–83, we noted, marked the first appointment of a professional prosecutor, and 1891–92 saw a new term (*mülâzim*) indicating that the member of the court was an apprentice or supernumerary official.[63] In the last yearbook published for the province in 1900–1, all but one of the figures on the court appear with professional titles, although two described there as member prosecutors were again familiar figures from the district.[64] Formally, and perhaps effectively, we see here the movement of regional leadership into the professional administration through a process of apprenticeship and association with administrators appointed from outside. This coincided with the entry of the next generation into the new elementary schools being opened in the locality and the rapid expansion of higher-level schools in the provincial capital, Damascus.

The year 1900–1 marks the publication of the last *Yearbook of the Province*. After this date, we do not have comparable lists of offices and their holders in the district administration. But if we turn back to the form of the attestation to property title, we can sense how property lay at the centre of the transformation in the *personae* of political administration which I have summarised above. By the beginning of the twentieth century, the *tapu* scribe's tours of the villages ceased. Any person who wished to register a mutation of title had to go him/herself (or dispatch a legally empowered agent), bearing the title document or, in the case that it had been lost, a document from the village headman and village council confirming continuous cultivation of the land. In the case of an inheritance, the person required a document from these same village authorities attesting to the death. In the *tapu* register, we find two types of attestation. The first is that of two civil, often semi-professional, witnesses, certifying the identity of the person(s) initiating the mutation of title. In earlier registers, identification of the subject of a right had never invited such attention – indeed the simplicity of naming in the title records is generally astonishing, a personal name followed by father's personal name being the most common form – but now the subject required witnessing in a mixed form of local and yet formal legal knowledge.[65] This witnessing was followed by the attestation (by signature and seal) of the major administrative figures of the district: the *kaymakam*, the deputy *kaymakam*, the scribe of the tax office (*vergi kâtibi*) and the *tapu* scribe. The elected civil members of the administrative council no longer appear. The presence of the *kaymakam* still speaks of the political centrality of title, but otherwise, his deputy being *ex officio* the head of the Court of First Instance, the seals belonged to *personae* holding formal administrative offices concerned with title to property.

As noted above, a full census, or more exactly registration of population for a civil registry (*nüfus*), was effected in the district only in 1910. It is thus in the difficult years just before and throughout World War I that the *tapu* registers reveal a yet more complete administration of title. In these last years of the Empire – and indeed beyond, as the systems of local administration continued in force well into the Mandate period – when an individual having inherited land sought to effect the legal mutation of title to the heirs, usually when he/she sought to sell, gift or mortgage some part of the property – the following paperwork was required: the original title document or, if that was lost, a confirmation from the village council to the title, a document from the same council attesting to the death of the person and the date of the death, a document from the civil registry (*nüfus*) to the effect that the death had been duly entered with them and noting the relatives of the person in question, a statement from the Islamic court detailing the heirs and their shares in *mülk* and *miri* property respectively, and a document from the tax-collection department to the effect that all back taxes due on the property had been paid. All these documents were noted in the column of the *tapu* register concerning the origin of the property under mutation, but now only the *tapu* scribe needed to attest that the transfer respected legal procedure.

Conclusion

An impressive bureaucratic achievement: distinct administrative departments provided certification of the subject (*nüfus*), the object owned (*tapu*) and the state's tax claim on the object of ownership. Furthermore, the court defined succession to the office of owner and devolution of rights in property as part of its legal definition of the familial relations framing a deceased person. The state of property rested on the administrative elaboration of these distinctions, rendered tangible by the separate registers and procedures of the administrative departments concerned. That they all came together on the page of the title register reveals the centrality of property in their articulation.

This narrative history of administration, dense in detail, nevertheless demonstrates just how much political work was required for the construction of an administration that, in the intrusive manner of the modern state, could finally appear as merely rubber-stamping evidently distinct entities: person, property, family and tax.

The narrative has sought to take seriously the 'moment of mediation' in political administration by revealing property to be as much a part of the state, of relations between administrative *personae*, as of civil society and of relations between everyday persons in everyday villages. The notion of political administration adopted in this study harks back to classical nineteenth-century analyses of the modern state in which the distinction between state and civil society rested upon the identification of the latter with the society of property relations, a domain of contract between property holders – the good functioning of which the state assures through the rule of law.[66] In the Hegelian formulation, the state was hypothesised as law and the persons engaged in actual administration represented the 'universal estate' within the three estates of civil society. In the inversion effected by Marx, this administration became resolutely part of the state, itself a superstructural institution of a character that corresponds, in law and in administration, to the class rule of civil society arising from relations of production. Theoretical readings which, following Foucault, have sought to transcend the state–society distinction by analyses of discursive power and governmentality are simultaneously insightful yet problematic for the representation of agency and contradiction. The present analysis, concerned with the very construction of the property that forms the condition for civil society, has retained the notion of the state – not as a unity, but as formal rules and techniques of knowledge and enunciation in hierarchically ordered institutions composed of named legal *personae*. Thus, whereas institutions of the central Ottoman state, both the central bureaucracy and the rules of Tanzimat legislation, appear as if from on high, transcendent or super-structural in the language of Hegel or Marx, the local administration with which we have been concerned in this study appears as more evidently mediatory between the law and regulations sent down from the centre and the social dynamics, rules and idioms generated upwards, as it were, from the relations of production visible in the villages of the district. Hence the focus here has been on this site of mediation, the local administration, and on its transformation in the course of the gradual construction of a state of property. Through the mediation of political administration, a civil society of property owners is brought into being whose private entitlements appear technically and legally guaranteed by, but not in essence an inseparable part of, the public state.

Far from local political leaders being erased from this mediation, we have seen them transformed into formal professional administrators as part of the successful reordering of the relations of government around property. Indeed the condition of their mediation remained their ability to translate between two distinct fields or languages of right, that of village production, where they were still persons of prominence, and that of the administration, where they had become legal *personae* of government. The mediation is, however, not without contradiction. On one hand, certain of the rural leaders gradually lost their eminent places to figures who came to occupy the sites, clustered around the administrative centre of the *kazâ*, in the new market of the government of property. Yet these leaders did not vanish from political relations in their home regions, and at the end of Ottoman rule the figure of Kulaib Yusuf al-Sharaida, the brother of 'Abd al-Qadir, was to contest both the rule of Faisal in Damascus and then more famously British Mandate rule in Transjordan.[67] Nor did all village leaders take to heart the administrative form that they were meant to serve.[68] On the other hand, at a level less likely to enter a narrative history, the ambiguous mediatory site of village authority – particularly in this region where the translation of existing rights in the field of production into the legal terms of the Land Code took the form of registration of ownership in shares – was to reappear with clarity in the early Mandate years. Village leadership continued to mediate between government administrative form and the effective rights generated in production in the systems of open-field re-allotment agriculture practised in so many villages of the district. And so when British Mandate authority, armed with an ideological hostility to the regime that preceded it and with a century of dogmatic and practical commitment to fixed individual private property in land, proceeded to effect cadastral registration of land in villages of the district from the early 1930s, its officers turned to village authority in the definition of legal right, treating *tapu* title as valid but not as necessary evidence of right. Claiming that *tapu* registration did not define 'property' according to their understanding, the Mandate authorities once again invited village authority to define right. This time, however, marking the borders of each separate plot 'in steel' on the ground and on paper on the maps, they brought to an end that village 'estate of administration' which had survived under late-Ottoman rule less as an entitlement than as a moment of ambiguous mediation.

Notes

1 All terms of Ottoman administration and law are transcribed as in modern Turkish, in keeping with other articles in this volume. Place names, personal names and terms from documents in Arabic are transliterated following the IJMES system for Arabic, but without diacritical marks. Three forms of datation appear in the text. Gregorian Christian datation alone appears without further specification in the text, but in the footnotes in combination with other dates, it is indicated by 'AD'; the Islamic calendar is 'AH' and the Ottoman financial calendar is written in full.

2 The Jordanian research on which this chapter draws was conducted jointly with Richard Saumarez Smith while I was Research Fellow at the Institute of Archaeology and Anthropology of Yarmouk University, 1989–92. It was supported by grants from the Wenner Gren Foundation and the SSRC (New York), CERMOC and BIAAH (Amman), the British Academy (London), the Kerr Fellowship at the University of California (Los Angeles) and the CNRS and MRT (Paris/Lyon). The records that I consulted were kept by the Department of Lands and Surveys, the Civil Court and the Civil Registry in Irbid and, in the case of the Islamic Court records, by the Department of Historical Documents of the University of Jordan. My general understanding has also been enriched by work at the Asad Library and IFEAD (Damascus) and at the Başbakanlık Arşivi, Millet, Bayezit and Süleymaniye Libraries (Istanbul), supported by CAORC (Washington, DC) in 1997 and three months' sabbatical leave during summer term 1999 from the LSE. I am also grateful for comments on earlier versions of this argument when presented to the workshop section 'Norms and Oppositions' of the European Science Foundation programme on 'Individual and Society in the Mediterranean Muslim World' in Istanbul in July 1998, and to the Research Seminars of the Department of Social Anthropology at the University of Edinburgh, the Department of Anthropology at University College London and the Middle East Centre of the University of Cambridge, Autumn 1998. Lastly, I owe a debt to Richard Saumarez Smith, Alain Pottage, Albert Schrauwers, Engin Akarlı and Laurent Mignon for advice on style and content.

3 See the review of this literature in Hann, 1998.
4 My understanding of these issues is indebted to the work of Thomas, 1998.
5 The work of Alain Pottage forms an exception to this cursory generalisation; see his contribution to this volume.
6 In anthropology, this point has recently come to the fore in analyses of property restitution in the former socialist countries: see Verdery, 1996.
7 Reiterated in various forms throughout the important series of programmatic declarations in the Irâde-i Mesâ'il-i Mühimme series of the Başbakanlık Arşivi (hereafter BA) (particularly no 58 of 1261AH/1845AD); the central relation between the power of state and the secure wealth of individuals was also pronounced in the Gülhane Rescript.
8 Compare BA, Irâde-i Mesâ'il-i Mühimme no 78, dated 1261AH/1845AD, and the analysis of Huri İslamoğlu of Ottoman *temettuat* registration in this volume.
9 For the memoirs of this great man of state, see Cevdet Paşa, 1986. For his role in the discursive constitution of property rights in the Yanya province, see İslamoğlu, 2000.
10 '*... taşralarda arâzi-yi emiriyenin tefvîz ve ihâlesine mâl memûrlari yani defterdar ve mal müdürleri ve kazâ müdürleri mezûn olmalaryla bunlar sâhib-i arz hükmündedirler...*', *Düstur*, vol. 1, p. 200. (All subsequent references to volumes of the *Düstur*, the published compendium of laws and regulations of the central Tanzimat period, are to this same first arrangement.)
11 Young, 1905–6, vol. 6, p. 93, who reproduces the translation of Aristide.
12 In so doing, I do some violence to the original meaning of this term as it appears in Russian history. The term there refers to a local official post established in 1889 as part of reform measures to oversee issues related to land. See, for example, Pearson, 1989, p. 164. I am adapting the term here to express the political role of regional figures concerned with the administration of land and tax, and to avoid using the catch-all term 'notable' that is most common in the historiography of the Arab provinces.
13 Other terms used interchangeably with *sahib al-ard* in Arabic jurisprudence of the period are *mutakallim* and *sibahi*: see 'Abd al-Ghani al-Hanafi, ms. 4400; Ibn 'Abidin uses these three terms and *multazim* seemingly interchangeably: Ibn 'Abidin, 1280AH/1863–64AD, vol. 2, pp. 181–93.

14 For a study of such households in Northern Iraq during the period before the Tanzimat, see Khoury, 1997.

15 This term, like that of 'estate of production' used below, originated with Max Gluckman (1965, pp. 91–92), discussing levels of right in a rather different African context. The terms have earlier been adapted for the analysis of agricultural right in Palestine and North India. See Firestone, 1990, p. 115; Saumarez Smith, 1996, p. 41.

16 Cf. Ibn 'Abidin, *'Bab mashadd al-maska'*, 1280AH/1863–64AD, vol. 2, pp. 181–93.

17 Thus, in the high Ottoman period, agricultural land which was held as *mülk* had often entailed the payment of very little tax compared to the burdens on *miri* land. It was, in short, thought – or given the importance of real interests to the issue, we should perhaps say parties successfully claimed or imposed – that it stood outside the hierarchy of rights and servitudes framed by revenue obligations.

18 Clauses 91–102 and 130 of the Land Code, *Düstur*, vol. 1, pp. 188–91, 198.

19 Legislation dates from the 1870s and effective administration from the 1880s: *Düstur*, vol. 2, pp. 404–9; vol. 3, pp. 281–95.

20 Such were the principles as given in *Düstur*, vol. 2, 'Instructions Concerning the Correct Procedures for Title [*tapu*]', but in the statements drawn up by the *tapu* scribes of 'Ajlun, the documents were sometimes described as coming from the *lîvâ* and sometimes from the provincial headquarters.

21 This is the dominant formulation in the Code, but clause 131 on *çiftlik* marks something of an exception: Düstur, vol. 1, pp. 198–99.

22 Or at least this is true in theory and in the forms for registration, although in practice variable measures appear at times simply to have been translated into the new grid. See Mundy, 1992.

23 The relevant laws are published in *Düstur*, vol. 3, pp. 447–56.

24 Cf. on law as education, Cain, 1983.

25 The basic administrative programme is set forth in the Law of Vilayets, *Düstur*, vol. 1, pp. 608–24. In Mundy, 2000, through two case studies, I examine how the character of internal village forces marked the actual performance and *personae* of village administrative institutions.

26 Concerning the region in greater detail, see Mundy, 1994 and 1996.

27 Cf. Mundy, 1996, pp. 88–91 on the Bani Hasan.

28 Thus the Land Code permits *bi'l-istirâk-i tasarruf/al-tasarruf bi-'l-ishtirak*: see *Düstur*, vol. 1, pp. 168–69.

29 On the central Hauran, see Schilcher, 1981, 1991; Schäbler, 1996. For resistance to such acquisition in the *kazâ* of 'Ajlun, see Fischbach, 1994.

30 Compare, on Yanya province, İslamoğlu, 2000. The 1858 Land Code is explicitly phrased in terms of awarding right to cultivators. There is also evidence that this was policy among officials appointed from the centre at the Syrian provincial level. In correspondence with Istanbul, the governor writes of the dangers that could arise from cultivators losing rights to land through debt: BA, Şurâ-yi Devlet (henceforth ŞD), 2272\86.

31 That is, 1297 of the Ottoman financial calendar. See Mundy, 1992, pp. 226–27 for an earlier discussion of this document. The translation here is the more accurate.

32 The original document is in Department of Lands and Surveys, Irbid *tapu* registers, 1292–97 Ottoman financial calendar, *asas yoklama*, vol. 1, p. 153.

33 The term *nafar* may be used here to indicate only men, hence the lack of fit of the 13 names of whom one is a woman with the 12 *nafar* mentioned by the *tapu* scribe and the 13 mentioned by the regional authorities, when in fact 14 names appear.

34 *Salnâme-i Suriye*, x, 1295AH, p. 103; xi, 1296AH, p. 101; xii, 1297AH, p. 218.

35 *Düstur*, vol. 4, pp. 236–39.

36 I have termed these statements 'attestations', since when in certain cases their legal purpose is mentioned in the statements the term used is *tasdik*.

37 *Salnâme-i Suriye*, xii, 1297AH/1879–80AD, p. 218. On the Councils of the pre-Tanzimat nineteenth century, see Ortaylı, 1974.

38 *Salnâme-i Suriye*, ii, 1286AH/1869–70AD, p. 101.

39 This appears in BA, ŞD 2273/38.

40 I cannot identify this last person with certainty.

41 *Salnâme-i Suriye*, v, 1290AH/1873–74AD, p. 94; xi, 1296AH/1878–79AD, p. 104.

42 Salnâme-i Suriye, xiii, 1298AH/1880–81AD; xiv, 1299AH/1881–82AD, p. 193; xvii, 1302AH/1884–85AD, p. 183; xv, 1300AH/1882–83AD, p. 248.

43 *Salnâme-i Suriye*, xvi, 1301AH/1883–84AD, pp. 193–94.

44 One such person was Na'il al-Gharaiba from the neighbouring village of Hawwarah, who joined the municipal council for three years between 1885 and 1887 and who, later on, served on an educational commission established in 1894–95 and on the Board of the Agricultural Credit Bank in 1900. See *Salnâme-i Suriye*, xvii,

1302AH/1884–85AD, p. 185; xviii, 1303AH/1885–86AD, p. 173; xix, 1304AH/1886–87AD, p. 192; xx, 1305AH/1887–88AD, p. 123; xxvii, 1312–13AH/1895–96AD, p. 211 and *Suriye*, no 1785, 26 October 1316 Ottoman Financial Calendar/1900AD, p. 1. For a fuller discussion of this individual, see Mundy, 2000.

45 *Salnâme-i Suriye*, xvi, 1301AH/1883–84AD, p. 194.

46 In 1305AH/1887AD and 1306AH/1888AD, Husain Barakat was on the administrative council. In 1305AH/1887AD and 1306AH/1888AD, 'Abd al-Qadir Yusuf Sharaida was on the Court of First Instance; for the following two years, he served on the administrative council: *Salnâme-i Suriye*, xx, 1305AH/1887–88AD, p. 122; xxi, 1306AH/1888–89AD, p. 118; xxii, 1307AH/1889–90AD, p. 128.

47 *Salnâme-i Suriye*, xvii, 1302AH/1884–85AD, p. 185.

48 For example, Qasim Hijazi was himself elected to the administrative council in 1892–93: *Salnâme-i Suriye*, xxiv, 1309–10AH/1891–93AD, p. 189.

49 *Salnâme-i Suriye*, xviii, 1303AH/1885–86AD, p. 173. In 1307AH/1889–90AD, Jerash became the site of an honorary administrative director (*Salnâme-i Suriye*, xxii, p. 127) and in 1901 the Kura became an independent *nâhiye*. For the latter, *Salnâme-i Devlet* of 1319AH/1901–2AD, p. 525.

50 *Salnâme-i Suriye*, xx, 1305AH, pp. 122–23.

51 *Salnâme-i Suriye*, xxi, 1306AH/1888–89AD, p. 118–19.

52 *Salnâme-i Suriye*, xxi, 1306AH/1888–89AD, p. 118.

53 *Salnâme-i Suriye*, xxiv, 1309–10AH/1308 Ottoman financial calendar, p. 190.

54 *Salnâme-i Suriye*, xxv, 1310–11AH/1309 Ottoman financial calendar, p. 228; xxvi, 1311–12AH/1310 Ottoman financial calendar, p. 199.

55 *Salnâme-i Suriye*, xxviii, 1313–14AH/1312 Ottoman financial calendar, p. 197.

56 *Salnâme-i Suriye*, xxv, 1310–11AH/1309 Ottoman financial calendar, p. 228.

57 *Salnâme-i Suriye*, xxvii, 1312–13AH/1311 Ottoman financial Calendar, p. 21; the members included Yusuf al-Da'ud and Muflih al-Jabr of the 'Ubaidat from Hartha and Kufr Saum, Muhammad Shannaq of Saum al-Shannaq, Na'il al-Gharaiba of Hawwara, Muhammad al-Hamud of Aydun, 'Awwad al-Hijazi of Irbid and Ahmad al-Nu'man, whose origin I cannot identify.

58 *Salnâme-i Suriye*, xxviii, 1313–14AH/1312 Ottoman financial calendar, p. 198; xxix, 1313–14AH/1312 Ottoman financial calendar, p. 205.

59 *Salnâme-i Suriye*, xxviii, 1313–14AH/1312 Ottoman financial calendar, p. 198. A Sulaiman al-'Ali also served on the municipal council.
60 *Salnâme-i Suriye*, xxix, 1313–14AH/1312 Ottoman financial calendar, p. 204.
61 See BA, ŞD 2276\15, 2276\25, 2276\32, 2276\42.
62 See BA, DH.SN.THR, 1805 15\56, 2114 18\51, 3050 27\98.
63 *Salnâme-i Suriye*, xxii, 1306AH/1307 Ottoman financial calendar, p. 127 and xxiii, 1308–9AH/1307 Ottoman financial calendar, p. 128, where the *mülâzim* was Ibrahim Sa'd al-Din of the 'Ubaidat. In subsequent years, other major rural leaders served as *mülâzim.* In 1894–95, the number of *mülâzim* members was increased to two, with Yusuf al-Sharaida and Muflih ibn Jabr 'Ubaidat occupying the posts: *Salnâme-i Suriye*, xxvii, 1312–13AH/1311 Ottoman financial calendar, p. 211.
64 *Salnâme-i Suriye*, xxxii, 1318AH/1316–17 Ottoman financial calendar, p. 213.
65 The witnesses are described as *mu'arrif* and *şâhid* and their action as *tasdik.*
66 Cf. Neocleous, 1996.
67 See al-Madi and Musa, 1988, pp. 111–12, 156–64.
68 See Mundy, 2000 for a case history.

Bibliography

Abbreviations

BA: Başbakanlık Arşivi
DH.SN.THR: Dahiliye Nezareti Sicil-i Nüfus Tahrirat Kalemi
ŞD: Şurâ-yi Devlet

Unpublished primary sources

Damascus, Zahiriyya Library
'Abd al-Ghani al-Hanafi, Ubayd Allah, al-Nur al-badi fi ahkam al-aradi, 1211AH/1796AD, ms. 4400
Amman
Department of Lands and Surveys, Irbid tapu Registers, *asas yoklama* 1292–97 Ottoman financial calendar, vol. 1

Istanbul

Başbakanlık Arşivi, Şurâ-yi Devlet 2272\2286, 2273\38, 2276\15, 2276\25, 2276\32, 2276\42

Dahiliye Nezareti Sicil-i Nüfus Tahrirat Kalemi 1805 15\56, 2114 18\51, 3050 27\98

Irâde-i Mesâ'il-i Mühimme 58 and 78

Published primary sources

Düstur (1st printing), Istanbul, Matbaa-i Amire, 4 vols, 1289–96AH/ 1872–79AD.

Ibn 'Abidin, *al-'Uqud al-dhurriyya fi tanqih al-fatawa al-hamidiyya*, Bulaq, Dar al-Tiba'at al-Amira, 2 vols, 1280AH/1863–64AD.

Salnâme-i Devlet 1319AH/1901–2AD.

Salnâme-i Suriye: ii, 1286AH; v, 1290AH; x, 1295AH; xi, 1296AH; xii, 1297AH; xiii, 1298AH; xiv, 1299AH; xvii, 1302AH; xv, 1300AH; xvi, 1301AH; xvii, 1302AH; xviii, 1303AH; xix, 1304AH; xx, 1305AH; xxii, 1306AH; xxiii, 1308–09AH; xxiv, 1309–10AH; xxvii, 1312–13AH; xxviii, 1313–14AH; xxix, 1313–14AH; xxxii, 1318AH.

Suriye, no 1785, 26 October 1316 Ottoman financial calendar/1900AD.

Secondary sources

Cain, M., 'Gramsci, the State and the Place of Law', in D. Sugarman (ed.), *Legality, Ideology and the State*, London, Academic Press, 1983, pp.95–117.

Cevdet Paşa, *Tezâkir*, Ankara, Türk Tarih Kurumu Basimevi, 4 vols, 2nd edn, 1986.

Firestone, Ya'akov, 'The Land-Equalizing *Musha'* Village: A Reassessment', in Gad Gilbar (ed.), *Ottoman Palestine 1800–1914: Studies in Economic and Social History*, Leiden, E.J. Brill, 1990, pp.91–129.

Fischbach, Michael, 'Al-Mukhayba Village: A Tale of Shaykhs, Efendis, Peasants, and Land in TransJordan', *Dirasat* 21/1, 1994, pp.46–71.

Hann, C.M. (ed.), *Property Relations: Renewing the Anthropological Tradition*, Cambridge, Cambridge University Press, 1998.

Gluckman, Max, *The Ideas of Barotse Jurisprudence*, New Haven, Yale University Press, 1965.

İslamoğlu, Huri, 'Property as a Contested Domain: A Reevaluation of the Ottoman Land Code of 1858', in Roger Owen (ed.), *New*

Perspectives on Property and Land in the Middle East, Cambridge, MA, Harvard University Press, 2000, pp. 3–61.
Khoury, Dina Rizk, *State and Provincial Society in the Ottoman Empire: Mosul, 1540–1834*, Cambridge, Cambridge University Press, 1997.
al-Madi, M. and S. Musa, *Ta'rikh al-Urdun fi-'l-qarn al-'ishrin (1900–1959)*, 1st edn, 1959, Amman, Maktabat al-Muhtasib, 2nd edn, 1988.
Mundy, Martha, 'Shareholders and the State: Representing the Village in the Late Nineteenth Century Land Registers of the Southern Hawran', in T. Philipp (ed.), *The Syrian Land in the Eighteenth and Nineteenth Centuries*, Stuttgart, Franz Steiner Verlag, 1992, pp. 217–38.
– 'Village Land and Individual Title: *Musha'* and Ottoman Land Registration in the 'Ajlun District', in Eugene L. Rogan and Tariq Tell (eds), *Village, Steppe and State: The Social Origins of Modern Jordan*, London, British Academic Press, 1994, pp. 58–79.
– 'Qada' 'Ajlun in the Late Nineteenth Century: Interpreting a Region from the Ottoman Land Registers', *Levant* 28, 1996, pp. 79–97.
– 'Village Authority and the Legal Order of Property (the Southern Hawran, 1876–1922)', in Roger Owen (ed.), *New Perspectives on Property and Land in the Middle East*, Cambridge, MA, Harvard University Press, 2000, pp. 63–92.
Neocleous, M., *Administering Civil Society: Towards a Theory of State Power*, London, Macmillan, 1996.
Ortaylı, Ilber, *Tanzimattan sonra mahalli idareler (1840–1878)*, Ankara, Sevinç Matbaası, 1974.
Pearson, T.S., *Russian Officialdom in Crisis: Autocracy and Local Self-Government, 1861–1900*, Cambridge, Cambridge University Press, 1989.
Saumarez Smith, Richard, *Rule by Records: Land Registration and Village Custom in Early British Panjab*, Delhi, Oxford University Press, 1996.
Schäbler, Birgit, *Aufstände im Drusenbergland: Ethnizität und Integration einer ländlichen Gesellschaft Syriens vom Osmanischen Reich bis zur staatlichen Unabhängigkeit, 1850–1949*, Gotha, Justus Perthes Verlag, 1996.
Schilcher, Linda S., 'The Hauran Conflicts of the 1860s: A Chapter in the Rural History of Modern Syria', *International Journal of Middle East Studies* 13, 1981, pp. 159–79.
– 'Violence in Rural Syria in the 1880s and 1890s: State Centralization, Rural Integration, and the World Market', in F. Kazemi and J. Waterbury (eds), *Peasants and Politics in the Modern Middle East*, Miami, Florida International University Press, 1991, pp. 50–84.
Thomas, Yan, 'Le Sujet de Droit, la Personne et la Nature', *Le Débat*, 100, 1998, pp. 85–107.

Verdery, K., *What was Socialism and What Comes Next?*, Princeton, Princeton University Press, 1996, pp. 133–67.

Young, George, *Corps de Droit Ottoman: Receuil des Codes, Lois, Règlements, Ordonnances et Actes les plus Importants de Droit Intérieur, et d'Etudes sur le Droit Coutumier de l'Empire Ottoman*, Oxford, Clarendon Press, 7 vols, 1905–6.

CHAPTER 8

Negotiation of Property Rights in Urban Land in Istanbul[1]

Elvan Gülöksüz

This chapter addresses the process through which private property in urban land, and the nature of its component rights, are formed. The main argument is that this process is political, in that conflicts among actors, notably between those excluded from and included in property ownership and between private and public interests in the definition of property rights, shape the outcome. These conflicts are intensified by the substantial income to be obtained from urban land transactions. The work also examines the nature of the relationship between state law and property-based social relations unfolding in the process of the formation of private property in urban land.

This study is based on research on the evolution of property rights in two districts in the city of Istanbul: Kazım Karabekir and Yukarı Dudullu. The two districts developed in the 1970s on two farm estates, the Hekimbaşı and Şerif Ali, which in the early twentieth century were located on the periphery of the city. Throughout their development, land in both districts was subject to multiple claims of ownership and conflicting interests concerned with qualifications of property ownership, particularly public interest in environmental conservation and private interests in land rent appropriation. A second common feature of the two districts is that both were designated 'illegal' because their development did not conform to urban planning and/or property legislation. The research covers a 125-year period, starting from 1874, when land on the two estates began to be registered as 'private property', and examines changes in laws defining property rights over time, transfers of property in the two farm estates, and the conflicts among the various actors over property rights or ownership.

In the next section, the main arguments of the chapter are formulated. This is followed by a brief description of the broader context within which research areas evolved, a note on research methodology, the presentation of the findings of the research and, finally, the conclusion.

The theoretical context

The relationship between state law and property-based social relations in the so-called 'illegal' settlements has been addressed by many scholars.[2] Common to all of these researchers is criticism of the legalistic centrist perception of society in which law and social relations mirror each other so that illegal urban settlements are seen as violations of the legitimate property-rights system established by state law. Many of these scholars hold that property-based social relations in these settlements stem from the strategies of low-income groups for survival within the larger society and, further, that governments regard these settlements as a means of solving housing problems of the urban poor, and thus tend to tolerate them.

There are, nevertheless, differing views on the nature of the relationship between state law and property-based social relations. Razzaz,[3] for example, defines this relationship as one of legal plurality. He contends that there is a plurality of property claims established by a plurality of legitimate institutions, within which property rights enforced by the state are only a subset. Each group constitutes a 'semi-autonomous social field' that possesses its own rule-making capacity while remaining at the same time subject to the effects of surrounding social fields. The process of mutual adjustment continuously redefines both sides. However, this view underestimates the capacity of the modern state to regulate social activity by reducing the relationship between rule-making practices of the state and those of other social fields to a mutual interaction among equals. Santos[4] similarly separates state law and local legal systems, but unlike Razzaz he regards the relationship between the two as one of domination and subordination. State law remains the dominant legal system in society, and strategies in illegal settlements are shaped as a response to it. One reaction to state law is developing adaptive strategies against it. Such strategies can constitute selective borrowing from the official legal system and inverting the substance of state law while adhering to its forms and procedures. While Santos's analysis of such adaptive strategies can explain data about illegal settlements in Turkey, this work will argue against his view of the legal plurality involved in the two legal systems as thus defined.

Azuela[5] departs from a conception of legal plurality, and argues that illegal settlement processes are conditioned by state law. He proposes the concept of 'forms of legitimation' to refer to the series of social representations related to the control of land in particular situations. The forms of legitimation may contravene or substitute state law. However, they cannot be entirely independent of the overall legal system, since they have to convince the settlers and/or the authorities that the control exerted over land is legitimate under state law. Those who control land do this by incorporating certain aspects of state law into their practices, that is they use regulations selectively, redefine or re-interpret regulations in particular situations, or utilise loopholes or inconsistencies in the law. For Azuela, this fact, also noted by Santos, points to a compromise between state law and the different forms of legitimation which leads to changes in both.

Examining the transformation of land rights in the Ottoman Empire in the nineteenth century, İslamoğlu[6] develops a somewhat similar outlook to the relationship between state law and property relations to that of Azuela. She points to the constitutive role of the state in the establishment of private property and the fact that new laws aimed at establishing private property in the mid-nineteenth century were resisted by those who lost their former property rights as a result of the claims of private ownership. Resistance to changes in property rights, however, was expressed in the context and vocabulary of the very law that initiated the changes. That is the new property laws formed the sites of resistance and spaces in which social actors confronted each other over property rights. The terms of laws themselves, on the other hand, reflected the nature of these conflicts. İslamoğlu notes, for example, how the text of the new Land Code of 1858 carried the stamp of these conflicts and how special regulations were issued during its implementation in different regions. İslamoğlu's conception of the definitions of property rights as domains of resistance and contestation, imparting to these rights their highly contingent political and historical character (reflected in the fluidity of property relations), is central to this study. Besides subscribing to Azuela's outlook, the arguments presented here are based primarily on İslamoğlu's analysis.

This chapter has four objectives. The first is to show how the high revenues obtained from urban land transactions intensified confrontations among actors who claimed property ownership or who sought to improve their property rights at the expense of others. The second is to show that these confrontations took place within the context of property and urban planning laws, that is the terms and vocabulary of relevant laws determined the terms and vocabulary of property rights and ownership in the settlements. Thus, as both Santos and Azuela note, local actors set out to negotiate laws so that their activities would conform to the legal definitions of the state to the greatest extent possible. Third, this work aims to demonstrate that outcomes of local struggles were reflected in relevant laws when wide acceptance of local formulations forced the state to seek a compromise. Last, it examines the attitudes of the many state agencies involved in the process of private-property formation on urban land, and thus illustrates the non-monolithic structure of the state.

Development of the context

The Hekimbaşı and Şerif Ali Estates were registered as private property after 1874 according to the reformed Ottoman property legislation[7] aimed at transforming the definition of property as a bundle of rights over revenue, use and title of land into a single individual right of ownership. The Turkish Republic, successor to the Ottoman state after 1923, did not alter the basic principles of the property regime established by the late Ottoman state, but instead improved its technical apparatus so that property registered according to Ottoman legislation (which provided title deeds for an imprecisely defined piece of land) had to be re-registered after the revolution according to the legislation of the Republic. This legislation introduced cadastral surveying in the form of a forest cadastre carried out by the Ministry of Forests on forested lands and an urban cadastre carried out by the Department of Land Registry and Cadastre on all other lands. The Hekimbaşı Estate, covering an area of approximately 1800 hectares, was surveyed as part of the forest cadastre in 1940 and re-registered in the name of the Treasury of the Republic in 1943. The Şerif Ali Estate, approximately 900 hectares, was surveyed as part of the urban cadastre in 1953 and was re-registered in the name of the individual who owned the Ottoman title deeds at that time. After their re-registration by the institutions of the Turkish Republic, the Ottoman title deeds were deemed to have lost their validity.

Urbanisation within the boundaries of the two estates began in the 1960s. The legal status of the two estates, however, was different. Kazım Karabekir[8] developed within the borders of the Hekimbaşı Estate, which at the time belonged to the Treasury. Thus, the dwellings in this district conformed to neither property nor urban planning legislation. Part of Yukarı Dudullu, on the other hand, developed within the boundaries of the Şerif Ali Estate, which was privately owned. In this respect, the dwellings conformed to property legislation, although they were still illegal, as they contravened urban planning legislation. The former type of dwelling unit was called *gecekondu*, a Turkish word meaning 'landed overnight', and the latter an unauthorised building.

Kazım Karabekir and Yukarı Dudullu developed within the context of rapid urban population growth stemming from massive immigration from the rural areas to the cities. The population growth rate of the city of Istanbul, in particular, was very high, reaching its peak between 1965 and 1970 at 5.5 per cent.[9] Similarly, the Ümraniye region, of which the two research districts were part, experienced rapid population growth after 1970, due to an industrial area centred in the Dudullu Industrial Estate established in the 1970s, and in the 1980s the construction of the trans-European motorway which passes through the region. From the 1970s on, Ümraniye remained one of the major industrial regions in Istanbul and the home of immigrants from many regions of Turkey.[10] Although initially located on the periphery of the city, Ümraniye was rapidly enclosed, during the 1980s, within the expanding city boundaries. The growth of Istanbul and the location of the two estates within the city are shown in Figure 2.

The illegal housing built in Kazım Karabekir and Yukarı Dudullu were instances of the widespread self-help strategies of immigrants in the industrialised cities of Turkey after the late 1940s. As many scholars such as Öncü,[11] Şenyapılı,[12] Tekeli,[13] Buğra[14] and Yönder[15] agree, the construction of *gecekondus* and unauthorised buildings was a spontaneous response to the need for low-income housing in the face of the inability of the prevailing property and urban-planning regulations or housing policies to meet this need. The same researchers also agree, however, that soon after the beginning of *gecekondu* and unauthorised building construction the motivation of appropriating land rent was added to the motivation of acquiring shelter in

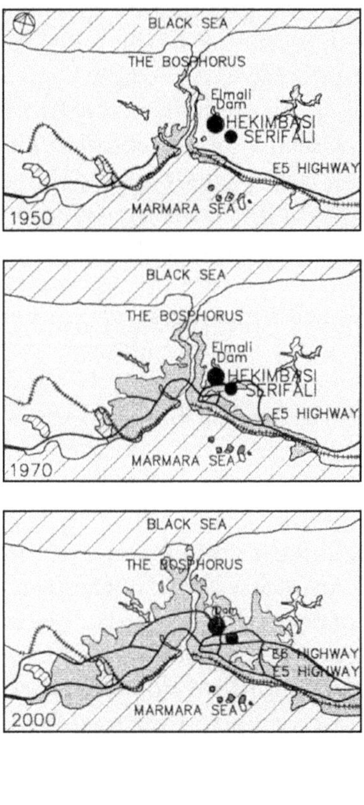

Figure 2
The growth of Istanbul

the city, so that the illegal land market was soon commercialised, creating its own agents and institutionalised practices.[16] The transformation of the self-help process into rent-seeking activity took place in the context of sharply increasing land rents in the cities as a result of rapid growth of demand for urban land and the rapid expansion of cities, changing the relative location of communities in the space of a few years. Rent-seeking was also triggered by the fact that an inflationary economy and a weak and undifferentiated financial sector made land rent a major channel of accumulation for a wide section of the society until the 1980s.[17]

The government's response towards this mode of housing provision was two-fold. On one hand, they were aware of its problem-solving capacity in the context of the general economy, where resources were scarce and cheap labour was required by the industrial sector, promoted by state macroeconomic policies.[18] The illegal mode of housing provision reduced the cost of the reproduction of labour, reducing wages. Moreover, the large electoral base formed by the inhabitants of such housing, coupled with the patron–client nature of the political system in Turkey and the lack of government resources that could be used as redistributive means[19] made both central and local governments sensitive to the demands of the populations of such settlements. Thus, successive governments tolerated these widespread activities by neglecting to implement the relevant legislation and periodically issuing amnesty laws. Between 1948 and 1984, 10 laws that included amnesty clauses for *gecekondus* and/or unauthorised buildings in specific geographical regions were issued.[20] The regularisation of illegal settlements entered a new phase in 1984 when the neo-liberal government of the time introduced an Amnesty Law (No 2981) as a redistributive measure in the face of the sharp decline in wages caused by the structural adjustment programmes at the beginning of the 1980s. This law extended amnesty to all buildings not conforming to the Development Law instead of restricting the amnesty only to the dwellings built on state land, as in previous laws. In addition, existing buildings were not only legalised, but were also given further construction rights by means of regularisation plans that provided title deeds for existing unofficial housing stock and granted the right of construction of up to four storeys in each building. Regularisation plans were prepared for the Kazım Karabekir and Yukarı Dudullu districts in the late 1980s.

The government's second approach was an effort to find 'official' solutions to the problem of low-income housing and to prevent the expansion of *gecekondu* zones. Many legal, institutional and financial policy tools were utilised to this end.[21] However, in spite of substantial achievements, in general these measures proved inadequate to solve the housing problem through official means. Supported by the regularisation schemes and the large income generated from land transactions, the illegal housing market remained an important means of housing provision.

Note on methodology

This study makes use primarily of relevant court cases, which provide two sets of information: information on property transfers and information on conflicts over property resolved in or outside the courts. These court reports, including expert testimonies, reports submitted to court by the disputing parties, and court judgements, provide a great deal of information on the history of the areas and the conflicts that arose there. Land registry documents, notary contracts of property transactions, urban plans and planning reports, municipal council decisions, correspondence between various state bodies, signed proceedings of the Ministry of Forests, and monographs prepared for nearby villages at various times provided further data. The research also made use of interviews with three municipal bureaucrats, one bureaucrat in each of the local branches of the Ministry of Forests, the state Treasury and the Department of Land Registry and Cadastre, as well as the headman of a nearby village.

The Hekimbaşı Estate

The Hekimbaşı Estate was registered after 1874 in the name of a member of the Ottoman royal family. The farm estate provided its owner with agricultural revenue until the late

1940s, when the early phases of massive rural immigration to the city of Istanbul and the parallel need for residential land made the prospects of much greater revenue from sale of the Hekimbaşı Estate in the form of urban subdivisions very appealing. The value of the estate as prospective urban land intensified the conflicts among several actors over ownership.

The seven heirs of the last individual landowner and the state agencies that took over the estate after the republican revolution, including the state Treasury, which owned the land, and the Ministry of Forests, which had jurisdiction over the forest, came into conflict over the ownership of the estate. Numerous *gecekondu* dwellers and a private firm became part of the conflict after the 1960s, as they bought land lots from the holders of the Ottoman titles. The conflict over the property was played out, first, in numerous court cases starting in 1940 and, second, through *gecekondu* construction in the Hekimbaşı Estate, which enhanced the *gecekondu* dwellers' power within the struggle. In the courts, land disputes were settled in accordance with the forms and procedures defining property. The changing laws, as well as the numerous past court decisions or other official statements on the legal status of the land, provided parties with tools for defending their claims. Throughout the 125-year period following the registration of the Hekimbaşı Estate, the context of the struggle for property rights changed a number of times, each change leading to the redefinition of the owner of the estate and the nature of the rights attached to ownership.

Some exclusions from property ownership

The republican revolution in 1923 exerted a substantial impact on the legal status of the Hekimbaşı Estate. A law issued in 1924 (No 431) excluded members of the royal family from the right to property ownership and transferred all their property to the treasury of the newly founded Republic. This law was implemented in the Hekimbaşı Estate in 1940, when the forest cadastre placed the estate within the jurisdiction of the Ministry of Forests, classified it as 'state forest' and registered it in the name of the state Treasury in 1943.[22]

The former owners of the estate, excluded from property ownership with their Ottoman title deeds cancelled, and deprived of the prospects of revenue from urban land transactions, actively contested these practices. They sued the Ministry of Forests in 1940[23] and the Treasury in 1944.[24] The decisions of the courts in both these cases were in favour of the suers, and the estate was re-registered in their names in 1946.[25] However, neither of these court decisions constituted a final resolution to the dispute, as the promulgation of a new law soon changed the definition of property once more.

The Nationalisation of Forests Act, and redefinition of property

The 1945 Nationalisation of Forests Act (Law No 4785) and its implementation in Hekimbaşı in 1947 re-defined property in the estate. The Hekimbaşı forest was registered in the name of the state Treasury for the second time, and this halted the dispute until 1950, when another two pieces of legislation were introduced, one providing for the exclusion of some types of forests from the jurisdiction of the Ministry of Forests (No 5653), the other providing for the return of nationalised forests of certain kinds to their previous owners (No 5658). These laws created a situation in which two previous landowners were able to bring a court case against the Treasury to have the nationalised forest area returned to them.[26] However, in 1978, the court rejected their claim[27] and the land remained in the hands of the Treasury.

Massive immigration to the city and change in land use

In the 1960s, the rapidly growing need for urban land was causing sharp increases in land rents in the city, and consequently the individual claimants to the Hekimbaşı Estate sought to sell the land in the form of urban subdivisions. However, despite their attempts to re-establish their ownership rights, the title of the estate still resided with the Treasury. Their response now was to sell the land to immigrants to the city while at the same time pursuing their title claims in the courts. Through these technically illegal sales, almost half the Hekimbaşı forest was first carved out by cultivators in the 1960s and then developed into an urban district in the 1970s.

The events in the Hekimbaşı Estate area during the 1960s and 1970s were shaped by two contradictory elements: the laws regulating property and urban development, to which individuals chose to conform, versus the desire of immigrants to buy land at low cost, and that of sellers to receive profits from land sales. Although the immigrants who acquired their land through unofficial sales were able to enjoy security of tenure and to benefit from various state investments without titles to land due to the clientalistic policies of governments in such types of urban settlements, they could not enjoy the fundamental advantage of state-defined private property: high land values accruing to 'owned land' as opposed to 'possessed land'. Owned land was clearly more desirable, since official title to land was a prerequisite for urban planning which, in turn, raised land values. Thus, the settlers in Hekimbaşı sought to acquire land in such a way as to enable them to sell it for profit.

The contradictory desires of actors in Hekimbaşı were resolved through the negotiation of laws in such a way as to enable actors to attain both. This negotiation was reflected in the way that all property transactions, including land sales and patterns of subdivision, were conducted as far as possible within the parameters of state laws. For example, transactions were made through notary contracts, so that sales would conform to official procedures. However, given the fact that the land was registered in the name of the Treasury, these transfers held no official status and were not declared in the Land Registry. These sales were made on the basis of the buyers' expectations of future legalisation, either through the sellers having their property title re-established as a result of their on-going court actions or through the declaration of a general amnesty for *gecekondus*. Thus, the presence of Ottoman title deeds attributed legitimacy to the sales and actually increased the probability of legalisation in the future. In fact, once the previous owners' title to property was re-established in courts, these contracts were accepted as valid documents and formed the basis of land registration. Another strategy that the settlers used to conform to legal forms was payment of real estate taxes for land to which they had no official title. Similar to the notary contracts, official documents demonstrating the payment of real-estate taxes provided the basis for property claims in the courts during the 1980s.

The legal status of the settlement in Hekimbaşı was also bolstered by the involvement of some local state agencies in development activities. For example, the neighbourhood authority of the central state (*muhtarlık*) was obliged to register new settlers as inhabitants of its territories no matter what the legal status of their dwellings. Moreover, the municipality, which was responsible for providing urban services only to legal settlements, always provided these services to illegal areas also. Various central state bodies also addressed the situation, albeit in different ways. The Treasury, which owned the land, and the Ministry of Forests, which had jurisdiction over the forest, both turned a blind eye to illegal settlement activities, despite the fact that they continued to claim ownership of the land in the courts. There were several reasons for this attitude. First, the bodies were not equipped with sufficient legal and technical tools to cope with the scale of illegal settlement. Second, their somewhat ambiguous approach to the problem was supported by governmental policies. The ministry responsible for regulating urban development was only to a limited extent capable of finding alternative solutions to the need for low-income housing. Parliamentarians and successive governments regarded the development of these settlements as a means of transferring resources to the weaker sections of society and thus gaining electoral support. It was in these circumstances that expectations of an amnesty and legalisation of the settlement in Hekimbaşı came to a peak during the 1970s.

Modification in the Law of Forests and redefinition of forest boundaries

In 1972, the first step towards legalisation of the Hekimbaşı settlement came from the Ministry of Forests, which enacted laws that excluded those parts of the forests that had already been destroyed from its jurisdiction (No 1744 and 3302). These laws reflected a major compromise by Parliament with the highly populated *gecekondu* settlements built on forested land adjacent to cities. Exclusion of this land from the jurisdiction of the Ministry of Forests meant that the area became subject to regulations governing urban areas. This change in the legal status of the land ruled out intervention by the Ministry of Forests, and thus a major tool that the Treasury could utilise in its ownership claims in the courts was rendered ineffective. In this sense, this act was a turning point in the redefinition of property in the Hekimbaşı Estate. The Commission for Forest Cadastre of the Ministry of Forests started work in Hekimbaşı in 1975 with the aim of establishing new forest boundaries in compliance with the requirements of the new law.

This commission excluded some parts of Hekimbaşı from forest jurisdiction, while other parts remained as state forest. The areas excluded from forest jurisdiction were submitted to an 'urban cadastre' procedure by the local branch of the Department of Land Registry and Cadastre. The commission, working under this department, re-registered the larger portion of the land excluded from forest jurisdiction in the name of the Treasury and registered the smaller remaining portion in the name of the *gecekondu* dwellers. The reports of the subsequent court decisions indicate that these *gecekondu* dwellers acquired property rights as a result of official acknowledgement of the ownership rights of the holders of the Ottoman titles from whom they had bought land by means of notary contracts. Hence, once this part of the Hekimbaşı Estate was excluded from the forest boundaries, removing the grounds for the nationalisation of the area, it was *de facto* returned to its owners prior to the Nationalisation of Forests Act. Registration of part of the land in the name of the *gecekondu* dwellers also constituted recognition of the fact that the notary contracts, which were once legally invalid as they were not based on titles to land, were now acceptable as valid documents for proving ownership rights.

The new scheme of property ownership in the Hekimbaşı area put in place by the change in the legal definition of forests marked only a temporary settlement of the problem, and triggered a new phase of confrontations over property rights. Parties excluded from property ownership as a result of the forest and urban cadastres of the late 1970s contested their exclusion in a vast number of court appeals. Similar to the court cases of the 1940s and 1950s, property was again negotiated within the terms of the law, its procedures and past official decisions. However, there was much confusion over the sequence and/or validity of the court decisions and cadastral applications dating back to the 1940s, which provided the parties with grounds for the defence of their claims. For example, in 94 cases finalised in 1978[28] in which the Treasury had contested the registration of 6 hectares of land in the names of the *gecekondu* settlers, the major consideration pertained to who owned the land before the Nationalisation of Forests Act. The court examined the evidence and decided that it had belonged to the holders of the Ottoman titles from whom the *gecekondu* dwellers had bought lots, and thus rejected all the cases brought by the Treasury. On the other hand, in a court case in 1982[29] brought by the holders of the Ottoman titles and a private firm (who had bought the land from them by means of a notary contract in 1975) involving 260 hectares of land registered as state forest, the suers claimed that the area was already excluded from the forest boundaries in 1954 by the Commission for Separating Areas Covered with Maquis according to a law enacted in 1950 and that, consequently, the forest cadastre of the late 1970s was unlawful. In 1989, the court declared that the case lay outside its jurisdiction. Another case brought by the Treasury concerning the same piece of land was still in court in 2000.[30]

The *gecekondu* dwellers who established their title to land as a result of the urban cadastre anticipated the extension of urban planning to these areas, so that they could have their plots transformed into urban property, thus commanding significantly higher rents than building subdivisions that did not conform to an urban plan. On the other hand, the *gecekondu* dwellers who still possessed Treasury land hoped for the finalisation of the relevant court case.

An amnesty law and regularisation practices

Legislative reforms during the 1980s opened the way for regularisation of urban settlements in Hekimbaşı. The Ümraniye District Municipality prepared regularisation plans for Hekimbaşı (1987) and Kazım Karabekir (1989), according to which individual building plots were to be registered and construction rights granted. The major obstacle for the implementation of these plans was the 260 hectares of land still under dispute in court. The building densities mandated by the plans constituted another domain of conflict with the *gecekondu* dwellers, who protested that the permitted densities were too low. As a result, the municipality revised the plans several times, allowing higher densities, each revision representing a new negotiated settlement. The Kazım Karabekir Regularisation Plan was revised in 1991, introducing an increase in the permitted number of floors per building, and the Hekimbaşı Master Plan of 1988 was revised in 1992, introducing an increase in the target population stipulated in the original plan. It should be noted that the struggle of property owners for higher densities demonstrated a departure from the conceptualisation of *gecekondus* as shelter, and their re-conceptualisation as income-generating investments. In 2000, the implementation of these plans was still suspended as problems with property titles persisted.

As can be seen from this outline of the process through which property rights in the Hekimbaşı Estate evolved over 125 years, negotiated settlements have been contested many times by various actors claiming property rights against a background context constantly altered by changes in laws or land use. The following case study of the Şerif Ali Estate highlights the fluid nature of property rights by focusing on the confrontations among multiple claimants of ownership, all private individuals (as opposed to Hekimbaşı, where confrontations occurred between public bodies and private individuals). It also illustrates conflicts between public interest in environmental conservation and private interest in land rent appropriation which arose after regularisation of the district.

The Şerif Ali Estate

The Şerif Ali Estate[31] was registered under 38 title deeds, most of which were issued in 1875. These title deeds were transferred as a package through sales or inheritance until 1941, when a transfer left one title deed in separate hands. The land was used for agricultural purposes until the 1950s. However, in 1950 an individual bought the estate in anticipation of urban development in the area and the potential rise in the value of the land. Immediately after he bought the land, he launched efforts to convert the estate into land ready for urban development, hoping to make significant profits. The first step was the cadastral registration of the land according to the property legislation of the Republic.

Efforts to enlarge the property

The report from a court case in 1976 clearly shows how the buyer of the Şerif Ali Estate in 1950 managed to enlarge his property by manipulating the new legal framework and exploiting the vagueness in the property definition of the Ottoman period. Having bought 37 title deeds amounting to one-third of the Şerif Ali Estate, he was aware that the remaining part of the estate (the thirty-eighth title deed) had not been registered according to the new legislation, which meant that it was not currently officially recognised. Moreover, in the title deeds issued by the Ottoman state, the borders of the estate were defined in imprecise ways (for example according to locations of bushes), almost allowing the landowner the liberty to determine the borders of his property himself. New legislation provided the landowner with the freedom to register his property through local courts, which focused on their particular cases only, rather than through the Department of Land Registry and Cadastre, responsible for the whole country. In this context, in 1953 the landowner went to a local court,[32] which combined 33 of the title deeds and subdivided this block into 830 cadastral plots, effectively enlarging the total area covered by the original title deeds from 225 to 400 hectares. The court refused to take action on the remaining four title deeds because of the existence of a registered shareholder not known to anyone.

The cadastral allotment of the land, however, still did not allow the sale of land to individuals intending to settle there. Such sales required that the large cadastral parcels be subdivided into small individual plots. Officially, this subdivision had to be carried out by means of urban planning, the responsibility of the Ministry of Redevelopment and Resettlement at that time. The owner of the Şerif Ali Estate, however, subdivided the land himself. As this subdivision had no legal grounds, the sale of subdivisions officially referred to shares of the entire cadastral plots instead of an identified building plot. This activity conformed to the legislation on property rights, which permitted shared ownership on cadastral plots. It did not, however, conform to urban planning legislation.[33]

After 1953, thousands of subdivisions were sold to individuals, and the subsequent development during the 1960s and 1970s formed part of the Yukarı Dudullu district. During these years, the Şerif Ali Estate remained one of the few places in the district which had been subject to cadastral registration.

New claims of ownership and negotiation of property in court

It was only in 1973 that the local branch of the Department of Land Registry and Cadastre submitted the environs of the Şerif Ali Estate to cadastral registration. During this procedure, the department confirmed the previous registration of the Şerif Ali area by the local court in 1953, and extended its jurisdiction to the four title deeds on which that court had refused judgement. At this decisive moment, the owners of the thirty-eighth title deed, registered in 1876 and originating from the same line of transfers as the other 37, claimed ownership rights to the Şerif Ali Estate. The land area designated in this title deed was almost twice as large as the total area covered by the other 37. Its owners claimed that the title deeds were duplicated and theirs was the only legally acceptable one. This was the first time that property rights in the Şerif Ali Estate had been contested.

These claims led to a court case lasting 14 years, from 1976 until 1990. The court was responsible for determining the owners, the exact borders and the total area designated by the title deeds, and for deciding which of the title deeds was legally acceptable. The court eventually decided that the title deeds were not duplicated but instead were complementary. Hence, the Şerif Ali Estate was not held in 37 title deeds but in 38, the thirty-eighth comprising 68 per cent of the estate's total area. This meant that of the area sold by the speculative landowner to thousands of people in the 1950s, 68 per cent belonged to a third party which had only recently claimed rights of ownership.

In the face of this new situation, the court made two decisions. It confirmed the 1973 registration of the 33 title deeds, to which no objections had been made within the official period assigned. By doing so, it narrowed the basis of its decision-making to procedural fact rather than to a substantive legitimacy argument. It registered 55 per cent of the remaining land – covering the four title deeds on which the 1953 court had refused to make a judgement – in the names of the owners of the thirty-eighth title deed. Thus, for an area of about 150 hectares, property rights that had been held for more than 30 years were re-established.[34]

At the same time that the legal battle over property ownership was being fought, property rights in the area were being contested in another domain: institutions representing public interests as opposed to the private interests of property owners. This conflict intensified at the urban planning stage.

Regularisation and conflict between public and private interests

During the 1980s, inhabitants of the Yukarı Dudullu district sought ways to have their settlement regularised, giving rise to conflict with public institutions seeking to protect the water catchment area of the Elmalı Dam located in the vicinity. While various departments of the Greater City Municipality of Istanbul, as well as the Istanbul Chamber of Architects, fought to minimise further urban development in the Dudullu area, the Ümraniye District Municipality in charge of urban planning in the area and sensitive to pressures from the voting population, aimed to satisfy the demands of property owners by manipulating urban planning laws.

At first, the Ümraniye Municipality tried to plan the area without infringing upon the Development Law (No 3194) which required that the area be developed in accordance with a *development plan* conforming to a higher-rank *master plan*. However, the existence of a settlement in the area created obstacles to conformance because land use designations of the master plan required that part of the settlement be demolished. In 1989, the municipality tried to resolve this difficulty by proposing a modification to a clause in the master plan which prohibited implementation of local plans, a legal tool allowing the planning of small parts of larger zones not to conform with the macro-level plan.[35] The Greater City Municipality rejected this proposal, mainly on the grounds that such a change would render the whole master plan unimplementable.[36]

Consequently, the district municipality gave up its efforts to solve the problem within the parameters of the Development Law, and prepared a 'regularisation plan' according to the Amnesty Law, which provided for the preparation and implementation of the regularisation plans by district municipalities independent of the control of the Greater City Municipality. In fact, this provision offered a loophole in urban planning legislation widely used by district municipalities to evade the control of the Greater City. However, the regularisation plan of 1989 faced renewed opposition, this time from the Istanbul Chamber of Architects, which was concerned that overcrowding in the Dudullu district would damage the Elmalı Dam.

In 1990, the Chamber challenged the regularisation plan in court,[37] arguing that it did not comply with the requirements of a regularisation plan, but rather had been prepared in a legal form designed to evade the control of the Greater City Municipality. Moreover, the argument claimed that the aim of a regularisation plan had to be to legalise and upgrade irreversible developments and to impede new unofficial developments in the environs of existing settlements. By contrast, the Ümraniye Municipality plan extended even over vacant land. In brief, the Chamber claimed that the district municipality had distorted the substance of the relevant legislation in order to avoid the control mechanisms.

The case lasted four years, during which the court twice rejected the Chamber's claims, but finally cancelled the plan in 1994. While the case was in court, another state body became involved in the conflict: the Water and Sewerage Department, a semi-autonomous body within the Greater City Municipality in charge of the developments in the Yukarı Dudullu district because of the settlement's location within a reservoir area. In 1993, this department cancelled all building permissions previously granted in the area, thus positioning itself at the side of the Greater City Municipality and the Chamber of Architects in the conflict.

To comply with the court's decision, the district municipality had to revise its regularisation plan in 1995 specifically to exclude vacant areas from the remit of the plan. Despite this, the revised plan still legalised all existing buildings, including those which should have been demolished according to the master-plan requirements. A report prepared by the Ümraniye Municipality in 1996 stated that title deeds for individual building plots had been provided for most of the planning area, and thousands of construction as well as settlement permissions had been granted. It should be noted that no title deeds could be provided through the regularisation plan for that part of the Şerif Ali Estate still under litigation, and it was only after the final decision of the Supreme Court in 1998 that the municipality began re-registering property according to the court's decisions.

Conclusion

It has been argued here that the high revenues obtained from urban land transactions intensified conflicts over property rights among many actors, including individuals claiming title to estates based on their Ottoman state title deeds, the *gecekondu* dwellers, the settlers in unauthorised housing and the state Treasury. These conflicts developed into a long process of negotiation and renegotiation of property rights against a changing background of reforms in Ottoman property legislation, new property laws enacted by the Turkish Republic, rapid urbanisation creating pressures for transformations in land use, and finally modifications in property and urban planning laws. Rights of ownership in the two estates discussed here evolved as each change in context triggered new property claims and resulting confrontations, and formed new negotiated settlements whereby ownership was assigned to one or another party. On the other hand, confrontations over property were not limited only to ownership, but also pertained to other rights attached to it. Hence the regularisation schemes implemented in the urban districts triggered confrontations among parties promoting private interests of land-rent appropriation and those promoting public interest in environmental conservation.

Conflicts over property rights took place within the context of property and urban-planning laws; that is, the orderings and practices of the relevant laws set up the terms and vocabulary of property relations in the urban settlements. Thus, the way that land in Hekimbaşı was transacted among parties who held no official title to land, or the way that a landowner in Şerif Ali invaded land which belonged to others by making use of loopholes in the legal–institutional setting, as well as the way that the district municipality in Ümraniye manipulated the urban planning laws in such a manner as to evade the control of higher-level administration illustrate how the actors sought to conform to state laws while, at the same time, achieving their own ends by negotiating those laws in particular situations.

When the local formulations of property rights became widespread, they were reflected in the relevant laws at the state level: for example, the specifications of the forest laws making possible individual ownership of the nationalised forests under certain circumstances, laws changing the definition of forests, and the Amnesty Law. The Amnesty Law, representing a negotiated settlement ending a long conflict between illegal settlers and the state, had particularly significant repercussions on property ownership, transferring a sizeable amount of public land to *gecekondu* dwellers and granting construction rights to unauthorised housing settlers, thus enhancing their property rights.

Various state agencies were involved in the development processes of the districts in different ways. Local administrations, specifically the district municipalities and village headmen, took the side of the illegal settlers and contributed to the development and regularisation of their settlements, as well as to the enhancement of private property rights in their districts. On the other hand, state bodies, including the Greater City Municipality of Istanbul, the Ministry of Forests, the Treasury and the parliament sought to control these settlements, and challenged them in the courts on a variety of grounds: for example, the claims of the Treasury and the Ministry of Forests to public ownership of Hekimbaşı and the claim of the Greater City Municipality to the right to restrict regularisation of the Dudullu district to a reasonable extent. However, as reflected in the enactment of the forest and amnesty laws, they simultaneously pursued a pragmatic long-term policy of compromise with the settlers.

Notes

1 This chapter is a reprint of Gülöksüz, Elvan, 'Negotiation of property rights in urban land in Istanbul', *International Journal of Urban and Regional Research* 26/3, 2002, pp.462–76. I am grateful to Huri İslamoğlu for her guidance during the research and the preparation of earlier versions of the work. My thanks are also due to three anonymous referees for their useful comments. Finally, I thank Judith E. Tucker for improving the text.

2 Including de Sousa Santos, 1977; Azuela, 1987; Razzaz, 1994; Razzaz, 1998; Azuela and Duhau, 1998; Durand-Lasserve, 1998; Fernandes and Varley, 1998.

3 Razzaz, 1994.

4 Santos, 1977.

5 Azuela, 1987.

6 İslamoğlu, 2000.

7 Three decrees (*irade*) enacted between 1874 and 1876 redefined the institutions establishing property. The first decree, dated 1874 (1290AH), replaced the evidentiary documents for property (*temelluk hücceti*) provided by the Islamic Law Courts (*Şer'iye Mahkemeleri*) with the title deeds provided by the Office of the Land Registry (Defterhane) for private property (Arazi-i Memluke). The second decree, in 1875 (1291AH), replaced the documents (*temessük*) provided by the trustees (*mütevelli*) of the pious foundations with title deeds provided by the Office of the Land Registry for Lands of Pious Foundations (Arazi-i Mevkufe). The third decree, in 1876 (1292AH), appointed the Office of the Land Registry as the authority for providing title deeds for built-up and non-built-up land of pious foundations (*musakkafat ve müstegallati vakfiye*) outside and within Istanbul: Esmer, 1990, p.11.

8 Within the borders of the Hekimbaşı Estate, the entire Kazım Karabekir and Hekimbaşı districts and a portion of Inkılap district developed. However, for the sake of simplicity, I use Kazım Karabekir to refer to all three urban settlements.

9 State Institute of Statistics, 1996.

10 See Erder, 1996.

11 Öncü, 1988.
12 Şenyapılı, 1992.
13 Tekeli, 1996.
14 Buğra, 1998.
15 Yönder, 1998.
16 See Yönder, 1998.
17 See Öncü, 1988; Tekeli, 1994.
18 See Tekeli, 1991.
19 See Öncü, 1988; Tekeli, 1994; Buğra, 1998.
20 See Uzel, 1987; Tekeli, 1996.
21 See Tekeli, 1996; Yönder, 1998.
22 Decision Report of the 14th Civil Court of the Supreme Court of Appeal Case No 978/2929, Decision No 978/4683.
23 The case was opened at the Üsküdar 15th Basic Civil Court with Case No 940/152 in 1940. In 1945, the case was transferred to the Üsküdar 1st Basic Civil Court with Case No 945/50. The suers claimed that the estate was private property and the Law of Forests of 1937 (No 3116) excluded private property from the jurisdiction of the Ministry of Forests, whether or not the land was covered with forests. (See the Decision Report of the Üsküdar 1st Basic Civil Court, Case No 978/69, Decision No 978/243.)
24 Üsküdar 1st Basic Civil Court, Case No 944/925, Decision No 944/280. This decision was also confirmed by the 1st Court of the Supreme Court of Appeal, Case No 5659/152 in 1945. The demands of the defendants for appeal was rejected by the same court with Decision No 2542/2249 in 1945. (See the Report submitted to the Decision Report of the Üsküdar 1st Basic Civil Court, Case No 978/69, Decision No 978/243.)
25 I have not been able to establish the reasons underlying this court decision. The basis of the classification of the estate as state forest was the law of 1924 excluding members of the royal family from the right to property ownership. The court makes no reference to this fact.
26 The case was opened in an Üsküdar Basic Civil Court with Case No 950/835. The court rejected the case, asserting that the location of the area remained out of its jurisdiction. The case was transferred to a Beykoz Basic Civil Court. The jurisdiction problem among courts was resolved by the 4th Court of the Supreme Court of Appeal, and the Üsküdar 2nd Basic Civil Court was authorised to take the case. The case was taken up as Case No 1955/489 in 1955. The court rejected the case, but this decision was cancelled by the Supreme Court of Appeal. Thus, the case continued in the

same court as Case No 973/923 in 1973. While the case was in court, the suers' claims were strengthened by the exclusion of 932 hectares of land within the Hekimbaşı Estate from forest jurisdiction by the Commission for Separating Areas Covered by Maquis in 1954. However, this decision was cancelled in 1960 both by the declaration of the area as 'protected forest' and by a decision of the General Directorate of Forests. (See the Decision Report of the Üsküdar 2nd Basic Civil Court, Case No 950/835, Decision No 978/711)

27 In 1978, the Üsküdar 2nd Basic Civil Court rejected the case on the grounds that the nature of this forest did not correspond to the kinds of forest defined by the law of 1950 because it displayed geographical continuity with the 'protected forest' in the north. This decision was confirmed by the Supreme Court of Appeal in 1979. (See the Decision Report of the Supreme Court of Appeal, Case No 979/3688, Decision No 979/6122.) In 1956, the holders of the Ottoman titles also legally challenged the declaration of the forest as protected forest. However, that case was also lost. In a parallel attempt, in 1956, some of the previous landowners brought another case (at the General Board of the State Council Litigation Offices, Case No 1956/344, Decision No 1957/289) against the General Directorate of Forests, demanding that the decision of the Council of Ministers classifying the land as 'protected forest' be cancelled. In 1957, the judge in this case refused to make a ruling, arguing that the matter concerned national security and was therefore outside the jurisdiction of the court. (See the Decision Report of the Üsküdar 2nd Basic Civil Court, Case No 950/835, Decision No 978/711.)

28 These cases were taken up by the Üsküdar 1st Basic Civil Court, which rejected them. However, these decisions were cancelled by the 14th Court of the Supreme Court of Appeal. Thus, the cases were taken up once more by the same court, which, in 1978, again rejected most of the cases. (See the Decision Report of the Üsküdar 1st Basic Civil Court, Case No 978/69, Decision No 978/243.) These decisions were confirmed by the Supreme Court of Appeal upon appeal of the suer. (See the Decision Report of the Supreme Court of Appeal, Case No 979/69, Decision No 979/137.)

29 Decision Report of the Üsküdar Basic Civil Court, Case No 982/221, Decision No 989/469.

30 In 1987, before the previous case was finalised (see footnote 29), the Commission for Forest Cadastre excluded the area in question from

forest boundaries, registering it in the name of the state Treasury. Thus, in 1992, the Treasury sued the shareholders and the private firm who were appealing its ownership rights through the courts, demanding that the land be registered in its name in accordance with the decision of the cadastre of 1987. (See the Expert Report for the Üsküdar 5th Basic Civil Court, Case No 992/61.)

31 For information on the property transfers in the Şerif Ali Estate, see the Decision Report of the Üsküdar Cadastral Court, Case No 1976/46, Decision No 1990/9.

32 Üsküdar 1st Basic Civil Court, Case No 1953/202. (See the Decision Report of the Üsküdar Cadastral Court, Case No 1976/46, Decision No 1990/9.)

33 The broad extent of this type of activity in the metropolitan cities led to legislative changes in the form of a new Development Law enacted in 1985, which introduced municipal councils or local branches of the central government as major decision-makers in cadastral registration and prohibited shared ownership in cadastral plots smaller than $5000m^2$.

34 The court's decision was appealed in the Supreme Court by the settlers, who sought to regain their previously established property rights. However, this application was rejected by the Supreme Court in 1998.

35 Decision of the Ümraniye Municipality Municipal Council, 21.6.1989, 989/46.

36 Decision of the Istanbul Greater City Municipality Municipal Council, 21.5.1991, 991/713.

37 Report submitted by the Chamber of Architects to the Istanbul 3rd Administrative Tribunal, Case No 991/143 (11.2.1991).

Bibliography

Abbreviations

IULA-EMME: International Union of Local Authorities, Section for the Eastern Mediterranean and Middle East Region

SIS: State Institute of Statistics

Unpublished primary sources

Hekimbaşı (listed according to case numbers and dates)

Decision Report of the Üsküdar 2nd Basic Civil Court, Case No 950/835, Decision No 978/711.

Decision Report of the 14th Civil Court of the Supreme Court of Appeal, Case No 978/2929, Decision No 978/4683.

Decision Report of the Üsküdar 1st Basic Civil Court, Case No 978/69, Decision No 978/243.

Decision Report of the Supreme Court of Appeal, Case No 979/3688, Decision No 979/6122.

Decision Report of the Supreme Court of Appeal, Case No 979/69, Decision No 979/137.

Decision Report of the Üsküdar Basic Civil Court, Case No 982/221, Decision No 989/469.

Expert Report for the Üsküdar 5th Basic Civil Court, Case No 992/61.

Şerif Ali (listed according to case numbers and dates)

Decision Report of the Üsküdar Cadastral Court, Case No 1976/46, Decision No 1990/9.

Decision of the Ümraniye Municipality Municipal Council, 21.6.1989, 989/46.

Report submitted by the Chamber of Architects to the Istanbul 3rd Administrative Tribunal, Case No 991/143 (11.2.1991).

Decision of the Istanbul Greater City Municipality Municipal Council, 21.5.1991, 991/713.

Published primary sources

State Institute of Statistics, Statistical Indicators 1923–1995, Ankara, SIS, 1996.

Secondary sources

Azuela, Antonio, 'Low income settlements and the law in Mexico City', *International Journal of Urban and Regional Research* 11/4, 1987, pp.522–42.

Azuela, Antonio and Emilio Duhau, 'Tenure regularization, private property and public order in Mexico', in Fernandes and Varley (eds), 1998, pp.157–72.

Buğra, Ayşe, 'The immoral economy of housing in Turkey', *International Journal of Urban and Regional Research* 22/2, 1998, pp.303–17.

Durand-Lasserve, Alain, 'Law and urban change in developing countries: trends and issues', in Fernandes and Varley (eds), 1998, pp.233–258.

Erder, Sema, *İstanbul'a bir kent kondu: Ümraniye*, Istanbul, Iletişm Yayınları, 1996.

Esmer, Galip, *Mevzuatımızda Gayrimenkul Hükümleri ve Tapu Sicili*, Istanbul, Kazancı Hukuk Yayınları No 82, 1990.

Fernandes, Edesio and Ann Varley (eds), *Illegal Cities: Law and Urban Change in Developing Countries*, London/New York, Zed Books, 1998.

– 'Law, the city and citizenship in developing countries: an introduction', in Fernandes and Varley (eds), 1998, pp.3–18.

İslamoğlu, Huri, 'Property as a contested domain: a reevaluation of the Ottoman Land Code of 1858', in Roger Owen (ed.), *New Perspectives on Property and Land in the Middle East*, Cambridge, MA, Harvard University Press, 2000, pp.3–61.

Öncü, Ayşe, 'The politics of the urban land market in Turkey: 1950–1980', *International Journal of Urban and Regional Research* 12/1, 1988, pp.38–64.

Razzaz, Omar, 'Contestation and mutual adjustment: the process of controlling land in Yajouz, Jordan', *Law and Society Review* 28/1, 1994, pp.7–39.

– 'Land disputes in the absence of ownership rights: insights from Jordan', in Fernandes and Varley (eds), 1998, pp.69–89.

Santos, Boaventura de Sousa, 'The law of the oppressed: the construction and reproduction of legality in Pasagrada', *Law and Society Review* 12, 1977, pp.5–126.

Şenyapılı, Tansı, 'A new stage of *gecekondu* housing in İstanbul', *Development of İstanbul Metropolitan Area and Low Cost Housing*, Istanbul, Turkish Social Science Association, Municipality of Greater Istanbul, IULA-EMME, 1992, pp.182–209.

Tekeli, Ilhan, 'Kentleşmeye kapital birikim süreçleri açısından bakmanın sağladığı açıklama olanakları', *Kent planlaması konuşmaları*, Ankara, Mimarlar Odası Yayınları, 1991, pp.166–70.

– 'The patron–client relationship: land rent economy and the experience of urbanization without citizens', in S.J. Neary, M.S. Symes and F.E. Brown (eds), *The Urban Experience: A People–Environment Perspective*, London, E. and F.N. Spon, 1994, pp.9–17.

– Türkiye'de yaşamda ve yazında konut sorununun gelişimi, Konut Araştırmalar Dizisi-2, Ankara, Toplu Konut Idaresi, 1996.

Uzel, Ahmet L., Imara Llişkin Bağışlamaların Gelişimi ve Değerlendirilmesi, Ankara, Batıkent Konut Üretim Yapı Kooperatifleri Birliği Yayını, 1987.
Yönder, Ayşe, 'Implications of double standards in housing policy: development of informal settlements in İstanbul, Turkey', in Fernandes and Varley (eds), 1998, pp.55–69.

CHAPTER 9

Politics of Administering Property: Law and Statistics in the Nineteenth-century Ottoman Empire

Huri İslamoğlu

James C. Scott, in *Seeing like a State*, poses legibility as a central feature of modern statecraft. In his perspective 'the pre-modern state was ... partially blind; it knew precious little about its subjects, their wealth, their landholdings and yields, their location, their very identity. It lacked anything like a detailed "map" of its terrain and its people ...'[1] Scott contrasts the opaque practices of the pre-modern state to those of modern statecraft aimed at subjugating land and population to state taxation, conscription and, most significantly, to state scrutiny. These practices, which were attempts at legibility and simplification, included the introduction of freehold tenure, establishment of cadastral surveys and standardisation of legal discourse. At the same time, for Scott, making society legible and simplifying the state functions of taxation, conscription and control is also the refashioning of modern social reality. Such simplifications were transformative and involved a reordering of social reality through categories which were generalised and given the force of law. Scott points to the character of modern society thus transformed as one robbed of its plurality and diversity, of the malleability of local or customary practices condemned to ineffective resistance to modern statecraft and to political emasculation. By contrast, pre-modern states, inefficient in carrying out their functions, allow for local and customary practices to flourish, representing the domain of politics where a plethora of local regulations relating to land and property vie with the ineffective attempts of central administrations to extend their control.

This chapter subscribes to the understanding that social reality is administratively and legally[2] constituted, which Scott's notion of 'transformative simplification' suggests. Yet it is critical of Scott's analysis, which positions statecraft or administration too readily in opposition to society which comprises a domain of politics involving negotiations among multiple and diverse actors. Administration for Scott simply refers to the reservoir of techniques the state employs to subjugate politics and social diversity to the singularity of taxation, conscription and surveillance. This chapter argues that the separation of administration from the local or the political detracts from the understanding of the political processes which characterise the legal and administrative constitutions of social reality. Viewed from this perspective, individual practices, including law, registration and cadastral mapping, represent power fields[3] where multiple actors, including administrative ones, confront each other to negotiate the terms of their existence. The understanding of administrative rules, regulations, procedures and law[4] as political power fields allows their conception in terms of the concrete strategies and concerns of actors (individual or social). No longer reified as disembodied tools of modern domination, they represent embodiments of society, of politics. Put differently, the functionalist perception of administration as a bundle of techniques geared towards the subjugation and control of society gives way to a perception of the politics of administration in which administrative technique is enmeshed in the societal relations which it orders. Above all, this chapter seeks to introduce an understanding of administration which stresses the political possibilities of administrative action and its historically contingent character which does not simply condemn such action to the political closure implied by its isolation from society.

The critique of Scott's analysis presented here suggests a blurring of the distinction between state and society. In doing so, it challenges the technicist conceptions of modern state domination, on one hand, and on the other hand, the impotence attributed to pre-modern states on the basis of the latter's technical ineffectuality. The emphasis on the political character of administration points to an understanding of state domination in terms of a context of power relations. That is, the state represents a hegemonic environment where a dominant group or groups seek to reconcile and mediate multiple interests, in the process eliminating some and including others. Hegemony or state power refers to those abilities of the dominant group or groups to affect the power configurations that would enable orderings of social reality (including property relations, which are responsible for allocation of resources) to achieve defined objectives. From the perspective of modern state domination, this understanding relativises that domination (by contrast with its technicist view, which absolutises it) and renders it contingent on the ability of central administrative actors to negotiate and to mediate in the multiple power fields which represent administrative practices. In this sense, the legal and administrative processes which are constitutive of social and property relations are also those through which the domination of the modern leviathan is politically realised or fails to be realised. Which actors are included and which are excluded and whose interests are mediated and whose are not, tell of the character of a given hegemony and are part of the struggle for domination.

Finally, hegemony is about 'framing' or defining the terms of negotiation and of contestation. Hegemonic vocabularies, or idioms of rule which articulate the objectives of domination, shape the character of the different outcomes. This is true of all hegemonic vocabularies whether they focus on the prevention of social strife, as was often the case with pre-modern states, or the provision of general prosperity represented by the interrelated goals of economic development and protection from external aggression, as has been the case with modern states. Legitimating idioms also impart a unity to the multiple orderings which make up the different hegemonic environments, so as to warrant their description as singular undifferentiated entities, that is, states.[5]

Viewed as contexts of power relations, pre-modern states cannot be characterised in terms of the inadequacy of their administrative techniques, which did not allow the centre or the ruler to exercise effective control over resources. They represented hegemonic environments in which central rulers sought to accommodate the interests of different groups by means of distributing access to resources. Administrative practices or rules and regulations represented negotiated settlements between the ruler and different groups regarding claims over access to resources, to their revenues or to their use. These practices were constitutive of the local or the customary as modern statecraft is constitutive of modern society. This chapter will show how in the pre-nineteenth-century Ottoman Empire administrative rules and regulations constituted the local in relation to power configurations which characterised the pre-modern-state environment. On the other hand, modernity represented a struggle to establish one kind of hegemony over another. Practices of modern states, including cadastral surveying, general laws or procedures which ordered social reality represented political processes in which the pre-modern and modern concerns and interests were entangled and continuously negotiated. The outcome was a modernity whose defining feature was, more often than not, its ambivalence.

This chapter will focus primarily on the administrative constitutions of individual property on land in the nineteenth-century Ottoman Empire through the practices of surveying land and property and through law. The establishment of individual property on land was inseparable from the formation of the Ottoman modern state in the environment of military and political competition in Western Eurasia, which began to intensify in the eighteenth century. Individual ownership developed as part of the process whereby the central administration emerged as the singular claimant to tax revenues, to the exclusion of the claims of members of the former ruling bloc. At the same time, individual ownership excluded multiple claims to land use in favour of use claims of the titleholder, thus making it possible for administrators to identify the person liable for payment of taxes on land. The establishment of individual property was strongly resisted. Regulations and procedures for compiling surveys which were constitutive of this form of property represented political power fields where negotiations and struggles of different groups left their imprint on the nature of property relations on land.

A primary target of resistance and contestation was the generality of rules and categories that were constitutive of individual ownership. For instance, the Land Code of 1858 included a general definition of individual property, but the text of the Code is replete with provisions which restricted individual property by allowing access to third parties and by imposing limits on disposability or alienability of land. The latter provisions not only reveal the highly contested character of the Code, but also point to attempts on the part of its drafters to mediate and reconcile the interests of groups which were affected by the introduction of individual ownership. These included the interests of holders of third-party claims, for instance those over buildings and trees on lands over which individual and absolute property rights were established, as well as interests of groups which were vulnerable to the vagaries of the land market if lands were to be transferred unconditionally in the event of indebtedness.[6] This chapter addresses the formation of individual property on land through the contested categories of land and property surveys and the procedures for their compilation. These categories and procedures, which were subject to continuous negotiations and re-formulation, are revealing of the attempts to mediate and reconcile different interests, including those of different state agencies, as well as to eliminate others.

What needs to be stressed here is that modern Ottoman state administration, in constituting individual ownership on land through legal practice or surveying, did not confront a society from which it was isolated and over which it sought to establish its unequivocal control. The resistance of different groups and the mediation as well as elimination of different interests in response to such resistance represented political processes which were constitutive of individual ownership. As such, resistance to administrative action was far from being ineffectual, nor can it be described simply in terms of an attempt to subvert an administrative domain which had an existence outside society or outside the control of social actors. These struggles were internalised to the administrative practices, and were part of the 'making' of individual property. Such internalisation involved incorporation of local knowledge, as witnessed in the recasting of procedures for surveying to emphasise the role of commissions consisting of local representatives in the gathering of information for tax assessment.

From the point of view of the modern administration's relation to society, this meant two things. First of all, procedures and regulations were continuously formed and re-formed as the central administration responded to the demands and the resistance of the different groups in the process of fashioning a rural society of freeholders. In that sense, the ability of the central administration to achieve its objectives of taxation and control was largely contingent on its abilities to mediate and reconcile different interests, including those of the different agencies of administration – that is, on its ability to consolidate its hegemony.

Secondly, local or customary practices did not disappear. Instead, they were reconstituted in terms of the hegemony of the modern administrative state. For instance, resistance to the general formulation of individual ownership in the Land Code of 1858 occasioned the issuance of special provisions, notably in the Balkan provinces where the revolts of cultivators showed a potential to develop into separatist nationalist movements. Special provisions represented negotiations of the category of individual ownership in response to local demand; it involved a recasting of the general precepts of the law in terms of local particularities with an infusion of local information. This did not, however, represent a subversion of the Code. The negotiations had as their reference point the general precepts of the Code; they were arguments that took place within categories set forth by the Code. In that sense, special provisions were part of the process of constituting the local in terms of the categories of modern hegemony. The bittersweet triumph of modern Ottoman statecraft perhaps lay in the fact that from the mid-nineteenth century onwards, contestations and challenges of its practices were taking place in terms of the categories and vocabularies which these practices introduced.

Historical constitutions of social reality

Starting from the premise that both pre-modern and modern social realities were administratively constituted, and that administrative practices were fields of negotiation and deliberation of multiple interests, this chapter emphasises the political character of administration in both contexts. Pre-modern and modern state contexts, however, represented distinct configurations of power or hegemonies. The 'making' of modern social reality, including individual property, involving re-allocation of resources, was also the 'making' of a new hegemony and the undermining of the old. In the process, the old and the new were entangled and administrative practices which were constitutive of modern social reality were power fields in which the old was cast in the terms of the new and the new was continuously formulated to accommodate and so transform the old. Thus the politics of modern administration were at the same time merged with and differentiated from the politics of the pre-modern administration. An understanding of this process presupposes an understanding of the politics of the pre-modern Ottoman administration.

The defining feature of administration in the early-modern Ottoman state was that rules and regulations ordering social reality represented settlements negotiated between the ruler and the different groups, both within the ruling bloc and outside it. These settlements were particularistic in that they addressed individual circumstances in a given locality or in relation to the status of a given person or group. In this sense, the rules and regulations did not have the character of the general rules or regulations of the modern state context. The particularity of administrative practices, however, referred to the distributive–accommodative concern of state power. This concern was articulated in the legitimating idiom of the state (represented by the ruler), which cast the ruler in the role of the dispenser of justice. The ruler's ability to dispense justice was, in turn, equated with his ability to prevent social strife and to ensure social order. Rules and regulations were accommodative of the claims of groups competing for control over sources of revenues (land, market dues, customs duties, mines, industrial installments) and the claims of producers over access to the use of resources, in particular land. In relation to the former, the ruler undertook the distribution of sources of revenue in the form of revenue grants to members of groups which formed the ruling bloc. Initially, the ruling bloc included military commanders, who acted as provincial administrators, as well as members of the religious establishment, and former rulers of conquered territories. Underlining the reciprocal character of the relationship between the ruler and holders of revenue grants, the latter were expected to provide mounted soldiers to provincial armies and social services, among which were the maintenance of infrastructural facilities and charity work.[7] From the point of view of the ruler, reciprocity also entailed the requirement of political allegiance from these groups in return for distribution of revenue grants. In the seventeenth and eighteenth centuries, under conditions of intensified inter-state competition, and faced with the increased importance of infantry armies and increased cash requirements, rulers turned to tax-farming as the preferred form of fiscal extraction. From the start, the Ottoman central government was engaged in incessant struggles over control of tax revenues, negotiating settlements with different groups of tax-farmers, including members of the religious establishments (Christian and Muslim), military commanders in the provinces, and provincial elites. In the late seventeenth century, possibly with the intention of disciplining groups which had become very powerful due to tax-farming contracts, the central government sought to circumvent and possibly eliminate the old guard by making tax-farming contracts with less powerful local actors,[8] that is, by attempting to reconstitute local practices.

Rules and regulations which were accommodative of the interests of rural cultivators and urban populations also subscribed to the distributive ethos of the early Ottoman state environment and were constitutive of a moral economy of subsistence and provisioning.[9] While state-wide famine relief was practised, Ottoman subsistence management emphasised regulations that controlled the movement of foodstuffs as well as raw materials and, in doing so, sought to ensure local provisioning through the formation of regional economies. Moreover, to ensure the continuity of food production, regulations restricted the alienability or divisibility of subsistence holdings, limited the freedom of movement of cultivators and regulated fallow practices. State rulings included in provincial regulations and in the ruler's edicts responding to individual complaints sought to protect subsistence producers from extortion by holders of revenue grants. To this end, these rulings delineated the use rights of producers as well as their obligations to different groups of revenue claimants. These obligations included specifications of the form in which dues were paid (in kind, in labour or in money), the rates at which they were paid, and exemptions from payments in return for services rendered. Finally, the different rulings and contracts which regulated actual land use represented multi-layered, shared claims that were negotiated over land use, including webs of grazing and planting rights on common lands as well as individual plots.

The argument that regulations or institutions which ordered social relations were settlements negotiated among different interests emphasises their historical and political character and does not treat the individual institutions as ahistorical entities emanating from an hypostatised ideal of a just order. Thus, the different orderings of social relations and the negotiated settlements which they represented were subject to change with variations in the power positions of the ruler and the different actors. For one thing, despite claims on the part of the ruler to divine powers, the legitimacy of the centre rested with its ability to negotiate settlements.[10] At the same time, 'customary', or indeed 'local', consisted of settlements which were negotiated among different groups – including revenue grant-holders, agents of the ruler and cultivators – and were summarised in texts of regulations. For instance, provincial regulations which were appended to tax surveys frequently described existing practices in a given region as dating from ancient times whereas they in fact referred to settlements negotiated only recently. Moreover, these settlements were subject to continuous negotiations and reformulation through the rulings of provincial courts of law, as well as through texts of the central government's responses to petitions submitted by individuals. In the sixteenth century, summations of new settlements reached among parties were entered in the margins of tax surveys as amendments to earlier settlements. Similarly, regulations directed towards the preservation of subsistence production were characterised by an administrative responsiveness to individual circumstances. They varied from one locality to another with conditions of production and with the political or military status of cultivators; they represented a series of settlements negotiated between the cultivators and the extractors of their surpluses over long periods of time. Finally, the courts of law provided the administrative spaces where these particularistic settlements were transacted. Until the nineteenth century, judges seem to have acted as power-brokers between local forces and the central government, and did not exactly conform to their image as devoted state servants.[11] In the nineteenth century, as part of its struggle for hegemony, the central government sought to replace local judges who belonged to former power networks with commissions or councils that were expected to take over the tasks of negotiating settlements as well as implementing procedures and rules.

In brief, early-modern Ottoman administrative practices were constitutive of a social reality of particularities and of localisms in a hegemonic environment where the ruler, representing the central government, could reproduce his dominance through accommodating multiple interests. This was achieved through negotiations of multiple settlements over shares of tax revenues and over access to land use. These settlements formed the substance of rules and regulations. They did not, however, form discrete local practices with an existence outside the state or its administration. Instead, the local, and rules and regulations which constituted it, partook in a state environment imbued with a specific understanding of social harmony that presupposed the ruler's role as upholder of social order and dispenser of justice. Reference to this role was the recurrent refrain in all regulations and all documents issued by the central government, as well as those addressed to the ruler and his government. It was the belief that rules and regulations contributed to social peace which was perhaps the substance of Ottoman 'stateness' and which imparted a unity to multiple orderings of social reality in terms of localities.

In the nineteenth century, there was a radical transformation of the understanding of state domination which rested on negotiations of particularistic settlements to accommodate the multiple claims to tax revenues and to subsistence. The new state was represented through the efficacy and generality of its practices, including legal codes and cadastres. These practices, instead of constituting particularistic claims (localisms or particularisms) through individually negotiated settlements, sought to obliterate those claims by subjecting them to general claims of the central government over tax revenues which involved constitutions of social reality in terms of general categories and general procedures. This did not mean an erasure of the local or society, nor did it mean that constitutions of social reality were no longer negotiated or contested. Simply, the administrative practices of the new state constituting social reality did so in relation to the generality and singularity of the interests of the state writ large, which were understood to encompass all groups or individuals that came under the jurisdiction of any one government. It meant that negotiations among different groups, including the agencies of the centre, were not summed up in particularistic rules and regulations. Instead, general categories, procedures and regulations were continuously negotiated and reformulated while the central government sought to ensure its hegemony through maintaining the generality and uniformity of its practices, seeking to subject all groups and regions to the generality of its claims. Thus, if ruler's justice, underpinning the hegemony of the early Ottoman state, was realised through addressing individual circumstances, the hegemony of the new state rested on its ability to address the general interests of society. Society, however, was constituted through state practices and in terms of general categories including those of tax-paying citizenry, of individual property which cut across particularistic categories responding to (and in doing so creating) differences in geographical location and in social status. As such, just as the early state practices were constitutive of particularisms and localisms, the practices of the modern state were constitutive of the generalities out of which modern society was made. The central bureaucratic government was embedded in society by virtue of its practices constituting it, and found its legitimacy in securing society and upholding its general interests. In the nineteenth century this took the form of protecting society from external aggression and ensuring its economic prosperity.

Historically, the transformation of the Ottoman state took place in the environment of intensified military and political competition among European states beginning in the seventeenth century. Inter-state competition and the requirement to maintain infantry armies, which in this period came to prevail over cavalry armies, were factors in empowering the central government at the expense of powerful groups in the provinces.

Confronted with the high costs of warfare as well as the financial burdens of an expanding bureaucracy, the centralising government sought to increase its revenues. Earlier territorial conquests had been a primary means of augmenting the revenues which accrued to the ruler. Conquests also enabled the ruler to accommodate rival political claims through the system of revenue grants. By the eighteenth century, the Ottoman state had reached the limits of its territorial expansion both in Europe and in the East, and in the nineteenth century it began losing territory in the Balkans and in Egypt.

Unable to expand outwards, the central government turned inwards to establish control over the revenues which had formerly accrued to members of the ruling bloc. This was a long-drawn-out process of incessant struggle between the central government and members of the religious establishment, provincial notables and the old-guard military establishment. In the nineteenth century, with the crystallisation of a central army and a central bureaucracy, the government undertook new orderings of taxation and property relations on land. These orderings aimed at establishing the general claim of the central government over revenues, to the exclusion of the entitlements of the different groups which formerly constituted the ruling bloc (including the ruler and his entourage, as well as different groups of tax-farmers). It meant the subjection to state taxes of these groups, together with others who were not holders of revenue grants or tax farms but, like them, were recipients of the particularistic privilege of exemption from taxes.[12]

At the same time, state centralisation took place in an environment of commercial expansion. This expansion prompted the individual states to see wealth generation not simply in terms of extensive measures, that is territorial conquests which enabled access to new sources of revenue or appropriation of resources controlled by rival political groups within individual territories. Taxation came to be perceived in more intensive terms of the state's regulation of economic activity in order to increase productive capacity, which would result in an expansion of taxable incomes.[13] This implied a coupling of concern for monopolising and increasing revenue with concern for increasing the productive capacity of the population, of land and of industry.[14] The central authority was not simply content to appropriate what was previously distributed, it also sought to create further wealth to be taxed. In the nineteenth century, this consciousness of the 'economy' on the part of the Ottoman government was revealed in the kinds of precise information about productivity levels and supply and demand for different products that the central government demanded from its officials charged with preparing surveys of landed property.[15]

In the nineteenth-century intellectual and political climate, two imperatives of modern state domination, taxation and economic growth, were expected to be realised through individual ownership in land.[16] In the utilitarian perception which permeated the makings of modern administrations, most eloquently articulated by Jeremy Bentham, property was entirely the work of law (by which Bentham meant administration). Bentham described property as an expectation on the part of the individual to derive certain advantages from a thing which he/she was said to possess. It was an expectation which developed in the environment of exchange (therefore historical) and which was to be realised in law. For Bentham, 'law created whatever [was] to be secured', hence individual property created in law provided the individual with a security and freedom which facilitated his/her decisions regarding production. It was instrumental in fulfilling an individual's expectations in realising his/her welfare. As such, by administratively constituting property, the government was realising the utilitarian ideal of achieving the 'greatest possible happiness of the community'.[17] It was also ensuring the production of surpluses to be appropriated as taxes. For the utilitarians, the legitimacy of modern administration was understood to rest on its ability to deliver in material terms. It was summed up in the notion of security, which referred to the government's ability to provide protection from external aggression (through the building of armies, which presupposed taxation) and to protect individual property. Thus, in the nineteenth century, when concerns for market expansion (arguably conceived in terms of maximisation of an individual's expectations) overlapped with concerns about increasing state revenues, it was evident to jurists and statesmen alike that the burden of the creation of the new economic order fell upon central administrations.[18] The history of how central administration constituted individual ownership is also the history of the constitution of the modern state. The struggle to generalise it and the resistance to it represented the processes through which modern social reality was fashioned.

How law constituted property

In the Ottoman Empire prior to the issuing of the Land Code in 1858, definitions of property rights on land consisted of a bundle of rights representing claims to land use, revenues and title.[19] The title to land (*rakaba*) generally lay with the ruler (or the Treasury). This did not represent a title of ownership in the modern sense, but an ability on the part of the ruler or the central government to distribute rights to revenues from land and, in so doing, to negotiate the conditions of allegiance with different groups or individuals. State 'ownership' also defined the boundaries of heritable use rights over plots of land. On agricultural lands to which the ruler or the Treasury had title, cultivators with use rights were expected to cultivate grains and thereby provide for their own subsistence and pay taxes, the most important of which was the grain tithe. In order to ensure continuity in grain production, state rulings introduced in provincial regulations and reiterated in numerous edicts imposed limits on the divisibility and alienability of use rights. They also restricted the time periods for which lands could be left uncultivated or left fallow.[20]

Different claims, however, were continuously negotiated and redefined. For instance, depending on the nature of the settlement negotiated among the parties, the rights to revenues could rest with a freeholder (*mülk*), a religious endowment or with the Treasury, while the title rested with the ruler or the Treasury. This should not suggest that the claim of the ruler to title was an absolute one. In areas where there was strong resistance to the Ottoman conquest, the Ottoman ruler often conceded the right to the title of land to former ruling groups. These groups included members of the religious establishment in the Muslim regions of Anatolia. The rights to revenues from such lands could be assigned to state officials and state regulations relating to subsistence production applied to them.

Just as state 'ownership' did not correspond to an understanding of ownership in the modern sense, in the pre-nineteenth-century Ottoman administrative universe, freehold (*mülk*) did not signify absolute ownership. Instead freehold was a category of entitlement to tax revenues which, like other types of revenue-grants, the grantee held by virtue of an official document from the ruler. The holder of the freehold grant could alienate his right to revenues, transfer it to his heirs or convert it into mortmain property or *vakıf.* Trees or buildings on agricultural holdings, as well as other produce, were also classified as freehold, which in this case referred to an entitlement to the fruits of land. These claims were differentiated from *miri* or state claims on fields, the ownership of which generally rested with the central Treasury. The cultivators of agricultural lands (on which the treasury had 'ownership' rights) had heritable usufruct rights, which they held by a deed issued for a fee by the local administrator-*cum*-revenue holder.

The bundle of claims which characterised property relations on land represented multiple settlements negotiated among different parties. Individual settlements took the form of court rulings or summaries of results of negotiations which the judges mediated. They were also cast as ruler's law (*kanun*), which included appropriations of local customary practice. One common feature of these formulations was that they sought to accommodate existing multiple interests and were not exclusive of them.

In the nineteenth century, the Ottoman central government did succeed in introducing individual ownership into the maze of multiple claims, but it did so following bitter struggles waged especially against those groups with claims over tax revenues from land. At the same time, the government sought to mediate the claims of subsistence producers who were threatened by the loss of their heritable usufruct rights through particularistic concessions. Introduction of individual ownership in land resulted in a recasting of power mappings that constituted the state context. It also signalled a reformulation of the legitimating idiom of state power that increasingly departed from the understanding of the distributive justice of the ruler, and focused on the ability of administrative procedure to mediate different property claims with a promise to deliver to all or uphold the general interest.

In the 'age of property',[21] a phrase which aptly describes the nineteenth century, the Ottoman environment had not fallen prey to the 'religion of property' which prevailed in post-revolutionary France, a country watched closely by Ottoman administrators. This was not due to any innate predisposition against private property stemming from state ownership in land, or to the lethal effects of state intervention in economic activity. Quite simply, the Ottoman administrators, in line with the conservative governments in Europe, were watching the disputes over the introduction of individual and absolute ownership which raged in the French countryside with a great deal of apprehension. Ottoman territories themselves were not, in any way, free of such disturbances. The liberal guarantees included in the reform edict of 1839 had encouraged provincial tax-farmers and notables to register their tax-farms as their private property. The decisions of provincial assemblies and of judges at provincial courts of law[22] served to buttress this new form of property. For instance, a decision of the provincial council of Vidin (in present-day Bulgaria), taken soon after the issuing of the 1839 edict and referring to the abolition of corvée impositions, stated that 'no person could cultivate or take over another's land without payment; he will have to pay by some other means [than corvée]'. In the course of the council's deliberations, a single rent was established by which the council acknowledged the abolition of corvée while at the same time seeking to establish the tenancy status of cultivators on lands owned by tax-farmers.[23] In 1851, when cultivators (mostly share-croppers) in Vidin broke out in open rebellion, they were voicing their claims vis-à-vis the tax-farmers in terms of demands for the issuing of title deeds to land, suggesting that those cultivators had already learned to employ the vocabulary of private ownership.

The rupture in the old order of property affected by actions of provincial groups resulted in widespread rebellions in the Balkans, not only in Bulgaria but also in Bosnia and Albania, by cultivators who also staked their claims in terms of individual ownership rights. The central government, in the mid-nineteenth century, attempting to contain these rebellions, found itself in a position of mediating the claims of different groups for absolute ownership. The capacity to do so increasingly differentiated the central government from other actors in the process of negotiating property claims; it imparted a degree of autonomy to the central administration. This was, in effect, the historical 'moment' when the central government took over the constitution of individual ownership through its administrative practices as none of the traditional propertied interests could claim to do.[24]

The 'moment' of property was inseparable from attempts on the part of a central bureaucracy to entrench itself at the expense of other groups within society. One important way of accomplishing this was to limit revenue claims to those of the central state while imposing the obligation to pay taxes on all, including the members of the ruling bloc. Other claims to revenue were thus eliminated, along with privileges in the form of tax exemptions. This also meant a de-linking of the property claim in the form of ownership claims from revenue and use claims on land.

The drafting of the Land Code of 1858 was a major political achievement. It attested to the Ottoman government's ability to establish its claim to mediate among different interests so as to set forth a general code that henceforth provided the reference point in all property matters. By contrast, the French state, throughout the nineteenth century, failed to pass a rural code primarily because the propertied classes insisted on viewing such a code as an instrument to strengthen their own hands at the expense of other groups including sharecroppers.[25]

The text of the Land Code has an intensely negotiated character, testifying to the diverse interests present which the drafting commission was compelled to mediate.[26] The Code introduced a definition of individual property on state lands alone. In doing so, it sought to establish the revenue claims of the central government to the exclusion of claims of other groups. On the other hand, by introducing a classification of lands, including *vakıf*, or lands of religious endowments and freehold, or *mülk* lands,[27] alongside *miri*, or state lands, the Code conceded the revenue claims of these groups outside of state lands. This also implied a change in the meaning of *miri*. Prior to the Code, state 'ownership' enabled the ruler to exercise his distributionist justice by allowing him to assign revenues to different groups in order to obtain their political allegiance and to ensure subsistence production. Under the Code, state ownership assumed a character which approximated a modern understanding of ownership in its emphasis on transferability by means of a sales contract and land registration. But when the central government attempted to extend the practices of registration and lease contracts which were applicable on state lands to non-state lands, it encountered strong resistance from former ruling groups. At the same time, state ownership was undergoing a further metamorphosis as public property, whereby the central government sought justification for its control over property in its claim of upholding public or general interest. An important form of public property which appeared towards the end of the nineteenth century was the setting aside of parts of state lands as forest lands. This meant the introduction of a new domain of contestation over land, whereby the boundaries of the public and private were continuously negotiated as state actors confronted private ones.[28]

I have shown elsewhere[29] the way that property relations in different localities were re-constituted in the nineteenth century within the context of struggles waged over general precepts of the Code. Here, I turn to the practice of compiling surveys and registration of lands and property for tax assessment as the political power fields which were constitutive of individual ownership in the nineteenth century.

Constitutions of individual property and land/property registers

The administrative constitution of individual property was underway prior to the issuing of the Land Code and following the declaration of the reform edict in 1839, which represented an internationally sanctioned statement about the new order of the state.[30] Steeped in the liberal ethos of the time, the edict assigned the central government the task of providing security of property and life for its subjects. In practice, this entailed the elimination of those groups who were perceived by the central government to be threatening that security through their onerous practices of taxation; primarily tax-farmers, including religious foundations. From the perspective of the central government, security of the property of its subjects was inseparable from the establishment of its specific claim to taxation to the exclusion of all other claims. Hence, the most desirable situation was to attach every parcel of taxable land to an individual who was then responsible for paying the tax on it. To this end, the central government sought to institute administratively individual property throughout the 1840s. The most significant of its attempts to do this was the surveying of lands and property for the assessment of individual incomes; it was followed by registration of individual title deeds.[31]

The new order of the state and/or of property was premised on an understanding that both land and other agricultural resources were productive assets exchangeable in the market. In order to capture the changes in productivity and in market values, the central government sought to tax the income from land and other resources. This was a departure from the earlier understanding premised on taxing pre-determined proportions of existing wealth in a given collectivity, most commonly the village. Absolute changes over time in this wealth were evaluated in taxes by means of periodic assessments, in the Ottoman case every 40 years. Assessment of taxes on individual incomes, however, presupposed the existence of individual property, and in the nineteenth century, surveying practices were instrumental in the constitution of this form of property. In this sense, the nineteenth-century surveys – unlike the earlier tax books, which simply recorded the estimates of taxes (both in kind and in cash) which a region was expected to deliver – sought to provide as accurate a depiction of the assets of the individual as possible in order to enable an assessment of his/her income. In relation to land, it meant descriptions, for instance, of the geographic location of fields, of the area under cultivation in standard units of measurement, as well as the quantity of seed cultivated and the yields for individual crops. It also meant systematic and ongoing recordings of changes in the extent and value of landed property, of its yield and its productivity.

Assessment of individual incomes proved to be particularly difficult on lands where individual property was not established. The earlier system of taxation had defined tax liability in terms of the tithe, or a proportion of yield which varied with locality, and of a land tax from the use of state lands, assessed on the basis of the extent of land ploughed by a pair of oxen. These taxes represented a tax/rent which accrued to the ruler and to the recipients of revenue grants from the ruler. This system, however, presupposed multiple claims on the use and revenues of land. Surveying officials in the nineteenth century were especially hard put to register and assess incomes from lands which were not the individual property of those who cultivated them but were part of the holdings of religious foundations and/or other types of revenue grants.[32] These lands were not part of state lands to which the precepts of the Code applied, and groups which had claim over revenues from these lands resisted the extension of the Code's jurisdiction, and in doing so evaded state taxation.[33] Thus, the practice of surveying became yet another scene where former claimants to revenues fought against the new order of the central administration and of individual property. It also became an arena in which individual property was constituted.

It is possible to trace the process of constituting individual property in the changes in the categories used to record land and resources in the surveys. The surveying of land and other agricultural resources for assessment of taxes had been practised since the inception of the Ottoman Empire, and was an important aspect of Ottoman statecraft. In keeping with the distributive logic of Ottoman state power in earlier periods, early tax surveys represented an administrative universe divided into the ruling bloc of claimants to taxes and the taxpayers. The members of the ruling bloc were present in the registers as recipients of different types of revenue grants. Surveys did not record them by their names, nor did they specify their population. Taxpayers, on the other hand, were recorded by their names; the amount of produce which was collected as tithe was also entered into the registers. Land was recorded as a category of taxation in relation to a tax that fell on the person as well as the land (*resm-i çift*). The unit of measurement was the *çift*, or the area ploughed by a pair of oxen. *Çift*, however, varied with climatic and ecological conditions. Its plasticity, in turn, made it amenable in an environment in which payment of taxes was subject to a process of negotiation.

Earlier surveys were signifiers of shifting power positions as they were transcribed in the continual distribution and redistribution of resources among different groups within the hierarchy of a distributive state environment. The information that they provided about population, production and land, in fact, represented a mapping of power relations in a given locality and the positioning of different actors vis-à-vis the ruler. As such, early Ottoman tax surveys (*tahrirs*) represented the bundle of claims on land to its use, title and revenues and the ways that these claims were negotiated in different localities. At the same time, these surveys bore witness to a recognition of the authority of the ruler, in that the power relations that they signified were described in the given format of the register and carried out by means of procedures determined by the centre. In that sense, old surveys provided an important vocabulary through which the Ottoman understanding of distributive justice was articulated.

The nineteenth-century surveys represented a radically different state environment, and Ottoman bureaucrats increasingly saw having access to information on population, income, land and property as an intrinsic part of realising the dual modern aspirations of state taxation and increased production-*cum*-economic growth. To this end, beginning in the 1830s, the central government undertook the preparation of statistics, including population censuses, income registers and cadastral surveys. The *temettuat* registers, or registers of income-yielding assets, compiled between 1840 and 1845[34] are first in a long series of land and property registers. Though *temettuat* surveys were possibly the least developed in terms of the categories that they embodied, and perhaps the least successful in that the tax assessments that they included were not used in actual taxation, they are, at the moment, the only surveys from the nineteenth century to which researchers can have full access.

The central government put a great deal of effort into the preparation of the *temettuat* surveys. These preparations included the carrying out of pilot projects in selected districts and the establishment of numerous local commissions to conduct collecting and recording of information. These efforts involved the mobilisation of society from the bottom up. That this was an urgent matter for the central government is attested by the fact that 18 thousand income registers were completed within a span of two years, covering all imperial territories outside Arab lands.

Temettuat registers included a system of classification and categories which situated the different actors on the land in relation to the singular claim of taxation of the central government over the annual income of the individual property holder. To this end, income registers did not classify information for different regions on the basis of the holders of revenue grants, as did the earlier registers. *Temettuat* registers rested on the assumption that the central state was the primary recipient of taxes and that members of the former military class, together with ordinary households, were subject to state taxes. As such, instead of devoting separate surveys for the assessment of revenue proceeds for the different types of revenue grants (*timar defterleri, mukataa defterleri, vakıf defterleri*), the income registers represented a single survey, with the household as the basis for classifying information on production and landholding. In the old surveys, the unit of recording had been the village; they recorded the different shares of tax revenues apportioned to different revenue grant-holders from a given village. Payment of taxes (in cash and in kind) was the collective liability of the village, and product taxes were divided amongst households on the basis of negotiated arrangements within the village.

In the *temettuat* registers of the 1840s and the subsequent property and land surveys of the nineteenth century, the individual household, as the unit of recording, was to be taxed on the basis of its annual income. The *temettuat* registers included inventories of lands, animals and other resources in the possession of the head of the household. The central government regulations emphasised that taxes were an obligation of the individual and not a collective liability of the village. This emphasis on individual obligation manifests itself in the registration of more than one taxpayer in a single household in the 1845 registers, in contrast to the practice in the registers of 1840.[35]

The practice of numbering and classification by numbers in what were called 'numbers registers' was important to the process of individuation of ownership, as well as for facilitating central government access to information compiled in the surveys. The practice of numbering was initiated in the *temettuat* of 1840–45 through the affixing of numbers to individual households. On the other hand, *Regulation for the Surveying of Property and Population*, issued in 1860,[36] stated that fields, orchards, pasturelands and vineyards were to be recorded in property listings in terms of general and particular numbers.[37] However, registers compiled according to these instructions are not at present available to researchers. As a result, it was not possible to ascertain what the general and particular numbers assigned to land or property meant. But there is little doubt that the procedure of numbering properties and individual households sought to facilitate an administrative crystallisation of individual householders as property owners. At the same time, the assigning of numbers to properties assisted in the fashioning of land or property as a 'thing' to be owned, exchanged and taxed on its income. Moreover, the recording of land in registers presupposed that documents of ownership – the title deeds (*tapu*) – were shown to the scribes in charge of recording. In the event that these were not available, they were to be renewed in the courts of law. The title deeds were to include the general number of property or land as it was recorded in the property register, together with descriptions of its borders and of its shape.[38] The procedures for registering land which are described in the *Regulation* of 1860, in correlating the information in multiple registers by means of a system of numbering and tables, lay before the eyes of government officials an order of landed property which these procedures were, in fact, shaping. Land or property was being made accessible for the realisation of central government's goals of taxation and economic development. In this sense, it can be said of the procedures of recording land in registers that they represented a snapshot of the Ottoman administrative universe of the nineteenth century. This was, however, a contested universe, where the achievement of both goals was seriously frustrated. The new order of property and of the state were 'made' in the context of incessant struggles among different groups representing multiple interests in land. The new order carried the imprints of these struggles and it owed its specificity to these struggles and confrontations. The categories of the surveys and practices of surveying were sites for these confrontations.

The remaining part of this chapter is devoted to the 'makings' of individual property in relation to these confrontations. Before that, however, it is important to note that the categories introduced in the *temettuat* surveys were also constitutive of an 'economic' imperative which was inseparable from the taxation imperative.

Temettuat registers suggest a thinking about land as an 'economic' category, as an income-yielding asset and not simply as a category of taxation-*cum*-use, that is, as territory to be taxed and/or leased for use. The *temettuat* registers recorded the different phases of productive activity, that is they recorded the extent of lands under cultivation, those left fallow and those leased out, together with the income from land leases, as well as the cash income that accrued from the land for the year before the registration and also during the year of registration. Moreover, the conceptual disentangling of land from the tangle of taxation/property relations which characterised the earlier distributive–accommodative environment becomes manifest in the adoption in the registers of *dönüm* (919.30 square metres), an areal unit of measurement, instead of the *çift*, a unit of measurement characterised by its plasticity and, therefore, variability in different localities. This was, no doubt, a step in the direction of standardising and making uniform the measurement unit, which was integral to the central government's effort to simplify property relations on land. The introduction of the areal unit of measurement was important from the point of view of the objectification of land as a 'thing', as the object of ownership and as an asset exchangeable in the market.

Equally important, taking incomes of individuals as the basis for taxation occasioned the central government's interest in evaluating the productive capacity of land and its resources, in the variations in that capacity as well as in market conditions which determined the value of assets. Beginning in the 1840s, the increase in the productive capacity of land and resources became a central preoccupation of the Ottoman government. This was expected to result in increased tax revenues and, perhaps just as significant, in an improvement in the ability of the central administration to deliver services to the population. In January 1857, the Ottoman government issued the *Instructions to Property Officials in the Provinces*,[39] asking property officials in different provinces to compile answers, on a yearly basis, to a list of questions related to agricultural production. Property officials were also expected to enter the results of their queries in registers and send them to Istanbul every year in February, or at the latest in early March.[40] The *Instructions* opened with the statement that 'the generosity of the ruler dictated that he rendered services for the progress of agriculture which would benefit the country and his subjects'. To this end, exact information was to be had for all villages in all districts and sub-districts concerning the measurements of areas of cultivated fields and figures concerning seed–yield ratios during harvest time.[41] For individual farms, information was requested on the area for each farm in areal units of measurement, the area sown and the amount of seed cultivated, the area of land left fallow, the yields from vineyards and grape presses as well as the amount of grape produce consumed in the locality of the farm and the amount exported. Finally, the *Instructions*, in the spirit of market management which was characteristic of nineteenth-century political economy, asked for comparative figures. Thus the property officials were to note yearly variations in production or yields and in prices. The central government wanted to know how the changes in the supply of a given good were reflected in its price, and which factors affected its supply or production. Any factor that caused a fall in production was to be counteracted by administrative intervention. In this regard, property officials were instructed to enlist the assistance of agricultural officials to combat diseases which damaged vines and thus caused a fall in revenues both to the state and to the owners of the vineyards.

From the above discussion, it is clear that compilation of statistics on the full extent and productive capacities of agricultural land for assessment of individual incomes was an exercise in the extension of governmental scrutiny into domains which government recording had not previously penetrated. This involved a considerable intrusion into individual lives, as evidenced by detailed descriptions of the physical appearance of heads of households, including whether those persons had a beard or were afflicted by a limp. It also meant accounting for all the assets of the individual household, sometimes down to personal belongings. In brief, it signalled an increased rigour in tax assessment and met with strong resistance. Recent work by Ottoman economic historians shows the period beginning in the 1840s was one of incessant tax revolts and resistance to the process of information-gathering directed towards the assessment of taxes on the basis of individual incomes.[42] The most dramatic outcome of this resistance was that notwithstanding the effort that went into their preparation, the central government was unable to use the information recorded in the *temettuat* registers in the collection of taxes.

For one thing, this information was often glaringly defective and showed serious discrepancies in the distribution of taxes among regions and individuals.[43] Above all, individual heads of household had been less than candid in declaring their assets. The central government was well aware that village headmen (*muhtars*) and prayer leaders (*imams*) who received and recorded the declarations of assets from these individuals tended to overlook the inaccurate statements. Another problem related to faulty assessment was the behaviour of *muhassıls*, or public servants appointed by the central government, responsible for the preparation of the income surveys, as well as for tax collection. These officials were found guilty of either over-assessing individual incomes to endear themselves to Istanbul or under-assessing them to endear themselves to certain local groups.

Misdemeanours on the part of individual officials, however, are revealing of the nature of surveying (including gathering information and tax assessment) as an arena in which numerous battles were waged over the establishment of the domination of the Ottoman central bureaucracy over members of former ruling groups with entrenched interests in land. The establishment of the hegemony of the central government implied the recasting of property and taxation relations, amounting to a radical revision in the allocation of resources on land. From the point of view of the central government, gathering of information with the objective of assessing taxes on the basis of individual incomes would make possible a more equitable distribution of taxes among regions and individuals. Central government officials blamed the heavy tax burdens felt by ordinary people on tax evasions on the part of members of former ruling groups, rooted in the resistance of those groups to recording of their assets.[44] Equity in taxation or relief from the excessive tax burden rested on the generality of the assessment and the collection of taxes. The government must have had some success in achieving that generality given the fact that in the second half of the nineteenth century taxes rose in absolute terms and per capita throughout the Empire's lands, increasing five-fold.[45] On the other hand, powerful groups in the countryside, including former tax-farmers and/or members of religious foundations and former holders of revenue grants, did resist the surveying process by withholding information about their assets. In many cases, these groups constituted the force behind local rebels, if they did not actually incite rebellion themselves.[46]

Traces of these struggles are to be found in the continuous reformulation of the categories used in surveying, as well as in changes in surveying methods and in the personnel who undertook the task. The strongest resistance was expressed in relation to the individuation of taxation. A government regulation issued in 1845 addressed to local administrative and financial officers emphasised that taxes were the obligation of the individual, to be paid on his/her income, and not the collective liability of the village.[47] Yet the 1845 surveys, and the 1840 surveys before them, recorded the totals of household and individual incomes for each village, suggesting that taxes were assessed on the basis of the income from the entire village. This slip into assessment on the basis of collective income was a way of allowing individuals to escape the full burden of taxation. It also allowed for the distribution of the tax burden among individual households on the basis of distributive processes characteristic of the earlier era, which pitted the strong against the weak in the village community. Similarly, the continued recording in the surveys of both 1840 and 1845 of the tithe on grains as a tax assessed on the total yield of grains in the village attests to the strength of the resistance to the individuation of taxation. Furthermore, the resetting of the tithe at the general standard rate of one tenth in all regions, instead of former rates which varied from region to region, may be seen as an acknowledgement on the part of the central government that the tithe was there to stay and the only alternative to abolishing it was 'modernising' it. Of course, collection of the grain tithe, which continued to be collected in kind, proved to be a highly lucrative business. In fact, many complaints about *muhassıls*, responsible for surveying as well as for tax collection for two years between 1840 and 1842, relate to their abuses regarding tithe collection.[48] These grievances were further fuelled by their rivals in the business of tithe collection, the former tax-farmers who, after 1842, resumed the task of collecting the tithe, while the collection of other taxes was entrusted to provincial governors and their financial officers, both appointed by the central government.

In fact, *temettuat* surveys represented an arena which encompassed the old and the new as the old categories insinuated themselves alongside the new. This was true for the category of tithe, which is often entered in the surveys sideways, almost in the margin above the entry of the name and the description of the head of the household. The assets of the household were listed, in even lines, under the name and the description of the head of the household. The sheep tax, which was levied in kind and was the collective liability of the village, was recorded, like the grain tithe, in an awkward fashion. On the other hand, survey entries included detailed inventories of sheep, describing individual sheep in their various stages of growth, including pregnancy and nursing, possibly directed towards the assessment of the sheep's worth and income-yielding capacity. Collection of the sheep tithe was also a very profitable business; it continued to be farmed until 1859–60, when surveys began to include assessments of the sheep tax on the basis of the value and/or the income yielded from individual sheep.[49] Finally, the transitional character of the *temettuat* registers is revealed in debates and discussions over what was to be considered income or which items yielded income liable to taxation and which did not. Central government officials often pointed out that the notion of *temettuat*, or what constituted taxable income, was misunderstood, resulting in abuses and/or frictions in the recording and assessment processes.[50]

Another major area of contestation had been regarding who was to take charge of the surveying of property, land and population as well as of tax assessment and tax collection, with the consequence that the surveying of property and land came to be carried out by a curious mix of local groups or individuals and state officials. The content of that mix, however, was suggestive of the ways that local society was being formed in relation to the practices of surveying. Initially, in 1840, the central government directly appointed *muhassıls* to be in charge of surveying of income-yielding resources, of tax assessment and collection. The central government also delegated to these officials the mission of propagating its reforms throughout the empire. *Muhassıls* were not accountable to other high-ranking government officials in the provinces, but reported directly to central government bureaux in Istanbul; they had considerable autonomy in carrying out their activities with the assistance of councils, the members of which the *muhassıls* appointed from among local personages. Salaries of *muhassıls* were paid by the central government, but the level of these salaries was determined by the councils. This measure was no doubt intended to give these bodies some control over the activities of *muhassıls*. The latter, in carrying out the registration of property and population, were to be assisted by two scribes: one was responsible for recording the population, the other for recording property. Both scribes came from the districts where the *muhassıls* served; they were appointed and paid by the *muhassıls*. The actual process of registration, as described by the central government instructions issued in January 1840, took place when the *muhassıl*, accompanied by his scribes, visited the different localities (towns, villages) in the region over which he had jurisdiction. The procedures to be followed in the registration of property and population were to be established by the councils in these localities in collaboration with the *muhassıl* and his scribes.[51] The abuses of *muhassıls*, and their entanglements with local groups through the system of councils – which seem to have resulted in serious misrepresentations of taxable incomes, ranging from fraud in the measurements of grain tithe to the measurements of areas of land[52] – appear to have been a factor in provoking the revolts in Anatolia and the Balkans. The central government might have intended that employing the *muhassıls* and the new local councils that they established would counterbalance the power of former revenue-holders in the provinces. But this objective was frustrated by the fact that former power groups either managed to attract the *muhassıls* to their ranks or resisted their activities to the extent of rendering them ineffectual. As a result, the central government was compelled to abolish the office of *muhassıl* in 1842.

This marked the end of grand posturing on the part of the central government in its attempt to affect the balances of power in the provinces by setting different groups against each other. It also marked the beginnings of a process of bureaucratisation in the registration of property, land and population. Above all, bureaucratisation presupposed mobilisation of diverse local groups through a system of commissions formed at all levels of provincial administration, down to the villages. The commissions or councils were channels through which local knowledge came to bear on the bureaucratic processes of registration carried out by government-appointed officials. Commissions were also the arenas in which different interests were negotiated with the central government and its representatives mediating among different groups.

Thus, in 1845, a regulation addressed to the senior administrative and financial officers of the central government assigned the responsibility for compiling registers and gathering information to administrators (*kaymakam*) and financial officers (*defterdar*) appointed by the central government in the provinces. These officials were to act under the auspices of 10 councils of reconstruction, which included local personages as well as central government officials, established throughout the empire. The actual task of information-gathering, however, was assigned to village headmen and village notables.[53]

While we have little information regarding procedures of surveying and the personnel in charge of registration in the case of surveys compiled in the late 1850s, the *Regulation for the Surveying of Property and Population*, issued in 1860, suggests that performance, in terms of effective taxation, was not entirely to the satisfaction of the central government.[54] The *Regulation* told the administrators in the provinces to persuade the population to provide information on their property and on members of their family; it declared that failure to do so which resulted in the evasion of taxes merited severe punishment, including three years of chained imprisonment.[55]

From the perspective of the central government, the most effective way of eliminating the information deficit was to elicit the co-operation of local populations in the process of gathering information and in the registration of property and population. To this end, the *Regulation* stipulated the appointment of commissions at different levels of the provincial administration. At the level of the province (*eyalet*), grand commissions included 22 scribes (*muharrir*) who were members of the *ilmiye*, or scholarly class, and who were appointed by the central government,[56] four estimate-makers (*muhammen*),[57] who were chosen from among the respected persons in individual localities, and one chairman. The scribes were responsible for the issuing of certificates of property for tax purposes as well as birth certificates. Commissions formed at the different levels of the administrative hierarchy were expected to provide information to keep these certificates up-to-date, keeping track of births and deaths, of sales and acquisitions of property, and of taxes paid. At the village level, a commission was to be appointed for a group of six villages, with each village providing one member. The village commissions were expected to meet weekly in the summer and bi-weekly in the winter on a given day of the week. They decided on the distribution of taxes among households according to their abilities to pay; they were responsible for reporting births and deaths, persons who moved in and out of the area of the six villages, as well as for reporting buildings that were constructed without permission of the provincial council. It appears that village commissions stood above the administrations of individual villages, represented by the headmen. In the compiling of the 1840–45 income registers, the village headmen had played a very important role, with poor results from the point of view of the government. The *Regulation* of 1860 stated that village headmen came from lower classes, and that people from respectable backgrounds deemed it below their dignity to hold this position. In order for reform and restitution to be executed properly, the *Regulation* specified that headmen had to be appointed from among persons who were considered to be trustworthy both by the central government and the local population. To this end, the *Regulation* stipulated that scribes appointed by the central government to the provincial councils should dismiss the existing headmen and appoint new ones from among trustworthy and respected persons in the village. Finally, in 1866, an addendum to the *Regulation* of 1860 introduced property commissions in districts (*sancaks*) and subdistricts (*kazâs*).[58] The scribes of the new property commissions, who were appointed by the central government and who came under the jurisdiction of the chief scribes of grand provincial commissions, took over some of the tasks, including that of issuing of property and birth certificates, from the scribes of grand commissions. This development suggests a deeper intrusion of the central government's administration of property and population registration into smaller administrative units while, at the same time, the format of the commission ensured the participation of local personages in that administration.

Despite, or perhaps because of, continual administrative adjustments which sought to reconcile (and in the process, recast) diverse local interests with those of the administration, the Ottoman state did not succeed in producing cadastral maps, which were central to the process of cadastral surveying. Cadastral maps remain the single greatest achievement of the modern state in constituting individual ownership on land. They enable the maze of property relations to be cut through in order to establish administrative controls over the land, its resources and population. Above all, cadastral maps draw boundaries and leave no ambiguity as to who owns what. Scott states that cadastral maps 'are designed to make a local situation legible to an outsider'.[59] This may explain the remarkable success of cadastral mapping in the colonial contexts of the nineteenth century, where the map provided an outsider-state with a 'bird's-eye view'.[60] In the case of the non-colonial Ottoman state, its ability to be an outsider, that is to abstract itself from the context of power relations within the empire, was far more limited. As a result, the central government conceded to local demands in curbing its practices of registering wealth and land. One reason that it did so was probably because in the absence of a reserve army of administrators located in a colonial homeland, the Ottoman state depended largely on the services of local groups and notables in the instituting of the new administrative order, as witnessed in the case of the establishment of commissions for the preparation of surveys. This was also true in the manning of the new administrative courts. Following the issuing of the Land Code, matters related to property and land came under the jurisdiction of administrative courts which, however, continued to be manned by the judges of the old courts of justice. The latter, more often than not, belonged to local networks of power relations represented by religious foundations and other local claimants to revenues.

The concessional politics of property which characterised Ottoman administrative practice in the second half of the nineteenth century, however, can be better understood in relation to the attempts of the central government to mediate different interests while at the same time eliminating some and including others in the hegemonic order of the new state. Commissions established on different levels of provincial administration were arenas in which a new order of the state was cast and recast as both the old and new power groups confronted each other. For instance, in relation to the administration of property and land, the central government appears to have sought to counterbalance the power of the judges at the courts of justice with that of the commissions, which, for a brief period between 1840 and 1842, were appointed from among local personages by *muhassıls.* Under the *ancien régime,* judges were responsible for mediating conflicts relating to land and taxation. Judges often entered the individual agreements negotiated among parties in the form of amendments to survey entries, frequently by scribbling the details in the margins of a survey page. Finally, the judges and their courts had been responsible for implementing regulations included in provincial codes. In the nineteenth century commissions appear to have usurped the tasks formerly performed by judges and their courts. These included the registration of property as well as the settling of disputes over land.[61] At the same time, commissions became arenas into which the former elites could be co-opted, and their influence diffused, as in the case of the membership of judges in commissions at the level of provincial administration.

Conclusion

Given the picture of Ottoman state practices which constituted individual property mired in the concessional politics of commissions and marked by an inability to define, in specific terms, land as an object of taxation and exchange on cadastral maps, could one speak of a failure of Ottoman modernity? The answer is no. For one thing, in the second half of the nineteenth century, the new hegemonic order of the central bureaucracy was in place. The central government's ability to tax had increased considerably, and through policies of welfare and reconstruction, the government sought to secure the interests of its subjects.[62] That the Ottoman central government failed and the Empire collapsed during the First World War in the face of inter-state competition in Europe does not alter the fact that a modern state order had emerged in the Ottoman setting. The lynchpin of the modern state environment in the nineteenth century was the formation of individual ownership in land. The Ottoman government, through its legal practices as well as through practices of surveying and registering, was able to constitute individual ownership in land. This chapter has addressed the political processes which characterised the 'making' of individual property as different groups or individuals, including administrative actors,[63] confronted each other to negotiate the terms of their existence in a new hegemonic environment where the central bureaucracy strove to establish its dominance. In emphasising political constitutions of individual property, this discussion has questioned those understandings of administrative and legal constitutions of individual property which identify the constitutive process with that of the subjugation of society to the imperatives of central government, including taxation, conscription and control for developmentalist ends. Instead, I have sought to problematise the domination of modern government as exercised through its various practices. As such, that domination did not imply so much an annihilation, but rather a reconstitution of the local or the society, albeit in terms of the new hegemony. Reconstitution involved confrontations among different interests and attempts at mediating those interests on the part of the central government. The politics of commissions in relation to registration and the surveying of landed property was one such arena in which the local was constituted and re-constituted. It was also the arena of the constitution of a new hegemony of the central bureaucracy.

Law and practices of surveying and registration constituted individual property in terms of general and uniform rules and categories. Such generality and uniformity articulated the demands of the central government for taxation and for control over resources, to the exclusion of other groups which formerly had access to these. The central government sought to justify the generality of its demands by its claim to serve the general interest. The self-definition of the new hegemony came to rest on an understanding of justice which no longer relied on the recognition and accommodation of particular circumstances, but referred to a justice of administration. The latter rested on a claim to administer effectively and equitably on the basis of the generality and the uniformity of rules, regulations and procedures transcending individual circumstances. This allowed for an ideological distancing by the central government or the bureaucracy, and cast it in the role of a third-party mediator among multiple interests.

Attempts to mediate through the generality of procedures and regulations, and reconcile the different interests, as witnessed in relation to the politics of commissions, was the substance of administrative justice. The central bureaucracy sought to dispense this justice through the efficacy of its administrative procedures. It tirelessly turned out procedures relating to the administration of landed property, seeking methods to survey property and population which could reconcile its own interests in taxation and economic development with those of different groups in society. For the most part, the outcome was a spate of compromises and grand undertakings which could not be put into practice, as was the case with the income registers of the 1840s. Yet a new order of the state and of property emerged out of these mediations, carrying the imprints of the political struggles waged by the different groups, including multiple agents of the central administration.

The new hegemony was no longer represented by the just ruler, but rather by the generality and uniformity of administrative practices that imparted the role of mediation to the bureaucrat. The figure of the bureaucrat, upholding general rules and regulations, came to embody the entity of the new hegemony. The administration sought an identity in keeping with the multinational character of the Empire, aspiring to effect an erasure of all national identities. As importantly, and not clouded by the romance of nationalism, it was a thoroughly modern (in the Weberian sense) identity. This identity, which survived until the 1980s most notably in the Turkish Republic, the immediate successor to the Ottoman state, has since been undermined by radical changes in the context of power relations or in the conditions of hegemony, both domestically and globally. This has meant a shift in the balance of power to commercial groups and an introduction of new forms of government outside those of the central state administration, which have also set in motion a search for a self-definition in the new state context. This is, perhaps, not very different from the situation in other regions of the world which, within their own trajectories of modern transformation, seem to be engaged in similar searches.

Notes

1 Scott, 1998, p.2.
2 For an eloquent description of the legally constituted character of social reality *à propos* property on land: Thompson, 1990, pp.261ff.
3 For the notion of power fields, see Bourdieu, 1987. Differing from Bourdieu's view, here the understanding of the power field is closely associated with the notion of a state context of power relations or hegemonic environment, a context which shapes the power fields while at the same time is shaped by them. Hegemonic environment is about 'framing' of providing or defining the terms of contestation, mediation, negotiation: İslamoğlu, 2000, pp.11–12.
4 Law here refers to governance. Cf. İslamoğlu, 2004.
5 Abrams, 1988, pp.58–89.
6 İslamoğlu, 2000.
7 On these relations of reciprocity in the context of the French state of the seventeenth century, see Guery, 1984.
8 Saltzman, 1993.
9 For a discussion of a moral economy of the Ottoman state, see İslamoğlu-İnan, 1994.
10 For discussion of this point in relation to the activities of French kings in the seventeenth century, see Parker, 1981.
11 Such characterisations of judges, or *kadıs*, prevail in mainstream Ottoman historiography; see, for instance, İnalcık, 1943. From the perspective of this article, it may be important to re-situate the *kadı* courts in the environment of power plays which characterised the Ottoman state context and not simply treat them as arms of an imaginary, omnipresent state.
12 Among these privileges were the exemptions granted to the poor. The generalisation of state taxes to the poor was a contested issue in the nineteenth century. Çakır, 2001, p.123.
13 For a physiocratic (Quesnay) version of the line of reasoning which linked private property to increased productivity, increased production of wealth and to the interests of state in terms of increases in taxable wealth, see Genovese-Fox, 1976, pp.110–33, especially 112–14; also for a discussion of 'productive principle' in

relation to the definition of private property rights in British India, see Dirks, 1986, p.316.

14 On measures in the nineteenth century by the Ottoman government to protect and render population more productive, see Dursun, 2001. On population politics of the modern state, see Foucault, 1991.

15 An indication of the Ottoman interest in political economy is the translation in 1852 of Jean Baptiste Say's *Economie politique*, one of the most popular political economy texts of the nineteenth century.

16 Also see İslamoğlu, 2004.

17 Bentham, 1931, pp.111–13, presented an impassioned critique of the eighteenth-century natural law formulations of property. According to Bentham, 'property and law are born together, and die together. Before laws were made, there was no property: take away laws and property ceases': Bentham, 1931, p.113. Bentham then proceeds to link property to security: 'law creates whatever is to be secured'. In this sense, Bentham established a direct link between property and law as governance.

18 Kanth, 1986, pp.132–39.

19 For the understanding of property as a bundle of claims in premodern settings, see Maine, 1920.

20 İslamoğlu-İnan, 1994.

21 Forster, 1997.

22 The practice of issuing certificates (*hüccets*) by judges in establishing property rights was a common one. In the earlier period this practice was used to establish *mülk* claims over revenues. Such freehold claims included the ability to exchange freely and to bequeath to heirs, rights to revenues from land and other taxable resources. In the nineteenth century, it appears that the practice of establishing property rights through issuing of court certificates was a means of establishing absolute ownership claims.

23 İnalcık, 1943, p.95

24 Decisions of provincial councils in the Balkans played an important role in the formulation of individual ownership rights. Ottoman historians know, in fact, very little about the decisions of *kadı* courts on property matters in the nineteenth century; after all there is no reason why *kadıs* in the provinces would not support property claims of tax-farmers and other local groups, as did English magistrates and French jurists with their close affiliations to local propertied groups. For the English case, see Arthurs, 1985; for the French case, Kelley and Smith, 1984.

25 Aberdam, 1982.

26 The commission of drafters consisted of jurists headed by Ahmet Cevdet Paşa. For the text of the report of the commission presenting the Code, see Akgündüz, 1986, pp.683ff.

27 For a discussion of *mülk* as a claim over revenues in the Ottoman context, see above and İslamoğlu, 2000.

28 For the shifting of boundaries between the public and the private on land in relation to the institution of forest lands, see the chapter in this volume by Gülöksüz.

29 For a detailed discussion of the Code in this perspective, see İslamoğlu, 2000.

30 The debate around Ottoman reform often points to its being forced upon the Ottoman government, especially by the British. This study disagrees with this position. Reform edicts of the nineteenth century, although embodying elements of the prevailing liberal discourse as this came out of Great Britain, were cast in the context of struggles among the members of the Ottoman ruling class and of attempts by the central bureaucracy to establish its hegemony. This struggle for the making of the Ottoman modern state had begun in the latter part of the eighteenth century and was rooted in the competition among the European states.

31 Registration of property in the name of individuals began in 1847: Ortaylı, 1983, p.159.

32 These included the *has*, or the domains of the ruler and his family, and *tımar*, or revenue-grants assigned to military personnel. It is interesting to note that *tımar* grants and their holders or *sipahis* are mentioned among holders of revenue grants who resisted the central government as late as the second half of the nineteenth century. For instance, Çakır, 2001, p.125. Given the fact that historians have written about them as extinct since the 'decline' of the Ottoman classical system, their frequent recurrence in documents from later periods may indicate that *sipahis*, while acting as tax-farmers, may have maintained a distinct identity which differentiated them from other tax-farmers. What exactly that identity was may be a subject of future research.

33 Çakır, 2001, p.121.

34 At present, researchers have full access to these registers, which represent sets compiled in 1840 (1256AH) and in 1845 (1260–61 AH). Our access to the surveys compiled in 1859–60 and in 1881–94 is at best patchy. Of these surveys, the 1859–60 sets appear to be the most comprehensive. The instructions issued by the central government regarding their preparation suggest that

these surveys sought to approximate to the character of modern cadastre. For further information on these surveys prepared under the auspices of *Tahrir-i Emlak Nezareti* (Ministry of Property Surveys), see Şener, 1990, pp.105–6, and Çakır, 2001, p.50. For a discussion of *temettuat* surveys, see Saraçoğlu, 1998, and for a comparison of the data of these surveys with French surveys of the same period, see Kaya, 1999. Pioneering work on *temettuat* surveys has been done by Güran, 1998, and Kütükoğlu, 1995.

35 See the text of the regulation issued in 1845 and addressed to high ranking administrative and finance officials in the provinces. BOA, *İrade, Mesa' il-ı Mühimme,* No 58/15, 1261 (1845).

36 *'Tahrir-i Emlak ve Nüfus Nizamnamesi', circa* 1866, pp.889–902.

37 Changes in the status of property due to sales and leases as well as births and deaths were entered in daily registers (*yevmiye defterleri*) and were subsequently recorded in the main registers, where each household was assigned a number. This may suggest a preliminary step in the direction of proper cadastral surveys.

38 *'Tahrir-i Emlak ve Nüfus Nizamnamesi', circa* 1866, First section, Article 12: *'defter-i emlakde muharrer umumi rakamlar ve eşkal ve akyise ve hudud tarif ve tahrir olunacak'.*

39 *'Taşra Mülkiye ve Mal Memurlarına Talimatdır', circa* 1866, pp.555–58.

40 *'Taşra Mülkiye ve Mal Memurlarına Talimatdır', circa* 1866, pp.555–58: article 5 on corrupt practices in the process of registration. Changes in production were to be reported every month to the new Treasury by property officials, or *mülkiye memurları.*

41 The catalogues of the Finance Ministry (*Maliye Nezareti Defterleri* No 797, 1272/1856) include a register of cultivated lands for villages in the sub-district (*kazâ*) of Çan, located in the district (*sancak*) of Biga. This register, different from those of earlier years, contains information on the area of cultivated lands, the geographic location of fields, quantities of seed planted and yields for individual crops for the years 1856 and 1857. The figures given are those of quantities measured in *kiles* and they are not monetary values (1 *kile* = 25.659 kg). The format of individual entries in the register is as follows: the name of the head of the household is followed by the numbers of animals he owns, the lands he cultivates. The land is measured in the areal unit of measurement of *dönüm* (919.30 square metres, under the Turkish Republic 1000 square metres), while the quantity of seed cultivated and yields for individual crops are measured in *kiles.* At the end of the recordings for each village, the quantities of seed and yields for individual crops are totalled. I am grateful to

my doctoral student Alp Yücel Kaya for providing me with this information.

42 For instance, Çakır, 2001, and Uzun, 2002.

43 In a number of cases, the tithe payments were recorded as nearly 45 per cent of total income from cultivated area.

44 *'Taşra Mülkiye ve Mal Memurlarına Talimatdır', circa* 1866, pp.555–58: article 2 on the failure of notables to register their sons in order to exempt them from military service and to pay less tax. A number of decrees issued by the central state prior to or at the time of compilation of the 1844 survey, as well as accounts referring to a failed attempt at compiling a survey in 1838, point to complaints about the heavy tax burdens on ordinary people, and to situations where notables did not pay taxes.

45 According to Şevket Pamuk, between 1750 and 1914 the taxes that accrued to the Ottoman Treasury increased five-fold and, by the end of this period, taxes amounted to 12 per cent of gross national product. I am grateful to Professor Pamuk for this information.

46 See Çakır, 2001, pp.130–40, and Uzun, 2002.

47 BOA, *İrade, Mesa' il-ı Mühimme*, No 58/15, 1261 (1845).

48 For a detailed description of the procedures of tithe collection in the nineteenth-century Ottoman empire and abuses involving *muhassıls*, see Çakır, 2001, pp.124–26.

49 I would like to thank Dr Ahmet Uzun for a very informative discussion of the sheep tax. When the central government could not do away with tax-farming as the mode of collection, it tried to get rid of the former tax-farmers and assign the farming of taxes to other groups. The experiment with *muhassıls*, who were central government officials, with respect to the farming of the grain tithe was part of this attempt. In the 1840s, the farming of the sheep tax was assigned to state officials or *mübaşir.*

50 Çakır, 2001, pp.118–20. Çakır refers to reports by the inspection commissions of the central government, which state that the concept of *temettuat* was poorly understood by *muhassıls.* It would be interesting to look at the cognitive changes forced upon Ottoman agricultural society by the introduction of the notion of income. Some of the problems referred to regarding the recording of all items may be a result of simply not understanding what the central government meant by income-yielding assets or *temettuat.*

51 For the instructions (*Muhassılan Yedlerine İ'ta olunan Talimat-ı Seniyye*) issued by the central government on January 1840 and sent to *muhassıls*, see BOA, *İrade, Dahiliye*, 260, 20 Zilkade 1255/25 Ocak 1840 and BOA, *Maliyeden Müdevver Defterleri*, No 9016, pp.2–4. For a discussion

of the text of instructions which included a listing of areas under the jurisdiction of *muhassıls*, see Çakır, 2001, pp.42–47 and 239–48.

52 I am grateful to Dr Ahmet Uzun for the information that one of the main abuses of *muhassıls* was related to tampering with strings used to measure land area.

53 İrade, *Mesa' ıl-ı Mühimme*, No 58/15, 1261 (1845).

54 Remnants of a survey dating from 1856 include categories of information which did not exist in the 1840–45 *temettuat* surveys. See note 41 above. The kind of information included in this survey closely approximates that in the 1859–60 surveys.

55 *'Tahrir-i Emlak ve Nüfus Nizamnamesi', circa* 1866, Second Section: in the process of the recording of population, persons failing to present birth certificates were not to be allowed access to courts and their travel certificates were to be revoked.

56 *'Tahrir-i Emlak ve Nüfus Nizamnamesi', circa* 1866, Second Section.

57 *'Tahrir-i Emlak ve Nüfus Nizamnamesi', circa* 1866, Second Section.

58 *'Tahrir Nizamnamesine Zeyl olunmak üzere Fıkra-ı Nizamiyyedir', circa* 1866, p.904.

59 Scott, 1998, p.45.

60 For successful cadastral mapping in British India in the mid-nineteenth century, see Saumarez Smith, 2004.

61 For the establishment on the spot of a commission for the settlement of a property dispute in Yanya in the 1870s, see İslamoğlu, 2000; for commissions attending cases which were formerly referred to courts of justice, see Çakır, 2001, p.114.

62 Özbek, 1999/2000.

63 For an understanding of administrative actors as legal *personae*, see Mundy, 2004, as based on Thomas, 1998.

Bibliography

Primary sources

Istanbul, Başvekalet Osmanlı Arşivi

İrade, Dahiliye, No 260, 20 Zilkade 1255 (25 January 1840).

İrade, Mesa' il-ı Mühimme, No 58/15, 1261 (1845).

'Muhassılan Yedlerine İ'ta Olunan Talimat-ı Seniyye', *Maliyeden Müdevver Defterleri*, No 9061,19 Zi'l-kade 1255 (24 January 1840), pp.2–4.

'Tahrir-ı Emlak ve Nüfus Nizamnamesı', 14 Cumade'l-ula 1277 (28 November 1860), *Düstur*, I. *Tertib*, v.1, 2nd ed., Istanbul, Matbaa-ı Amire, 1282 (*circa* 1866), pp.889–902.

'Tahrir Nizamnamesine Zeyl olunmak üzere Fikra-ı Nizamiyyedir', 27 Şaban 1282 (15 January 1866), *Düstur*, I. *Tertib*, v.1, 2nd ed., Istanbul, Matbaa-ı Amire, 1282 (*circa* 1866), p.904.
'Taşra Mülkiye ve Mal Memurlarına Verilen Talimatdır', 15 Cumade'l-ula 1273 (11 January 1857), *Düstur*, I. *Tertib*, v.1, 2nd ed., Istanbul, Matbaa-ı Amire, 1282 (*circa* 1866).

Secondary sources

Aberdam, Serge, *Aux Origines du Code Rural, 1789–1900: un siècle de debat*, Paris, Institut National de la Recherche Agronomique, 1982.
Abrams, Philip, 'Notes on the Difficulty of Studying the State', *Journal of Historical Sociology* 1/1, March 1988, pp.58–89.
Akgündüz, Ahmet, *Mukayeseli İslam ve Osmanlı Hukuk Külliyatı*, Diyarbakır, Dicle Üniversitesi Hukuk Fakültesi Yayınları, 1986.
Arthurs, H.W., *Without the Law: Administrative Justice and Legal Pluralism in Nineteenth Century England*, Toronto, University of Toronto Press, 1985.
Barkan, Ö.L., 'Türk Toprak Hukuku Tarihinde Tanzimat ve 1247 (1858) Tarihli Arazi Kanunnamesi', in *Tanzimat I*, Istanbul, Maarif Matbaası, 1940, pp.321–421.
Bentham, Jeremy, *The Theory of Legislation*, ed. C.K. Ogden, London, Routledge & Kegan Paul, 1931.
Bourdieu, Pierre, 'The Force of Law: Toward a Sociology of the Juridical Field', *Hastings Law Journal* 8, 1987, pp.805–53.
Çakır, Coşkun, *Tanzimat Dönemi Osmanlı Maliyesi*, Istanbul, Küre Yayınları, 2001.
Dirks, Nicholas, 'From Little King to Landlord: Property, Law and Gift under the Madras Permanent Settlement', *Comparative Studies in Society and History* 28 (1986), pp.307–33.
Dursun, Selçuk, *Population Policies of the Ottoman State in the Tanzimat Era: 1840–1870*, MA thesis, Sabancı University, March 2001.
Forster, E.M., *Howard's End*, New York, St Martin's Press, 1997.
Foucault, Michel, 'On Governmentality', in Gordon Burchell et al. (ed.), *The Foucault Effect: Studies in Governmentality*, London, Harvester Wheatsheaf, 1991, pp.87–104.
Genovese-Fox, Elizabeth, *Origins of Physiocracy: Economic Revolution and Social Order in Eighteenth Century France*, Ithaca, Cornell University Press, 1976.
Guery, Alain, 'Le roi dépensier, le don, le contrat et l'origine du système financier de la monarchie française de l'ancien regime', *Annales* 39, no 6 (November–December 1984), pp.1241–69.

Gülöksüz, Elvan, 'Negotiation of Property Rights in Urban Land in Istanbul', in Huri İslamoğlu (ed.), *Constituting Modernity: Private Property in the East and West*, London, I. B. Tauris, 2004, pp.248–75.
Güran, Tevfik, *19. Yüzyıl Osmanlı Tarımı*, Istanbul, Eren, 1998.
İnalcık, Halil, *Tanzimat ve Bulgar Meselesi*, Ankara, Türk Tarih Kurumu Basımevi, 1943.
– *The Ottoman Empire: The Classical Age 1300–1600*, New York, Orion Publishing Co., 2000.
İslamoğlu, Huri, 'Property as a Contested Domain: A Reevaluation of the Ottoman Land Code of 1858', in Roger Owen (ed.), *New Perspectives on Property and Land in the Middle East*, Cambridge, MA, Harvard University Press, 2000, pp.3–61.
– 'Towards a Political Economy of Legal and Administrative Constitutions of Individual Property', in Huri İslamoğlu (ed.), *Constituting Modernity: Private Property in the East and West*, London, I. B. Tauris, 2004, pp.3–34.
İslamoğlu-İnan, Huri, *State and Peasant in the Ottoman Empire*, Leiden, E.J. Brill, 1994.
Jones, Eric L., *Growth Recurring: Economic Change in World History*, Oxford, 1988.
Kanth, R.K., *Political Economy of Laissez-Faire: Economics and Ideology in the Ricardian Era*, Totowa, NJ, Rowman & Littlefield, 1986.
Kaya, Alp Yücel, *Les enquêtes agricoles de la France et de l'Empire ottoman au milieu du XIXe siècle*, unpublished mémoire du DEA, Paris, Ecole des Hautes Etudes en Sciences Sociales, 1999.
Kelley, Donald R. and Bonnie G. Smith, 'What was Property? Legal Dimensions of the Social Question in France (1789–1848)', *Proceedings of the American Philosophical Society* 128/3, 1984, pp.200–30.
Kütükoğlu, Mübahat, 'Osmanlının Sosyal ve Iktisadi Kaynaklarından Temettü Defterleri', *Belleten* 59/225, 1995, pp.395–418.
Mundy, Martha, 'The State of Property: Late Ottoman Southern Syria: the *Kazâ* of 'Ajlun (1875–1918)', in Huri İslamoğlu (ed.), *Constituting Modernity: Private Property in the East and West*, London, I. B. Tauris, 2004, pp.214–47.
Maine, Henry James, *Ancient Law*, London, John Murrray, 1920.
Özbek, Nadir, 'Osmanlı İmparatorluğunda "Sosyal" Yardım Uygulamaları, 1839–1918', *Toplum ve Bilim* 83, Kış, 1999/2000, pp.111–33.
Ortaylı, Ilber, *İmparatorluğun En Uzun Yüzyılı*, Istanbul, Hil Yayınları, 1983.
Palairet, Michael, *The Balkan Economies c.1800–1914: Evolution without Development*, Cambridge, Cambridge University Press, 1997.
Parker, David, 'Law, Society and the State in the Thought of Jean Bodin', *History of Political Thought*, v.2, 1981, pp.253–85.

Saltzman, Ariel, 'An *Ancien Régime* Revisited: Privatization and Political Economy in the Eighteenth Century Ottoman Empire', *Politics and Society* 21/4, 1993, pp.393–423.
Saraçoğlu, Safa, *'A Snapshot of the County of Kafirni through the Surveys of 1843'*, MA thesis, Middle East Technical University, October 1998.
Saumarez Smith, Richard, 'Mapping Landed Property: A Necessary Technology of Imperial Rule?', in Huri İslamoğlu (ed.), *Constituting Modernity: Private Property in the East and West*, London, I.B.Tauris, 2004, pp.149–79.
Scott, James C., *Seeing Like a State: How Certain Schemes to Improve the Human Condition Have Failed*, New Haven, Yale University, 1998.
Şener, Abdüllatif, *Tanzimat Dönemi Osmanlı Vergi Sistemi*, Istanbul, İşaret Yayınları, 1990.
Thomas, Yan, 'Le Sujet de Droit, la Personne et la Nature', *Le Débat* 100, 1998, pp.85–107.
Thompson, Edward P., *Whigs and Hunters: The Origins of the Black Act*, Harmondsworth, Penguin, 1990.
Uzun, Ahmet, *Tanzimat ve Sosyal Direnişler: Niş İsyanı Üzerine Ayrıntılı bir İnceleme* (1841), Istanbul, Eren, 2002.

Index

www.ingramcontent.com/pod-product-compliance
Ingram Content Group UK Ltd.
Pitfield, Milton Keynes, MK11 3LW, UK
UKHW020204290926
15470UKWH00001B/13

9 781860 649967